St. Mark's Episcopal Cemetery

Orange, Essex County, New Jersey

(Near the Southwest Corner of Main Street and Scotland Road,
Adjacent to the First Presbyterian Church of Orange)

History of the Cemetery;
Expanded List of Interments;
and
Early History of St. Mark's Church

—*Revised Edition*—

Compiled by
Carol Personette Comfort

HERITAGE BOOKS
2010

HERITAGE BOOKS
AN IMPRINT OF HERITAGE BOOKS, INC.

Books, CDs, and more—Worldwide

For our listing of thousands of titles see our website
at
www.HeritageBooks.com

Published 2010 by
HERITAGE BOOKS, INC.
Publishing Division
100 Railroad Ave. #104
Westminster, Maryland 21157

Copyright © 2008 Carol Personette Comfort

Other books by the author:

Cedar Grove Cemetery, Cedar Grove, Essex County, New Jersey
St. Mark's Episcopal Cemetery, Orange, Essex County, New Jersey

All rights reserved. No part of this book may be reproduced or transmitted in any form or by any means, electronic or mechanical, including photocopying, recording or by any information storage and retrieval system without written permission from the author, except for the inclusion of brief quotations in a review.

International Standard Book Numbers
Paperbound: 978-0-7884-4770-9
Clothbound: 978-0-7884-7531-3

ST. MARK'S EPISCOPAL CEMETERY
Orane, Essex County, New Jersey

Revised Edition

History of the Cemetery
Completed List of Interments from New Information
Inscriptions
Civil War Veterans
Map Transcript of the Cemetery
Early History of St. Mark's Church

Compiled by
Carol Personette Comfort

CONTENTS

History of St. Mark's Cemetery	Page 1
Expanded List of Interments and Inscriptions	Page 3
Church Plaques and Stained Glass Windows	Page 269
Early History of St. Mark's Church	Page 275
Sources	Page 281
Inscription Records of St. Mark's Cemetery	Page 283 (Appendix I)
Transcript of undated Map of the Cemetery	Page 291 (Appendix II)

HISTORY OF ST. MARK'S EPISCOPAL CEMETERY

* * * * *

Vincent P. Dahmen, Head Deacon of the Lamb of God Fellowship, has been devoted to the 2007-2009 restoration project at St. Mark's Cemetery. He has worked tirelessly to help preserve the history and to honor those buried there. The progress made from an overgrown, long abandoned and vandalized burying ground has been remarkable. It is an accomplishment which is still in process and will expand in the future. The efforts of the Episcopal Diocese of Newark and Vincent P. Dahmen should be appreciated and acknowledged with gratitude.

* * * * *

"On November 28, 1842, the corporation of St. Mark's (Episcopal) Church bought of Edward Condit a lot, eighty-six feet wide on the main street, lying west of the (Presbyterian) Old Ground, with the same depth as the latter. The price paid for the plot was $313.70; which was raised by subscription, and of which Samuel Williams gave $200.00. The corporation of St. Mark's, being desirous of retaining the whole width of its lot for purposes of interment, arranged with the old parish for a driveway on its west line, to be used by both corporations. The consideration for its use, on the part of St. Mark's was that it should erect the gates, and pay the expense of keeping them in repair." (*History of the Oranges*, Stephen Wickes, p.238)
(Note: A 2009 survey shows St. Mark's Cemetery, including the Negro Burial Ground, is now 80.91 feet wide on Main Street; 88.38 feet wide across the back; 625.22 feet deep on the driveway side, and 631.30 feet deep on the side opposite the driveway.)

- - - - -

"Over the years there was no line of demarcation between the two cemeteries and some copies of the inscriptions made of the Orange Burying Ground include a number of burials in the Episcopal section. It was not until 1927, when the First Church of Orange decided to erect their new edifice within the confines of the old burying ground, that the Episcopal Cemetery which belongs to St. Mark's Church of West Orange, was delineated." (*Orange Episcopal Cemetery*. Richard W. Cook. The Genealogical Magazine of New Jersey. Vol.67.1992.)

- - - - -

"The cemetery has always been a problem for St. Mark's. When it was first parceled out to St. Mark's, along with a number of other cemeteries in the Oranges to other churches, St. Mark's was wealthy and could handle it. From the mid 1960s, St. Mark's began a down hill slide that culminated with only seven parishioners remaining and its endowment spent. The cemetery, along with everything else, fell into serious benign neglect. Since my predecessor took over in 1980 the congregation has been slowly rebuilt to where we now (1992) number around 200 but we are still far from the wealthy congregation of the 19th century. Many records were lost, including most of the cemetery records.

"It is a very small cemetery which means that if the headstones have not been damaged by vandalism, individual graves and plots are relatively easy to find in the cleared section. It is not fenced so that there is access to it 24 hours a day. "(*Letter*, from The Rev. H. Robert Ripson, TSSF, Rector. St. Mark's Episcopal Church, St. Mark's Square, 45 Main Street, West Orange, New Jersey. May 8, 1992.)

- - - - -

On November 6, 1904, "An unidentified man about thirty-five years old was found late this afternoon lying on the grass near the tomb of the late Bishop Whittingham in St. Mark's Cemetery by Chester Robinson .... (he) notified Dr. Frances J. E. Tetrautt, (who) ....found that the man was dying and advised his removal to the hospital; the man died before reaching there. A three-ounce bottle, which had contained carbolic acid, drained of its contents and clutched in his right hand, told the story. ...A pawn ticket made out to the name of J. Parker, 327 Washington Street, Newark ... was found. Inquiry at that address by the Newark police developed the fact that no such person lived there. The man looked to be a person of refinement and good habits. His only possessions were a cheap watch and leather fob, and 5 cents in money...." (*New York Times)*

- - - - -

In 2004 the Episcopal congregation of St. Mark's Church was disbanded and the few remaining members started to attend other Episcopal Churches in the area. The ownership and control of the church and hence the cemetery reverted to the Episcopal Diocese of Newark. The Diocese then arranged for the removal of excess trees and overgrowth. In July of 2004 the Diocese leased St. Mark's Church to the Lamb of God Fellowship. In December of 2008 the Lamb of God Fellowship agreed to take over maintenance of the cemetery.

- - - - -

EXPANDED LIST OF INTERMENTS

"CAPITAL LETTERS" - indicate the person **has been recorded** as buried at St. Mark's Cemetery.

"*" - indicates this person has **not been recorded** as buried at St. Mark's Cemetery. Some of these may have been buried at St. Mark's with no marker or the marker did not survive; some may have been buried at St. Mark's and were later moved to other cemeteries; some may have been previously buried elsewhere and were moved to St. Mark's Cemetery; some were also recorded as buried at the Old Burying Ground of the adjacent Presbyterian Church.

Source information is noted below each capitalized, recorded name:
csl - Inscriptions on Tombstones in the Episcopal Cemetery
gmnj - Orange Episcopal Cemetery; sighting reports
map - map of interments of St. Mark's Church
nps - Soldiers and Sailors System, National Park Service

NOTE: - This is a collection of data found in the map, previous sighting records and recent observation of headstones. Notes for each interment are meant to be research clues. Please confirm and check carefully.

- - - - -

ADDY

Addy, Thomas S.*
b.
d. (before July 1832)

wife, ELIZABETH
(csl-E135)(map, Section D)
b. (abt. 1773)
d. July 20, 1832

relict
In her 59th year

daughter, JANE
(gmnj)(csl-E135)(map,Sect.D)
b. October 15, 1801
d. December 7, 1837

Addy, JOHN
(map, Section D)
b.
d. February 24, 1851

Notes:
--bur. map, Section D, near Daniel Babbitt, q.v. and Henry Stryker, q.v.
--1810 Census, p.144, 5Wd, New York City;Thomas Addy
--1815 NY Register and City Directory:Thomas Addy, hatter

Children of Thomas S. Addy and Elizabeth .....
Jane, b. 1801; d. 1837
Elizabeth, b. August 6, 1806; m. Henry Stryker,q.v.

- - - - -

ALLEN

Allen, John*
b. (abt. 1819)
d.

wife, Sarah* (Hampton)
b. (abt. 1820)
d.

son, JOHN
(csl - E80)
b. (November 15, 1862)
d. May 25, 1865.
Aged 2.6.10

Notes:
--See:Map: Section G: Plot of John Allen & John Jones
--John Allen was son of William Allen, q.v. and Elizabeth .....

--1850 Census, p.240, Orange: William Allen, age 67, b. Ireland, laborer; Elizabeth, age 60 b. Ireland; John, age 30, b. Ireland; Sarah (daughter-in-law) age 30, b. Ireland; Eliza J., age 8, b. Ireland (granddaughter); Emma, age 4, b. NJ (granddaughter); Mary A., age 2, b. NJ (granddaughter)
--1860 Census, p.394, 3Wd. Orange: John Allen, age 42, b. Ireland, laborer; Sarah, age 40, b. Ireland; Eliza J. age 18 b. Ireland, hat trimmer; Emma, age 14, b. NJ; Mary age 12 b. NJ; Sarah, age 10, b. NJ; Hampton, age 6, b. NJ
--1870 Census, p.401, 3Wd, Orange: John Allen, age 53, b. Ireland, works at felt hat factory; Sarah 57 b. Ireland; Sarah age 19, b. NJ; Hampton, age 16, b. NJ, hatter apprentice; Rachel, age 9, b. NJ

--1880 Census, p.266.1, West Orange, NJ: Wm. J. McGall, age 33, b. Bermuda, father b. Scotland, mother b. England, hat manufacturer (McGall, Allen & Co.); Mary (Allen), wife, age 31, b. NJ, parents b. Ireland; Emma, age 10 b. NJ; Grace, age 8 b. NJ; Alice, age 1, b. NJ; John Allen, age 63, father-in-law, b. Ireland, laborer; Sarah Allen, age 61, mother-in-law, b. Ireland; Rachel Allen, age 18, sister-in-law, b. NJ, works at hat shop; Mary Sullivan, aunt, widow, age 52, b. Ireland
--1880 Census, p.182C, Orange: Hampton Allen, age 25, b. NJ, hat finisher; Alice, wife, age 23, b. NJ; Katie, dau., age 3, b. NJ; Louisa McChesney, sister-in-law, age 25, b. NJ, hat trimmer

Children of John Allen and Sarah ......:
Eliza J., b. abt. 1842, Ireland
Emma, b. abt. 1846, New Jersey
Mary , b. abt. 1848 NJ, m. Wm. J. McGall
Sarah, b. abt. 1850 NJ
Hampton, b. August 28,1854; m. Alice Mathilda McChesney
Rachel, b. abt. 1861, NJ
John, b. November 1862, NJ; d. May 25, 1865

- - - - -

Allen, ELIZA (map, plot owner,Sect. G))	b. (abt. 1790) d. (aft. 1850
Allen, WILLIAM (map, Section G)	b. (abt. 1827) d. June 16, 1852 *Aged 25*
Austin, DAUGHTER of E. (map, Section G)	b. (abt. 1864) d. November 20, 1866 *Aged 2 years*
INFANT (map, Section G)	b. (abt. 1845) d. July 26, 1845
INFANT (map, Section G))	b. (1845) d. July 26, 1845
CHILD of Peter Sarony (map, Section G)	b. d. May 15, 1859

Notes:

--see John Allen, John McMullin
--1850 Census, p.240, Orange: William Allen, age 67, b. Ireland, laborer; Elizabeth, age 60 b. Ireland; John, age 30, b. Ireland; Sarah (daughter-in-law) age 30, b. Ireland; Eliza J., age 8, b. Ireland (granddaughter); Emma, age 4, b. NJ (granddaughter); Mary A., age 2, b. NJ (granddaughter)

- - - - -

Allen, ROBERT E. (map, Section M)	b. d. July 10, 1883

Notes:
(?)Served: Civil War, Co. A, 7th NJ Inf., 2nd Lt. (nps)
--bur. plot of James Crogan, q.v.

- - - - -

Allen, WILLIAM (map, Section G)	b. (abt. 1783) d. April 22, 1853 *Aged 70*
Allen, MRS. (map, Section G)	b. (abt. 1793) d. November 23, 1873 *Aged 80*
Allen, WILLIAM C. (map, Section G)	b. d. February 22, 1880
Allen, CHILD of William (map, Section G)	b. d.

Notes:
--See: Map, Section G: Plot of John Allen & John Jones

- - - - -

ARMSTRONG

Armstrong, JAMES (map, grave owned, Sect. I)	b. d. April 22, 1890
Armstrong, MRS.	b.

(map, grave owned, Sect. I)   d.

Armstrong, FREDERICK CLARK b.
(map, grave owned, Sect. I)   d.

Notes:
--?1880 Census, p.529A, Newark, NJ: James Armstrong, age 54, b. Scotland, business mgr. at newspaper; Margaret, wife, age 49, b. England; Robert J., age 21, b. TN; William, age 19, b. IA; Richard, age 17, b. MO
--?1910 Census, p.9A, 14Wd, Newark, NJ: Richard M. Armstrong, age 49 b. MO, father b. Scotland, mother b. England, m.26 yrs., painter; Agnes, age 47 b. Canada, 6 born 4 living; James A., age 25, b. NJ, painter; George L., age 23, b. NJ, blacksmith; Robert S.C., age 17, b. NJ, leather worker; Agnes M., age 9, b. NJ

- - - - -

ARNOLD

Arnold, MARJORIE(?)   b.
(map, ch. property)   d. December 19, 1895
(map, Section N)   *Aged 35(?)*

Notes:

- - - - -

ATCHISON

Atchison, JOHN   b. (abt. 1824)
(csl - E39)   d. October 26, 1876
(map, plot owner, Sect. K)   *In his 52nd year*

wife, Mary* (Woodruff)   b. (abt. 1826)
                              d. (aft. 1900)

daughter, EMILY J.   b.(November 29,1851)
(csl - E47)(map, Sect. K)   d. September 5, 1852
                              Aged 0.9.6

Notes:
Served: Civil War, Co. F, 7th NJ Inf., Pvt. (nps)

--John Atchison m. abt. 1850, Mary Woodruff, daughter of Thomas Ogden Woodruff of Caldwell, NJ and Hannah Markwith
--1850 Census, p.240, Orange Twp: John Atchinson, age 24, b. Ireland, shoemaker; Mary, age 24, b. NJ
--1860 Census, p.370, 3Wd. Orange: John "Olhcson", age 35, b. Ireland, shoemaker; Mary, age 34 b. NJ; Samuel, age 7 b. NJ; James, 5, b.NJ; Mary, age 2, b. NJ; Alfred Woodruff, age 27, b. NJ, boot fitter; Samuel Woodruff age 49, b. NJ, shoemaker; Herman Woodruff, age 19, b. NJ, carpenter apprentice
--1870 Census, p.395B, 3wd Orange: James Atchinson, age 43, boot/shoe factory, b. Ireland; Mary age 42, b. NJ; Samuel age 17, b. NJ; James age 14; Mary age 12; Benjamin, age 8
--1880 Census, p.164.3, Orange: Mary A. Atchison, widow, age 53, b. NJ, keeping house, James I., son, age 23, b. NJ, father b. Ireland, works in hat factory; Benjamin, son, age 17, b. NJ, telegraph operator
--1880 Census, p.152C.Orange: Mary A. Atchison, niece, age 22, b. NJ, hat trimmer, father b. Ireland, mother b. NJ; at res. of Thomas B. and Sarah J. Woodruff.
--1880 Census, p.178C, Orange: Samuel Atchison,age 27, b. NJ, father b. Ireland, mother b. NJ; Engraver; Maggy, wife, age 26, b. NJ, parents b. Ireland; Walter, son, age 2, b. NJ; Thomas, age 6 months b. NJ
--1900 Census, p.12A, 1Wd, Orange: George W. Baxter b. January 1854, b. NJ, father b. Scotland, mother b. England, grocer; Mary b. May 1858 b. NJ, father b. Ireland, mother b. NJ; Esther M. b. March 1884 NJ; Agnes H. b. January 1889 NJ; Mary Atchison, age 73, widow, mother-in-law, b. September 1826 NJ, m. 50 years, 6 born 4 living

Children of John Atchison and Mary Woodruff:
Emily, b. abt. November 29, 1851; d. September 5, 1852
Samuel H., b. abt. 1853, Orange; m. Margaret A. .....
James I., b. abt. 1857, Orange; m. Monnie J. .....
Mary, b. abt 1858, Orange; m. George W. Baxter
John, b. June 27, 1862, Orange; d.y.
Benjamin L., b. abt. 1863, Orange; m. Nettie E. .....

- - - - -

AYMAR

Aymar, John James*   b. (August 4 1800)
                                          d. (December 22, 1869)
                                          (bur. Trinity Cemetery, NYC)

first wife, SARAH (Babb) b. (abt 1800)
(gmnj)(csl-E37)(map,Sect. K) d. April 3, 1861

Notes:
--bur. plot of James Robbins, q.v.
--John James Aymar was baptised September 7, 1800 at Trinity Church Parish, New York City, son of James Aymar and Margaret Cahill. He d. Dec. 22, 1869;funeral at St. Ann's Church at 18th St. near Fifth Avenue; buried Trinity Cemetery, Manhattan; (Monument: Ann Myer 1800-1885; Eliza M. Boice 1811-1888; John J. Aymar 1800-1869; Mary C. B. Aymar 1808-1885)
--He married Sarah Babb September 24, 1833 at New York City. She died in New York; "funeral at St. Luke's Church NYC; interment at Orange NJ" (*New York Times*) (She was sister of William George Babb; a well known architect and dau. of John Babb and Sarah .....)
--He married #2 Mary C. B. Myer; b. October 30, 1808 and d. June 22, 1885 at New York City; bur. Trinity Cemetery; Manhattan NY (1850 Census p.321 18Wd Dist.2 NYC: Sarah Myer age 76; Ann Myer age 45; Sarah Myer age 41; Mary C. B. Myer age 38; Charles S. Myer age 5; all b. NY)

--1850 Census, p.235, Orange Twp: Henry S. Condit age 30, b. NJ, hatter; Sarah E. T. Condit, age 27 b. NY; James P. Robbins, age 55 b. NY; Matilda Robbins, age 40, b. NY; Robert P. Robbins, age 10 b. NJ; John J. Aymar age 52 b. NY, clerk; Sarah Aymar age 50, b. England; Eliza Babb, age 48, b. NY; Catherine Kelly, age 10, b. NJ
--1860 Census, p.813, 20Wd, Dist.4, New York City: Mrs. 'Robins' age 45 b. NY; Robert P. Robins, age 18, b.NJ 'D.G.' (dry goods?) clerk; Jno. J. 'Amays' (Aymar) age 50 b. NY, D.G. clerk; Sarah Amays age 40 b. England; Eliza Babb, age 46 b. NY; Sarah Thomas age 40 b. NY; Chas. Mott, age 19 b. NY, dry goods clerk; Jno. Mott age 17 b. NY, D.G. Clerk; Geo. Mott, age 15, b. NY; 1 servant

- - - - -

BABB

Babb, James* b.
  d.

wife, ... b.
  d.

daughter, ELIZABETH b. (abt. 1798)
(csl - E38) d. June 28, 1864
(map, Sect. K) d. July 8, 1864
Aged 66

Notes:
--See: Henry S. Condit; see: James Robbins
--?1860 Census, p.813, 20Wd, Dist.4, New York City: 'Mrs.' Robins age 45 b. NY; Robert P. Robins, age 18, b.NJ 'D.G.' (dry goods?) clerk; Jno. J. 'Amays' (Aymar) age 50 b. NY, D.G. clerk; Sarah Amays age 40 b. England; Eliza Babb, age 46 b. NY; Sarah Thomas age 40 b. NY; Chas. Mott, age 19 b. NY, dry goods clerk; Jno. Mott age 17 b. NY, D.G. Clerk; Geo. Mott, age 15, b. NY; 1 servant

Child of James Babb and Elizabeth ......:
Eliza, b. abt 1814; d. 1964

- - - - -

BABBITT

Babbitt, Dr. DANIEL b. August 3, 1788
(csl - E126) d. May 16, 1864
(map,plot owner Sect. D) d. June 19, 1864
(NJ Will #15861G,1864)

Daniel Babbit
entered into rest
May 16th, 1864
aged 75 years
The Lord preserveth
the souls of his saints

first wife, NANCY b. April 7, 1794,
(Matthews)(map, Sect. D) d. December 8, 1828
(gmnj)(shaw)(csl - E127)

Erected
to
The Memory of
Nancy
wife of
Dr. Daniel Babbit and loved child of

Noah & Phebe Matthews
who was born
April 7th 1794
and died
Dec.r 8th, 1828
Aged 34 years and 4 months
Could parental affection or connubial love have arrested the stroke of
death, our infant babes would not have been left motherless
Farewell, ye friends whose fond care
Has long engaged my love
Your fond embrace I now exchange
For better friends above

second wife, CHARLOTTE (Stryker)(csl-E125)(map,Sect. D) (removed to Rosedale Cemetery)	b. 1799 d. July 4, 1884
son, NOAH MATTHEWS (gmnj)(csl - E131)	b. June 20, 1813 d. November 15, 1832

In memory of
Noah Matthews
Son of
Dr. Daniel & Nancy Babbit
who was born
June 20, 1813
Graduated at Nassau Hall
Princeton in Sept.
and died Nov.r 13, 1832
In his 20th year"
Sic transit Gloria Mundi

son, DANIEL CLINTON (gmnj)(csl - E128) (map, Sect. D)	b. September 20, 1828 d. January 6, 1839 *In 9th year*
Babbitt, MRS. PHEBE (map, Sect. D)	b. d.
Babbitt, infant SON of Wm. (map, Section D)	b. d.

Notes:

--See: Noah Matthews
--Daniel Babbitt b. August 3, 1788, Mendham, NJ, son of Daniel Babbitt and Sarah Beach. He married Nancy Matthews, August 2, 1812 at Orange, NJ, daughter of Noah Matthews, q.v., and Phebe Harrison. He married second, Charlotte Stryker, October 11, 1839; she was daughter of Henry Stryker, and Esther Harrison; sister of Henry Stryker, q.v.
--Daniel Babbitt was a town council member at Orange in 1860-61 (Shaw, p.734)

--1850 Census: p.211, Orange Twp., NJ: Noah Matthews age 79b. NJ, no occupation; Willliam M. Babbitt age 29, b. NJ, lawyer; Frances Babbitt, age 24, b. NJ; Alice Babbitt, age 3 months, b. NJ
--1850 Census: p.211, Orange Twp., NJ: Daniel Babbit age 62, no occupation listed; Charlotte age 57; Phebe age 32; Charlotte age 9.
--1860 Census, p.405, 2Wd, Orange: 'Danl Babbit' age 69 b. NJ, physician; Charlotte age 59 b. NJ; Charlotte E. age 19, b. NJ (adj. to Stephen Wickes, age 49, physician, who wrote *History of the Oranges*)
--1870 Census, p.367, 2Wd, Orange: William H. Vermilye age 54, b. NY, banker; Phebe L. age 42 b. NJ; Daniel B. age 16, b. NJ; Catherine H. age 14, b. NJ; Charlotte Babbitt age 70 b. NJ; Charlotte E. Babbitt, age 26, b. NJ
--1880 Census, p.109A, Orange: William H. 'Virmilye', age 65, b. NY, banker; Phebe L., wife, age 51, b. NJ; Daniel B. son, age 25, b. NJ, lawyer; Mary P., dau-in-law, age 22, b. PA; Katharine H., dau., age 23, b. NJ; William M. grandson, age 4 mos.;Charlotte Babbit,mother-in-law, widow, age 81, b. NJ; Charlotte E. Babbit, sister-in-law, single, age 37, b. NJ; Margaret Dougherty, single, age 18, b. Ireland, servant

Children of Daniel Babbitt and Nancy Matthews:
Noah Matthews, b. June 20, 1813; d. November 15, 1832
William Matthews, b.August 28, 1821, d.Sept. 25, 1875;
      m.Frances P. Condit
Phebe Louise, b. September 30, 1828; d. Sept.17, 1907;
      m. William Henry Vermilye
Daniel Clinton, b. September 20, 1828;d.January 6, 1839

Children of Daniel Babbitt and Charlotte Stryker:
Charlotte Elizabeth, b. May 25, 1841

- - - - -

BALDRIDGE (?)

Baldridge(?), THOMAS
(map, Section I)

b. (abt.
d. (January 2_, 1869?)

Notes:
--map, Section I - illegible

- - - - -

BALDWIN

Baldwin, ISAAC
(gmnj)(csl-E185)(map,Sect.B)
(NJ Will #18997G, 1877)

b. July 1, 1791
d. March 16, 1877
In 86th year

wife, NANCY (Hopper)
(gmnj)(shaw)(csl - E184)
(map, Section B)

b. May 3, 1796
d. March 16, 1866
In 70th year

daughter, JANE AUGUSTA
(csl-E183)(map, Sect. B)

b. January 18, 1833
d. December 9, 1838
Aged 5

burned to death

Notes:
--Isaac Baldwin was son of Caleb Baldwin and Lydia Johnson.
--Isaac Baldwin m. Nov.16, 1815, Orange, Nancy Hopper. (*Baldwin Gen.*,p.553)

--1850 Census, p.234, Orange Twp: Caleb J. Baldwin, age 31, shoe cutter; Anna M. age 26; Clarence W. age 5; Alamina G. dau. age 3; Isaac, age 59, shoemaker; Nancy, age 53; Jep. Condit, age 43, blacksmith; all b. New Jersey
--1860 Census, p.416&417, 2Wd, Orange: Richard A. "Terham" (Terhune), age 42, master builder; Sarah M. age 40; Mary E. age 16; Theresa age 11; Harry R. age 9 months; Isaac Baldwin, age 68, shoe cutter; Nancy Baldwin, age 64; all b. New Jersey
--1870 Census, p.355, 2Wd, Orange: Richard "Therheme" (Terhune), age 52, b. NJ, carpenter; Sarah 51, b. NJ; Mary, 27 b. NJ; Addie, age 24, b. NJ; Harry, age 10, b. NJ; Isaac Baldwin, age 79, b. NJ, works at boot/shoe factory

Children of Isaac Baldwin and Nancy Hopper:
Caleb Johnson, b. January 9, 1817; m. Anna M. Gray
Sarah Maria, b. June 9, 1819,m. Apr. 26,1847, Richard Albert Terhune
Isaac Preston b. June 17, 1821, q.v.
Martha Ann, b. December 3, 1823, m. (Jeptha?) Harrison
Henry William, b. August 25, 1826, m. Caroline Foster
Lewis Mandeville, b. December 19, 1828 (q.v.)
Jane Augusta b. January 18, 1833
(*Baldwin Gen.*, Vol.II, p.553)

- - - - -

Baldwin, Isaac   b.
(map, plot owner, Sect. H)   d.

Notes:
--See: Map, Section H - surnames recorded as buried in this plot:
Canning, Cochran, Dangler, Doe, Edwards, Ferguson, Hanson, Hopkins, McCullough, Patterson, Pratt, Sheridan, Taylor, Weiss

- - - - -

Baldwin, Isaac Preston*   b. (June 17, 1821)
                                      d. (bef. December 10,1895)

wife, ABBY (Dean)   b. October 12, 1822
(gmnj)   d. March 5, 1891
(removed to Rosedale Cemetery?)

Notes:
--Isaac Preston Baldwin was born June 17, 1821, son of Isaac Baldwin, q.v., and Nancy Hopper. He d. before his daughter Arian Gertrude's wedding, December 10, 1895.
--Isaac Preston Baldwin married, October 23, 1842, Abby Dean daughter of Viner Dean
--March 6, 1891: *New York Times:* "At West Orange, on Thursday, wife of Isaac P. Baldwin in the 69th year of her age. Funeral service on Saturday at the residence of her son, Frank R. Baldwin, West Orange."

--1850 Census: p.228, Orange Twp., NJ: Isaac P. Baldwin age 28, hatter; Abby age 27; Jane A. age 6; Frank W. age 3, Jeptha H. age 1; all b. New Jersey

--1860 Census: p.405, Orange, NJ: Isaac P. Baldwin age 38, postmaster; Abby D. age 37; Jane A. age 16, postal clerk; Frank W. age 13; Jeptha H. age 11; Abby C. age 6; all b. NJ
--1870 Census, p.387, 3Wd, Orange: Isaac P. Baldwin age 49, clerk in office; Abby 47; Augusta 26; Frank W. 24, editor; Jeptha H. age 21, printer; Mary E. 18; Abby C. 15; Arien C. age 5; all b. New Jersey; 1 governess; 2 servants
--1880 Census: p.513.4, East Orange, NJ:Elma Reimer, widow, age 66, b. England, keeping house; Jeptha H. Baldwin, son-in-law, married, age 31, printer; Elma V. Baldwin, daughter, married, age 30, b. NJ, father b. Denmark;Merrick R. Baldwin, grandson, age 6;Cyrus P. Baldwin, grandson, age 4;Marion, granddaughter, age 3;Ralph B. Baldwin, grandson, age 1; Isaac P. Baldwin, age 58, hatter and Abby Baldwin, age 57, b. NJ

Children of Isaac Preston Baldwin and Abby Dean:
Jane Augusta, b. April 2, 1844; m.June 14 1871 Frank Arnold
Frank Wilfred, b. June 26, 1847;
    m. September 25 1871 Frances Eliza Love
    m. Harriet M. E. Cox
Jeptha Harrison, b. March 9, 1849;
    m. September 11, 1872 Elma Vale Reimer
    m. Hannah Reeves Edwards
Mary Estelle, b. August 14, 1851
Abby Caroline, b. November 2, 1854;
    m. September 15 1875 Sylvester Y. L'Hommedieu
Arian Gertrude, b. July 26, 1865;
    m. December 10 1865 Dr. Henry Allston Pulsford
New York Times: Dec. 11, 1895:Orange NJ, Dec. 10 "One of the large and fashionable weddings of the season in this vicinity was solemnized at high noon today in the Church of the Holy Communion, South Orange, when Miss A. Gertrude Baldwin, daughter of the late Isaac P. Baldwin, and Dr. Henry Allston Pulsford were married by the Rev. Louis Cameron, the rector of the church." etc.,
Elizabeth
Walter

- - - - -

Baldwin,
LEWIS MANDEVILLE
(gmnj)(csl-E182)
(map, Section B)

b. December 19, 1828
d. January 26, 1902
bur. January 28, 1902

(nps)	*Aged 72 years* *Co. C, 25 Inf. N.J.*
wife, EVA (Stope) (map, Section B)	b. (abt. 1835) d. February 5, 1912 *Aged 77.5.5*
daughter, LUCY IRVIN (map, Section B)	b. (April 29, 1860) d. (October 21, 1861)
Baldwin, ELLA JANE (map, Section B)	b. d. July 11, 1928

Notes:
Served: Co. G, 26th NJ Inf., Pvt. (nps) (gmnj)
--Lewis M. Baldwin was born Dec. 19, 1828 at Orange, son of Isaac Baldwin, q. v., and Nancy Hopper. Lewis married March 22, 1854, Eva Stope of Albany, New York.

--1850 Census, p.274, 11Wd, Brooklyn, NY: Lewis Baldwin, age 22, b. NJ, cabinet maker; at res. of Uriah VanVoorhees, carpenter (His first child was b. at Brooklyn, NY)
--1860 Census: p.356, 3Wd. Orange, NJ: Lewis M. Baldwin age 30; Eva age 24; Isaac E. age 4; Henry P. age 2, Lucy I. age 1 month.
--1870 Census: p.369, 3rd Ward, Orange,NJ: Lewis M. Baldwin, age 41, saw mill worker; Eva age 55; Isaac E. age 13, Henry P. age 10; Irene age 7; Lewis H. age 2.
--1880 Census, p.120.4, Orange: Lewis M. Baldwin age 51, b. NJ, carpenter; Eva, wife, age 44 b. NJ, father b. Prussia, mother b. France; Isaac E. age 24 b. NJ, glass stainer; Henry P. age 22 b. NJ, works jewelry mfg.; Leila A. age 17 b. NJ; Louis H. age 12 b. NJ; Walter Irving, age 8, b. NJ
--1900 Census, p.9A, 3Wd, Orange, NJ: Lewis M. Baldwin, b. Dec. 1828, NJ, m.46 yrs.; Eva, b. July 1834, Germany, 6 born 5 living; Louis H., b. April 1868 NJ, printer; Walter I. b. Sept. 1871 NJ, jeweler; 2 boarders
--1910 Census p.1A 3Wd Orange: Eva S. Baldwin age 78 b. Germany; Louis H. age 41 b. NJ printer; Walter I. age 38 b. NJ works at jewelry factory

Children of Lewis M. Baldwin and Eva Stope:
Isaac Engelbert b. October 14, 1855; m. abt. 1885 Sophie W.
Henry Preston b. January 16, 1858, m. Mary Ruth Crain

Lucy Irwin b. April 29, 1860, d. October 21, 1861
Leila Irene b. May 18, 1863; m.Charles Henry DeCoster
Louis Harrison b. April 2, 1868; d. aft. 1930 San Diego CA
Walter Irving b. September 1, 1871; d. aft 1930 San Diego
(*Baldwin Gen.*, Vol. II, p.594)

- - - - -

Baldwin, MARY
(gmnj)

b.
d. March 17, 183_

- - - - -

BANNISTER

Bannister, Stacy B.*
(map, plot owner,Sect. J)

b. (abt. 1822)
d. (aft. 1886)

1st wife, MARGARET (Perry)
(csl - E550)
(map, Section J)

b. (July 23, 1821)
d. March 31, 1870
d. April 6, 1872)
Aged 48.8.8

mother, DEBORAH
(gmnj) (Shaw)(csl - E54)
(map, Section J)

b.(April 9, 1790)
d. July 9, 1866
Aged 76.3.0

daughter, GERTRUDE
(gmnj) (shaw) (csl - E56)
(map, Section J)

b.
d. September 10, 1874
Aged 12.4.3

Notes:
--Stacy B. Bannister was the son of ..... Bannister and Deborah ..... He m. #1, Margaret Perry, b. 1821, New York; he m. #2, before 1877, Jessie Ryder, b. abt. December 1855, England.

--1850 Census, p.244, Orange: Stacy B. 'Bannister', age 28 b. NY; Margaret age 28 b. NJ; Mary E. age 4 b. NJ; Dewitt age 3 b. NJ; Deborah age 60 b. NY; Lewis Condit, age 19, b. NJ, shoemaker; Henry Myer, age 18, b.Germany, cigar maker
--1860 Census, p.366, 3Wd, Orange: Stacy B. 'Bannister' age 38 b. NY, shoemaker; Margaret age 38 b. NJ; Mary E. age 14; Dewitt 12; Caroline 9; Ann E. 6; Charles 4; Frank 2; all children b. New Jersey

--1870 Census, p.334, 10Wd, Newark: Stacy 'Bannister', age 49 b. NY, shoemaker; Carrie, age 19, b. NJ; Elizabeth age 16 b. NJ: Frank age 12, b. NJ; Carrie Lang, age 19, b. NJ
--1880 Census: p.307C, Newark, NJ: Stacy B. 'Bannister', age 59, b. NY, boot fitter; Jessie, wife, age 25, b. England; Charles son, single, age 25, b. NJ boot fitter, mother b. NY;
Frank, son, single, age 23, b. NJ, engraver, mother b. NY; Horace M. son, age 3, b. NJ,mother b. England.
--1900 Census, p.6B, 6Wd, Newark, NJ: Jessie Bannister, widow, b. Dec. 1855 England; Horace M., son b. Feb. 1877 NJ, clerk in cutlery; Elsie M. dau. b. Sept. 1885 NJ; Rebecca Ryder, mother, widow b. Feb. 1819 England; Lizzie M. Ryder, sister, b. Oct. 1860 England

Children of Stacy B. Bannister and Margaret Perry:
Mary E. b. abt. 1846
DeWitt, (q.v.)b. abt 1847
Caroline, b. abt 1851
Anne Elizabeth, b. abt. 1854
Charles, b. abt 1856
Frank b. abt 1858
?Gertrude, b. .....; d. September 10, 1874

Children of Stacy B. Bannister, and Jessie .....:
Horace M. b. abt. February 1877; married and divorced
Elsie M., b. abt. 1885

- - - - -

Bannister, DeWitt*   b. (abt. 1847)
                               d. (aft. 1900)
                               bur. (probably Rosedale Cem.)

wife, Emily A*   b. (abt. 1854)
                               d. (1917)
                               Aged 63, widow

son, FREDDIE DEWITT   b. (March 16, 1874)
(csl - E59) (map, Sect. J)   d. July 16, 1880
                               Aged 6.4.0

Notes:
Served: Civil War: Co. C, 39th Reg't, NJ Inf.,Pvt. (nps)
--DeWitt was son of Stacy B. Bannister, q.v.

--1850 Census, p.244, Orange: Stacy B. Bannister, age 28 b. NY; Margaret age 28 b. NJ; Mary E. age 4 b. NJ; Dewitt age 3 b. NJ; Deborah age 60 b. NY; Lewis Condit, age 19, b. NJ, shoemaker; Henry Myer, age 18, b.Germany, cigar maker
--1860 Census, p.366, 3Wd, Orange: Stacy B. Bannister age 38 b. NY, shoemaker; Margaret age 38 b. NJ; Mary E. age 14; Dewitt 12; Caroline 9; Ann E. 6; Charles 4; Frank 2; all children b. New Jersey
--1870 Census: p.349, 2nd Ward, Orange, NJ: DeWitt Banister, age 23, b. NJ, carpenter, boarder at res. of Abram D. Brower, q.v.
--1880 Census: p.274 B, West Orange, NJ: Dewitt Bannister, age 32, b. NJ, milkman; Emily, wife, age 26, b. NJ; Clara, dau., age 6; Ella, dau., age 4; Margaret, dau., age 3; Albert, son, age 2; Frederick, son, age 4 mos.; all b. NJ
--1900 Census, p.7B, West Orange: 'Witt Banister' b. Dec. 1847 NJ, father b. NY, mother b. NJ, m.27 yrs.,house builder; 'Emelly', b. Aug. 1854 NJ, father b. England, mother b. NJ; Margrett b. June 1877 NJ; William b. Dec. 1883, NJ
--1910 Census, p.8B, 2Wd, West Orange: Emily A. Bannister, age 55 b. NJ; William S. age 26; Margaret, age 33; Elizabeth, age 15; all b. NJ (census page faded)

Children of Dewitt Bannister and Emily A. ......:
Freddie Dewitt b. 1874, d. 1880
Clara, b. abt 1875
Ella, b. abt. 1876; m.1898 George L. Dascam
Margaret, b. June 1877
Albert Perry, b. abt 1878; m. Sarah E. Steiner?
Frederick, b. 1880
William S., b. December 1883
Elizabeth, b. abt 1895

- - - - -

BARD

Bard, Samuel W.*	b. (abt. 1838)
	d.
wife, Mary L. *	b. (abt. 1840)
	d.
daughter, GRACE ESTELL (csl - E74)	b.(April 3, 1872) d. July 3, 1872

(map,ch.property, Sect. H) *Aged 0.3.0*

--(?)1850 Census, p.252, Eastchester, Westchester Co., NY: Samuel Bard age 42 b. NY, laborer; Abagail age 38 b. NY; Samuel age 13 b. NY; 3 other children, b. NY
--1870 Census, p.486, Woodside Twp., Essex Co., NJ: Samuel W. Bard age 32 b. NY, grocer; Mary L., age 30 b. ...; Emily Judson age 20, at home, b. ....; Amos Judson age 16, b. ..., grocer clerk; Fredk. Stevens, age 44, physician b. .....
--1880 Census, p.503.4, Columbia Twp.,Ellsworth Co., Kansas: S. W. Bard age 40 b. NY, parents b. NJ, farmer; Mary L. age 39 b. NY, parents b. NY; Mary L. Judson, age 17, niece, b. Michigan; Chas. Crane age 20, b. OH, father b. MA, mother b. NY, farm labor

Children of Samuel W. Bard and Mary L. ......:
Grace, b. 1872; d.1872

- - - - -

BEACH

Beach, CHARLES b. (January 3, 1816)
(gmnj)(Shaw)(csl-E97) d. February 28, 1864
(map, Section F) *Aged 49*
(removed to Rosedale Cem.)

wife, Susan (Losey) b. (January 28, 1817)
  d. (October 13 1898)

Notes:
--See:bur. plot of David Beach
--Charles Beach was b. January 3, 1816, son of William Beach and Susan Smith. He married May 15, 1838, Susan Losey b. January 28, 1817; she d. October 13, 1898,
daughter of Ichabod Losey and Sarah Condit. Susan Beach, Ichabod Losey and Sarah Losey are all buried at Rosedale Cemetery, East Orange, New Jersey. Charles Beach's daughter, Sara Louisa Beach b. July 4, 1842 m. Elias Mulford Condit. (*The Harrisons of New Jersey, p.78)(Condit Gen.*, p.33)

--1850 Census: p.239, Orange Twp., NJ: Charles "Black" (Beach), age 34, shoemaker; Susan age 33; Sarah L. age 7.

--1860 Census: p.425, 2Wd, Orange NJ: Charles Beach age 44, shoemaker; Susan age 43; Sarah L. age 17.
--1870 Census: p.478, West Orange, NJ: Susan Beach age 54, b.NJ; Sarah L. 28, b. NJ, teacher;
--1880 Census, p.246.2, West Orange: Elias M. Condit 39, surveyor; Sarah L. 37; Chas. B. 7; Phebe A. 6; Clara L. 4; Wilbur 1; Alberk K. age 3 months.; Susan 'Bach' age 63, widow, mother-in-law; all b. NJ, all parents b. NJ

Child of Charles Beach and Susan Losey:
Sarah Louisa, b. July 4, 1842, m. Elias Mulford Condit

- - - - -

BELL

Bell, ALEXANDER b. December 6, 1809
(gmnj) (Shaw)(csl - E99) d. May 27, 1857
(map, plot owner, Sect. F) *Aged 47.5.21*

Notes:
--?Alexander Bell was born 'December 4, 1809' at Abby Parish, Renfrew, Scotland.(IGI)
--Names on stone of Alexander Bell: Louise Bell, q.v.; Catherine Elizabeth Bell, q.v.; Ellen Bell, q.v.; Ann Bell, q.v; Mary Ann Bell, q.v.; Louise Bell, q.v.; Mary Buchanon, q.v.; Mary Dight (Dykes), q.v.; Peter Dight (Dykes), q.v.
--See also: David Watson, bur. in plot of Alexander Bell

- - - - -

Bell, David* b. (abt. 1819)
(map,plot owner, Sect. J) d. (bef. 1870)

wife, Eliza* (Smyth) b. (abt. 1827)
  d. (aft. 1900)

daughter, ISABELLA b. (abt. 1860)
(map, Sect. J) d. December 4, 1860

Bell, JAMES b. (abt. 1848)
(map, Sect. J) d.

Bell, ...	b.
(map, Sect. J)	d.

Notes:
--David m. Nov. 1845, Eliza Smyth
--1850 Census, p.235, Orange Twp., NJ: David Bell, age 32, b. Scotland, carpenter; Eliza, age 23, b. NJ; James, age 3, b. NJ; Ellen, age 1, b. NJ
--1860 Census, p.382, 3Wd, Orange, NJ: David Bell, age 41, b. Scotland; Eliza, age 33, b. NY; James, age 12; Ellen, age 10; Eliza, age 8; Mary, age 6; Eveline, age 4; David age 2; Isabella, age 1 month; all children b. NJ; (near James Bell, q.v.) (near George Stother, q.v.)
--1870 Census, p.409, 3Wd, Orange, NJ: Eliza Bell, age 44; Ellen, age 21, works felt hat factory; Eliza, age 18, works felt hat factory; Mary, age 16, works felt hat factory; David, age 12; Abby, age 8; Sarah, age 6; John, age 4; Lilly, age 3; all b. New Jersey
--1880 Census, p.194.4, Orange, NJ: Eliza Bell, widow, age 53, b. NY; David, age 22,b.NJ, blacksmith; John, age 14, NJ; Lilly, age 12, b. NJ
--1900 Census, p.1A, West Orange, NJ: Eliza Bell, b. Feb. 1826 NY; David, b. Jan. 1852 NJ, laborer; John, b. Jan. 1866 NJ, teamster; 2 boarders

Children of DAVID BELL and ELIZA .....:
James, b. abt. 1848
Ellen, b. abt. 1850
Eliza, b. abt. 1852
Mary, b. abt. 1854
Eveline, b. abt. 1856
David, b. abt. 1858; unm. in 1900
Isabella, b. 1860
Abby, b. abt. 1862
Sarah, b. abt. 1864
John, b. abt. 1866; unm. in 1900
Lilly, b. abt. 1868

- - - - -

Bell, James*	b. (abt. 1825)
(?NJ Will #27776G, 1899)	d. (1880-1900)
wife, Ellen*	b. (October 1831)
	d. (1910-1920)

daughter, LOUISE
(gmnj)(csl - E99)
(on stone of Alex. Bell)

b. (August 12, 1856)
d. August 24, 1856
Aged 12 days

CHILDREN of James Bell
(map, Section E)

b.
d.

Notes:

--1860 Census: p.382, 3Wd, Orange, NJ: James Bell age 35, stone cutter, b. Scotland; Ellen age 28, b. England; Isabella age 3, b. NJ; Emma A. age 4 months.

--1870 Census, p.409, 3Wd, Orange: James Bell, age 45 b. Scotland, stone & brick mason; Ellen 39 b. England; Isabelle age 13 b. NJ; Emma age 10 b. NJ

--1880 Census:p.154D, Orange, NJ:James Bell, age 54, b. Scotland, stone mason; Ellen, wife, age 48, b. England;Isabella, dau., age 23, b. NJ; Emma, dau., age 20, b. NJ; Alister, son, age 5, b. NJ (adj. to Henry S. Condit)

--1900 Census, p.13A, 3Wd, Orange: Ellen Ball b. Oct. 1831, England, widow, 13 born, 3 living; Emma dau b. Jan 1860 NJ, father b. Scotland; Allister M. b. Dec. 1874 NJ, father b. Scotland; (Chas. W. Dexheimer, b. Jan. 1856 NJ, parents b. Germany, housemover; Isabelle b. Sept. 1856 NJ, father b. Scotland, mother b. England; Louise b. Apr 1884 NJ; Marion b. Apr. 1892 NJ; James b. Jan. 1894, NJ.)

--1910 Census, p.12B, 1Wd., Newark: Ellen B. Bell age 78, widow, b. England, 13 born 3 living; at res. of Anna Annin, age 64, widow, b. NJ, parents b. England

--1920 Census, p.1A, 2Wd, Orange: Isabelle Dexheimer age 62, widow; Louise Dexheimer 37, single, bookkeeper; Isabella, age 35, single; James, age 25, single, printer; Emma Bell, sister, single, age 59; all b. Orange, NJ, father b. Scotland, mother b. England

--1930 Census, p.11A, East Orange: Emma A. Ball age 70, single, lodger, b. NJ

Children of James Bell and Ellen .....:
Louise, b. 1856; d. 1856
Isabelle, b. September 1856; m. Charles W. Dexheimer
Emma A., b. December 31, 1862
Alister M., b. December 1874

- - - - -

Bell, JOHN
(map,plot owner,Sect. F)
b. (abt. 1803)
d. November 23, 1873
Aged 70

Notes:
--See: map, plot of Morris Condit
--See: Louisa Hennessey

--1870 Census, p.467, West Orange, NJ: Jane Hennessey, age 37, b. Ireland, keeps grocery; Thomas J. Hennessey, age 10, b. NJ; Mary J. Hennessey, age 8, b. NJ; Nellie, Hennessey, age 6, b. NJ; Martha Hennessey, age 1, b. NJ; John Bell, age 70, b. Ireland, no occupation; Mary A. Hennessey, age 40, b. Ireland, no occupation

- - - - -

Bell, Jonathan*
(map, Sect. F)
b.(abt. 1820)
d.

wife, Ellen*
b. (abt. 1820)
d.

daughter,CATHERINE ELIZABETH
(gmnj) (csl - E99)
(map, Sect. F)
(on stone of Alex. Bell,q.v.)
b. (abt. July 30, 1846)
d. December 30. 1851
Aged 5.5.0

daughter, ELLEN
(gmnj)(csl - E99)
(map, Sect. F)
(stone of Alex. Bell)
b. (abt. May 2, 1851)
d. April 21, 1853
d. (April 3, 1852?)
Aged 1.11.8

Bell, ANN
(map, Sect. F)
(on stone of Alex. Bell, q.v.)
b.
d. September 1888(?)

Bell, Mrs. M. A.
(map, Sect. F)
(on stone of Alex; Bell, q.v.)
b.
d. April 17, 1851

Notes:

--1850 Census, p.180, Harrison, Hudson Co., NJ: John Bell, age 28, b. Scotland, printer; Ellen age 28 b. NY; Catherine E. age 4 b. NJ; Isabella, age 2, b. NJ
--?1860 Census, p.826, Bowmansville PO, Lancaster Twp., Erie Co., NY: John Bell age 40, b. Scotland, tanner/tinner(?); Ellen age 40 b. PA; Isabella age 12, b. NJ; William J. age 6, b. NJ; Hannah age 5, b. NJ; Jeanette or Jean M.W., age 2, b. NY; 2 labor
--?1870 Census, p.372, Lancaster, Erie Co. NY: John Bell, age 50, b. Scotland; Ellen, age 50, b. PA; William John, age 16, b. NJ; Hannah Taylor, age 15, b. NJ; Jenette Ward, age 12 b. NY; Ransey V.P. age 8, b. NY
--?1900 Census, p.1A, Lancaster, Erie Co. NY: "Rancey W." Bell, b. May 1862, single, b. NY, father b. Scotland, mother b. PA, real estate salesman; Isabel, sister, single, b. June 1848 NJ, father b. Scotland, mother b. PA, nurse; William, brother, single, b. Oct. 1855 NJ, father b. Scotland, mother b. PA

Children of Jonathan Bell and Ellen......:
Catherine Elizabeth, b. 1846; d.1851
Isabella, b. June 1848, NJ
Ellen, b. 1851; d. 1853
William John, October 1855, NJ
Hannah Taylor, b. abt. 1855, NJ
Jenette Ward, b. abt 1858, NY
Ransey V.P., b. May 1862 NY

- - - - -

Bell, Nicholas*	b. d.
wife, ANN (gmnj)(csl - E99)	b. April 15, 1822 d. May 17, 1850 *Aged 28.1.2*
daughter, MARY ANN (gmnj)(csl - E99)	b. May 14, 1850 d. October 14, 1852 *Aged 2.5.0*
Bell(?),INFANT of Nicholas (map, Section I)	b. d.

- - - - -

BENNETT

Bennett, Mary Anna b. (abt. 1863)
(map, Section J) d. 1882

Notes:
See: Thomas E. Brown

- - - - -

BENSON

Benson, CHARLES b.
(map, Section J) d.

Benson, MRS. b.
(map, Section J) d.

Notes:
--See: Map, Section J, plot of Mrs. Bentley, q.v.

- - - - -

BENTLEY

Bentley, Mrs. b.
(map, plot owner Sect. J) d.

Notes:
--See: Charles Benson, George Palmer, Mrs. Gilman

- - - - -

BILL

Bill, JOHN b.
(map, Section G) d. November 23, 1873

Notes:
--bur. map, Section G, plot of Morris Condit, q.v.

- - - - -

BIRCH

Birch, THOMAS
(map, Section O)

b. (abt. 1840)
d.

Notes:
--Map says: "Section O., Row 5, Negro Burial Ground"
--1870 Census, p.469&470, West Orange, N: Sarah E. Force, age 30 b. OH; William L., age 14, b. GA; (Mary)Adelia, age 7 b. GA; John P., age 4, b. (Augusta) GA; Thomas Birch, age 30, b. SC, black, coachman; Ellen Flaherty, age 38, b. Ireland, domestic (see: Alfred C. Force, age 40, b. NJ, boot & shoe dealer in Augusta, Georgia)

- - - - -

BISHOP

Bishop, WARREN S.
(map, plot owner, Sect. G)
(gmnj) (csl E78) (nps)

b. (abt. 1821)
d. January 9, 1882
(*Co. B, 26th NJ Inf.*)

Bishop, WARREN S.
(gmnj) (map, Sect. G)

b. (September 17, 1848)
d. April 7, 1862

Bishop, EMILY
(map, Sect. G)

b.
d. November 17, 1851

Bishop, MARY A.
(map, Section G)

b.
d. May 15, 1871

Bishop, PHEBE E.
(map, Sect. G)

b. (1850?)
d.

Bishop, RACHEL
(map, Sect. G)
(second wife)

b. (abt. September 1822)
d. bur. December 2, 1905)
Aged 82

Williams, LAURA
(m. ...Casey; m. .....Williams)
(map, Sect. G)(step dau.?)

b. (abt. January 1848)
d. bur. July 8, 1919
Aged 76.5.8

King, JOSEPH   b.
(map, Sect. G)   d. bur. May 26, 1899
                                 Aged 3 days

Notes:
Served: Civil War, Co. B, 26th NJ Inf.
Served: (?) also, Co. D, 39th NJ Inf.
--Gov't headstone provided
--1850 Census: p.223, Orange Twp, NJ. Warren S. Bishop, a. 29, b. NY, shoemaker with wife, Catherine, a.20; Mary J. age 4; Warren S. age 1; Phebe E. age 2 months
--1860 Census, p.733, 9Wd, Newark: Warren S. Bishop age 39 b. NY, shoemaker; Catherine, age 30 b. NJ; Mary age 13 b. NJ; Warren, age 11 b. NJ
--1880 Census, p.274.2, Newark, NJ: Warren S. Bishop, age 59, shoemaker b. NY; Rachel, age 56, b. NJ; Laura Casey, age 32, 'daughter', widow, b. NJ; John Hopper, age 26, son-in-law, b. NJ, works button factory; Lorena Hopper, age 24, 'daughter', b. NJ
--1900 Census, p.7B, 13 Wd. Newark, NJ: Rachel Bishop, age 77, b. Sept. 1822, NJ, parents NJ, widow, 2 born 1 living; Laura Williams, dau., age 53, b. Jan. 1848, widow, b. NJ, parents NJ, 1 born 1 living, janitoress
--?1910 Census, p.36A, Alms House, 9Wd, Newark, NJ: Laura Williams, age 59, widow, b. U.S.,occup: domestic.

Children of Warren S. Bishop and Catherine L. .....:
Mary J., b. abt. 1846
Warren S., b. 1848; d. 1862
Phebe E., b. abt. 1850

- - - - -

BLAKE

Blake, MABEL   b.
(map, Section O)   d.

Notes:
--Map says: "Section O., Row 5: Negro Burial Ground"

- - - - -

BLANCHARD

Blanchard, JOHN
(map, Section O)

b. (abt. 1824)
d.

Blanchard, JOHN E.
(map, Section O)

b.
d.

Notes:
--Map says: "Section O, Row 5: Negro Burial Ground"

--1850 Census, p.236, Orange Twp., NJ: John H. Matthews, age 42, b.NJ,farmer; 'Elima' age 40; Charlotte age 18; Sarah, age 16; Ambrose, age 14; John H., age 8; Caleb, age 6; Alfred, age 4; Arthur, age 1;all b. NJ; Emma Blanchard, age 12, black, b. NJ; Henry Childs, age 30, b. England, laborer
--1870 Census, p.324, 1Wd, Orange, NJ: John Blanchard, age 46, black, b. NJ, teamster; Margaret, age 28, b. NJ; Ellen, age 13, b. NJ; John, age 11, b. NJ
--1880 Census, p.469.4, East Orange NJ: John Blanchard, age 62, black, b. NJ, parents b. NJ; Margaret, wife, age 38, black, b. NJ, parents b. NJ
--?1880 Census, p.465.4, East Orange, NJ: Sarah Blanchard, age 77, black, widow, b. NJ, parents NJ; Louisa Smith, age 50, black, single daughter, b. NY, parents b. NJ, goes out to work; Charles H. Blanchard, age 18, black, grandson, b. NJ, parents b. NJ; works at grocery store
--?1900 Census, p.8A, 1Wd, Orange, NJ: Margaret Blanchard, age 68, widow, b. NJ, parents b. NJ, black, 2 born 0 living, janitress; Oliver Blanchard, b. June 1877, grandson, single, b. NJ, father NJ, mother b. VA, driver; Mary White, b. Feb. 1830, sister, widow, b. NJ, 2 born 0 living

Children of John Blanchard and Margaret.....:
Ellen, b. abt. 1857
John, b. abt. 1859

- - - - -

BODWELL

Bodwell, PHILANDER J.
(csl-E163)
(map, plot owner, Sect. C)
(NJ Will #17252G,1871)

b. (abt. 1807)
d. July 14, 1871
In 64th year

wife, SARAH (Wilmot) b. (May 4, 1800)
(gmnj)(shaw)(csl - E163) d. November 3, 1870
(map, Section C) *In 71st year*

son, CHARLES A. b. (abt. 1844)
(csl - E162)(map,Sect. C) d. March 24, 1862
　　　　　　　　　　　　Aged 19.5.0

son, WILLIAM b. (abt. 1849)
(csl - E161)(map,Sect. C) d. October 26, 1876
　　　　　　　　　　　　Aged 27

Notes:
--Philander Joseph Bodwell was born in Connecticut, son of Joseph Bodwell and Sabra Stocker
--?Philander Bodwell m. Sarah Milmot, b. May 4, 1800, Southbury, New Haven Co., CT, dau. of Walker Wilmot and Millicent Hitchcock; niece of Charity Wilmot
--Philander 'A.' Bodwell was warden of Grace Protestant Episcopal Church which was carved out from **St. Mark's** Church in March 1854.
--October 28,1867 *New York Times:* "Orange,NJ., on Saturday, October 26th, William, son of Philander and Sarah Bodwell, (died) aged 28 years."

--1850 Census: p.219, Orange Twp., NJ: Philander Bodwell age 42, hatter, b. Connecticut; Sarah age 49, b. CT; William age 10,b. NY; Charles age 7, b. NJ; Sabra Bodwell (mother) age 68 b. Conn.; Charity Wilmot, age 50, b. CT; John Harrison, age 15, b. Germany
--1860 Census: p.326&327,Orange, NJ: Philander J. Bodwell age 52, hat manufacturer, b. Conn; Sarah age 59; William age 20, clerk; Charles age 17, clerk; Charity Wilmot age 62, b. Conn;(Caroline)Amelia Carson age 55 b. Conn; Henry Carson age 10; Philander Carson age 8; Henry Kent age 17, apprentice hatter, b. NJ
--1870 Census: p.314, 1st Ward, Orange, NJ: Philander Bodwell age 63, retired hat manufacturer, b. Conn; Sarah age 70 b. Conn; Caroline A.(Amelia) Carson age 43, b.Conn; Henry (Carson) age 20, printer apprentice; Philander (Carson) age 18, printer apprentice; Charity Wilmot age 75 b. Conn.

Children of Philander Bodwell and Sarah Hitchcock:
Charles A. b. abt 1844, d. 1862
William, b. abt 1849, d. 1876

BOEHNER

Boehner, JOHN B.
(map, Section L)

b. (abt. April 1850)
bur. August 23, 1933
Aged 84.4.17

Boehner, KATHERINE E.
(Heer) (map, Section L)

b. (abt. January 1851)
d. May 1, 1925
Aged 71

Notes:
--bur. map, Section L, plot of Charles Heer, q.v.
--John B. Boehner m. abt.1873, Katherine 'Victoria' Heer.
--1850 Census, p.256, South Ward, Newark, NJ: John 'Bohner' age 28 b. Germany, shoemaker; Barbara (nee Bauer), age 28, b. Germany; John, age 4 months, b. NJ
--1860 Census, p.513, 4Wd, Newark, NJ: John "Bohner" age 39 b. Bavaria, shoemaker; Barbara, age 39 b. Bavaria; John, age 10; Andrew, age 9; Francis, age 7; Sebilla, age 5; Agnes, age 3; all children b. NJ
--1860 Census, p.420, 2Wd, Orange, NJ: Catherine Heer, age 40, b. Ireland; Catherine, age 7, b. NJ; Emily age 3 b. NJ; Ellen, age 3, b. NJ
--1870 Census, p.468, West Orange, NJ: Catharine Heer, age 50 b. Ireland; Catharine, age 18, b. NJ, hat trimmer; Emily Heer, age 16, b. NJ, hat trimmer; Nellie, age 14, b. NJ
--1880 Census, p.252A, West Orange: John Boehner age 30 b. NJ, parents b. Germany, hatter; Cath. wife, age 27 b. NJ, father b. Switzerland, mother b. Ireland; Chas., son, age 7, b. NJ; Ella M., dau., age 4, b. NJ; Ellis, son, age 2, b. NJ
--1900 Census, p.14A, West Orange, NJ: John "Bahner" age 48, policeman; Katherine, age 48; Ellis, age 21, r.r. brakeman; all b. NJ
--1910 Census, p.5A, 3Wd, Orange, NJ: John B. Boehner, age 58, m.37 yrs., twp. policeman; Kate E., age 54, 7 born 3 living; Courtney L. Early Sr. age 30, m. 10 yr. b. KY, electrician at phonograph; Ella M., age 28; Courtney L., Jr., age 6; Lucile, age 4; Bettie, age 1 yr 11 mos.; John B., age 2 mos., all exc. Courtney Early Sr., b. NJ
--1920 Census, p.9B, 2Wd, Orange, NJ: John "Bonvie" age 70, nightwatchman; Victoria, age 66; Ella M. "Barley" age 35, dau.; "Christin" L., age 16, grandson, moving pictures; "Frielle" M., age 14,granddau.; Bette B., age 11,granddau.; Joseph B., age 9 yr. 11 mos.grandson; Ellis B. "Bonvie" age 37, son, brakeman Erie RR; all b. NJ

--1930 Census, p.5B&6A, West Orange, NJ: Ella M. Early, age 45, widow, dressmaker, b. NJ; Cortney,age 26 b. NJ, chauffeur;Elizabeth, age 22, b. NJ model at dress shop; John, age 20, b. NJ, works at park; John Boehner, age 80, father, widower, b. NJ, policeman

Children of John B. Boehner, and Katharine E. Heer:
Charles J.,q.v., b. 1872; m. Catharine V. .....
Ella M., b. abt. 1876; m. Courtney L. Early, Sr.
Ellis B., b. abt. May 1879; m. May......

- - - - -

Boehner, Charles J.*   b. 1872
(map, Section L)   d. (date not inscribed)

Boehner, CATHERINE V.   b. (June) 1877
(stone visible in 2009)   d. 1955

Notes:
--bur. map, Section L, plot of Charles Heer, q.v.
--Charles was son of John B. Boehner, q.v.
--1880 Census, p.252A, West Orange: John Boehner age 30 b. NJ, parents b. Germany, hatter; Cath. wife, age 27 b. NJ, father b. Switzerland, mother b. Ireland; Chas., son, age 7, b. NJ; Ella M., dau., age 4, b. NJ; Ellis, son, age 2, b. NJ
--1900 Census, p.13A, West Orange: Charles Boehner (indexed as 'Bolhuis') b. May?, 1874 NJ, parents b. NJ, m. 3 years, r. r. brakeman; Katherine b. June '1879', b. NJ, parents b. Ireland; John, son, b. Feb. 1899 b. NJ
--1910 Census, p.8B, 2Wd, West Orange: Charles 'Brenn', age 35, b. NJ, conductor?; Catherine age 27; John, age 14; 'Ellihue'? age 7; (page faded and illegible)
--1920 Census, p.14A, 2Wd, West Orange: Charles J. 'Bochorn' age 43, b. NJ, parents b. U.S., conductor, Erie R. R. ; Katherine, age 41, b. NJ, parents b. Ireland; John, age 19, b. NJ, chemist at factory; 'Ellia', age 16, dau., b. NJ

Children of Charles J. Boehner and Katherine V. .....:
John, b. Feb. 1, 1900; d. July 1985 Colorado?
Ella?, b. abt. 1903

- - - - -

BOND

Bond, DANIEL (gmnj)(shaw)(csl-E187) (map, Sect. B, plot owner) (Will #19009G, 1877)	b. (September 15, 1795) d. December 11, 1877 *Aged 82.2.26*
wife, PHEBE (Mitchell?) (csl - E188)(map,Sect. B)	b. (August 14, 1796) d. May 16, 1872 *Aged 75.9.2*
child (CATHERINE M.?) (csl - E190)	b. (July 3, 1820) d. August 10, 1866 *Aged 46.1.7*

Notes:
--Daniel Bond was a West Orange chosen freeholder 1866-78. (Shaw, p.806)
--"John" Bond m. Phebe Mitchell October 3, 1819, Essex Co., NJ.(IGI)
--Phebe Mitchell was bapt. April 14, 1799 at Hanover, NJ. She was daughter of Joseph Mitchell. (IGI)

--1840 Census, Orange Twp: Daniel Bond
--1850 Census: p.239, Orange Twp., NJ: Daniel Bond age 54, NJ, shoemaker; Phebe age 53 b. NJ. (near Charles and Susan Beach)
--1860 Census: p.406, Orange, NJ: Daniel Bond age 64, machine operator; Phebe age 63. Adj. to Joseph A. Condit and John H. Sharp.
--1870 Census: p.467, 3rd Ward, Orange, NJ: Daniel Bond age 74, shoe shop worker; Phebe age 73; William A. Reeve (q.v.) age 23, carpenter.

Child of Daniel Bond and Phebe (Mitchell?):
?Catherine M., b. abt 1820; d. 1866

- - - - -

BONNELL

Bonnell, CHARLES P. (gmnj) (nps)	b. 1838 (March 11, 1836) d. 1911 (October 8, 1914?) *Co. G., 26th NJ Inf.*
wife, Sarah Jane*(Mitchell)	b. (abt. 1837) d. (before 1900)

Notes:
Served: Civil War; Co. G., 26th NJ Inf., Pvt.
--Government stone; he may be buried elsewhere;see below
--Charles was son of John Bonnell, q.v. and Lucinda Edwards.
--Charles m. 1859, Sarah Jane Mitchell; she was born 1837, New York

--1850 Census: p.220, Orange Twp., NJ: John Bonnell age 45, shoemaker, b. NY; Lucinda age 42, NJ; John W. age 19,NJ, shoemaker; Charles P. age 14; Mary E. age 8; Sarah H. age 5; Elizabeth J. age 6 months; Elizabeth, age 20, b. Ireland
--?1870 Census, p.542, Rutland Twp., Dane Co. Wisconsin; Charles 'Bonnel' age 34 b. NJ, farmer; Jane age 23 b. NY; Luella age 2 b. WI; William 5 b. WI; Emma age 2 months, b. Wisconsin
--?1880 Census, p.310.2, Rutland, Dane Co., Wisconsin; "Chas. Bonnel" age 47, b. NJ, farmer;Jane, age 34 b. NY; William 15, labor; L. J. dau. age 13; Edith M. age 10; Anna 8; Charles B. age 4; Llewellyn, son, age 7 mos. b. October; 1 boarder
--1900 Census, p.31B, Jefferson Twp., Montgomery Co., OH; National Home for Disabled Soldiers; Charles 'B' Bonnell, age 64, b. March 1836, NJ, widower
--1910 Census, p.19B, Jefferson Twp., Montgomery Co., Ohio; National Military Home: "Charles B. Bonnel" age 73, widower, b. NJ, inmate
--?1910 Census, p.1B, Rutland, Dane Co., WI: Jane "Bounell" age 63, 'widow', b. NY, parents b. NY, farmer;
Charles B., age 33, b. Wisc., parents b. NY, farm labor; 1 boarder, farm labor.

?Children of Charles Bonnell and Sarah Jane Mitchell:
Luella J., b. abt. 1868
William, b. abt. 1865; m. Rosie G. .....
Edith Emma, b. abt. 1870
Anna, b. abt. 1872
Charles Bertell, b. November 2, 1875
Llewellyn, b. October 1879

- - - - -

Bonnell, JOHN (gmnj)	b. 1805 (October 1805) d. 1890 (April 28, 1890)
wife, LUCINDA (Edwards) (gmnj)	b. 1808 (December 16, 1808) d. 1887 (November 16,1887)

Notes:
--The members of this family are also recorded at adjacent, Old Burying Ground of the First Presbyterian Church. The large headstone is at St. Mark's Cemetery.
--Lucinda Edwards m. John Bonnell November 19, 1825, Essex Co., NJ. She was b. December 16, 1808 at Livingston, daughter of Joseph Edwards and Phebe Cook.(IGI)
--1850 Census: p.220, Orange Twp., NJ: John Bonnell age 45, shoemaker, b. NY; Lucinda age 42, NJ; John W. age 19,NJ, shoemaker; Charles P. age 14; Mary E. age 8; Sarah H. age 5; Elizabeth J. age 6 months; Elizabeth, age 20, b. Ireland
--1860 Census: p.413, 2Wd, Orange, NJ: John 'Bonnd' Bonnell, age 53, shoemaker, b. NJ; Lucinda age 50; Mary E. age 19; Sarah age 15. All b. NJ
--1870 Census: p.350, 2nd Ward, Orange, NJ: John Bonnell age 64, b. NY; Lucinda age 61; Sarah age 26; Charles age 32, jewelry worker.
--1880 Census, p.475.4, East Orange: John Bonnell, age 74 b. NJ; Lucinda, wife, age 71 b. NJ; Sarah, daughter, age 25, b. NJ

Children of John Bonnell and Lucinda Edwards:
Joseph W.q.v., b. 1831?; d. 1871?; m. Amanda Treadwell
John Wesley, q.v., b. 1835; d. 1890; m. Eliza Jenkins
Charles P. q.v., b. 1838; d. 1911?; m. Sarah Jane Mitchell
Mary E., b. 1842; m. Charles R. Lyon
Sarah H. b. 1845
Elizabeth J. b. 1849

- - - - -

Bonnell, JOHN WESLEY b. June 19, 1835 (1830?)
(gmnj)(map, Section O) d. October 12, 1890
(nps)(pension to Eliza) *Drum Major, 7th NJ Vols.*

wife, MRS. J. W. b. (March 1821?)
(Eliza Jenkins) d. (December 2, 1913)
(map, Section O)

Notes:
Served: Civil War; Drum Major, 7th NJ Volunteers
--John was son of John Bonnell, q.v. and Lucinda Edwards.
--John m. Eliza Jenkins May 8, 1848. She was born March 1821, Ireland and d. December 2, 1913, NJ

--1850 Census: p.220, Orange Twp., NJ: John Bonnell age 45, shoemaker, b. NY; Lucinda age 42, NJ; John W. age 19,NJ, shoemaker; Charles P. age 14; Mary E. age 8; Sarah H. age 5; Elizabeth J. age 6 months; Elizabeth, age 20, b. Ireland
--1860 Census, p.413, 2Wd, Orange: John M. 'Bonnd' age 29 b. NJ, shoe cutter; Eliza, age 30 b. Ireland; Elizabeth age 10; Emma 6; William 4; Frederick 1; all children b. NJ
--1870 Census, p.350, 2Wd, Orange: John W. Bonnell, age 38, works at boot/shoe factory; Eliza, age 40, b. Ireland; Emma age 16, dressmaker; William age 13; Frederick age 12; Stephen age 4; Frank age 1; all children b. NJ
--1880 Census, p.96.2, Orange: John W. Bonnell, age 48, hatter; Eliza age 49; Emma, age 25, works at hat mfg.; William F. age 23, age 23, bookkeeper; Frederick A. age 21, hatter; Stephen A. age 13; Benjamin F., age 11; all b. NJ
--1900 Census, p.1B, 2Wd, Orange: Eliza "Bunnell" b. March 1821, Ireland, widow; Emma, b. January 1855 NJ, hat tip maker; William F., b. December 1860, widower, bookkeeper at hat office
--1910 Census, p.18B, 2Wd, Orange: Eliza Bonnell, age 84, b. Ireland, widow; William F. age 51, m.26 yr, b. NJ, bookkeeper at horseshoeing shop; Frank J., age 41, widower, b. NJ, bookkeeper at retail liquors

Children of John Wesley Bonnell and Eliza Jenkins:
Elizabeth I., b. 1849; m. Laurence T. Fell
Emma, b. January 1855
William H. Bonnell, b. 1856; d.1923
Frederick Aloysius, b. 1859; m. Bridget Evangeline Gilluley
Phebe, b. abt. 1866
Stephen A., b. 1867; m. Mary Ann Chambers
Francis John b. 1869; m. Emma Trabold

- - - - -

Bonnell, JOSEPH W.
(gmnj)(csl - EC3)(nps)
(map, Section O)
(pension to widow, Amanda)

b. 1831
d. 1871 (May 16, 1873)
Co. G. 26 NJ Inf.

wife, Amanda* (Treadwell)

b. (abt. October 1828)
d. (September 18, 1914)

CHILD of Joseph W.

b.

(map, Section O)   d.

CHILD of Joseph W.   b.
(map, Section O)   d.

Bonnell, THEODORE   b. (abt. 1849?)
(map, Section O)   d. August 5, 1876

Notes:
Served: Civil War: Co. G., 26th NJ Inf., Pvt. (nps)
--Gov't headstone provided
--see: map, Section O, plot of Mary A. Bonnell
--Joseph W. Bonnell was son of John Bonnell,q.v., and Lucinda Edwards.

--1850 Census, p.222, Orange Twp: Joseph Bonnell, age 24 b. NJ, boot fitter; Amanda age 22 b. NY; Theodore, age 1 b. NJ; David Treadwell age 10? b. NY; boarders
--1860 Census, p.364, 3Wd, Orange: Joseph W. Bonnell, age 33 b. NJ, boot fitter; Amanda age 32 b. NY; Theodore age 11 b. NY; Alviretta, age 5 b. NY; Edward age 9 months b. NY
--1870 Census, p.325, 1Wd, Orange: Joseph W. 'Bonnel' age 44 b. NJ, works boot/shoe factory; Amanda, age 41 b. NY; Theodore age 22, b. NJ, works at felt hat factory; 'Alvarida' age 15, b. NJ; 'Edwin', age 11 b. NJ; David, age 8, b. NJ; Alida, age 3 b. NJ
--1880 Census, p.83.2, Orange: Amanda Bonnell, age 52, b. NY, father b. CT, mother b. NY; Edwin, age 20 b. NJ, butcher; David age 17 b. NJ, clerk; Lydia, age 14 b. NJ; Henry M. Camp, age 33, son-in-law, b. PA, parents b. NJ, clerk in store; Alvaretta Camp, age 25, daughter, b. NJ
--1900 Census, p.2A, 3Wd, Orange: "Amitola" Bonnell, b. Oct. 1828, NY, father b. CT, mother b. NY, widow, 7 born 3 living; Alvaretta Camp, b. Mar 1855, daughter, m. 27 yr, 0 born; Henry M. Camp, b. Apr. 1847, PA, parents NJ, son-in-law, hostler; Alida Lait, dau., b. May 1866 NJ, m. 15 yr, 2 born 2 living; Ruth Lait, b. Sept. 1891, granddaughter, b. NJ, parents b. NJ
--1910 Census, p.4A, 2Wd, Orange: Alvaretta Camp, age 55, widow, b. NJ, 0 born 0 living; Amanda Bonnell, mother, widow, age 82

Children of Joseph W. Bonnell and Amanda Treadwell:
Theodore, b. abt 1849 (see: Thaddeus Edwards)
Alviretta, b. abt 1855; m. Henry M. Camp
Edwin, b. abt 1859
David, b. abt 1862

Alida, b. abt. 1867; m. ..... Lait

- - - - -

Bonnell, Mary A.*   b.
(map, plot owner, Sect. O)d.

Notes:
--In this plot see: Amanda, wife of Joseph W. Bonnell, John W. Bonnell, Theodore Bonnell, etc.

- - - - -

BOYD

Boyd, George N.   b.
(map, plot owner, Sect. J)   d.

Notes:
--See: map, Sect. J, Mrs. Gilman

- - - - -

BRADY

Brady, James S.   b. (abt. 1814)
(map,plot owner, Sect. K)   d.

wife, Apphia Caroline(Ball)   b. (abt. 1822)
                                    d.

son, JAMES E.   b. (abt. March 29, 1851)
(csl - E34)   d. February 13, 1852
(map, Section K)   *Aged 0.10.15*

son, ELLIS M.   b. (abt. 1861)
(map, Section K)   d. August 18, 1905?
                                    Aged 48

Brady, EUGENE(?)   b.
(map, Section K)   d.

Brady, F.....ette (map, Section K)	b. d. August 15, 1863(?)
son, MARSHALL BERTRAND (map, Section K)	b. (abt. 1854 d. November 9, 1893
Brady, EMILY (map, Section K) (wife of Ellis M.Brady)	b. (abt. Dec. 1858) d. October 17, 1917 *Aged 47.10.0*

Notes:
--Apphia was dau. of Noah Ball and Fanny Edwards
--1850 Census, p.239, Orange Twp., NJ: James Brady, age 35, b. Ireland, hatter; Caroline, age 28, b. NJ (same house as Nicholas Miller, q.v.)
--1860 Census, p.391, 3Wd, Orange, NJ: James Brady, age 45, b. Ireland, merchant; 'Affal" C. age 36 b. NJ; Marshall B. age 6, b. NJ; Granville C., age 4, b. NJ; Ellis M., age 1, b. NJ
--1870 Census, p.468, West Orange, NJ: James Brady, age 54, b. Ireland, hatter; "Abby" C. age 46, b. 'Ireland'; Marshall B., age 17 b. NJ, clerk at savings bank; Granville C., age 14, b. NJ; Ellis M., age 10, b. NJ
--1880 Census, p.250.2, West Orange, NJ: Jas. S. Brady, age 66, b. Ireland, hatter; Affie C., age 58 b. NJ; Marshall B., age 26, NY, insurance clerk; Granville C., age 24, works in hat shop, b. NJ; Ellis M., age 19, b. NJ, hatter apprentice; Thomas, age 58, brother, b. Ireland, laborer (same page as John H. Sharp, q.v.)
--1900 Census, p.14A, West Orange NJ: Ellis Brady, b. June 1858 NJ, m.10 yrs., real estate; Emily b. Dec. 1858 NJ, father b. Switzerland, mother b. Ireland

Children of James Brady and Apphia Caroline Ball:
James E., b. abt. 1851; d. 1852
Marshall Bertrand, b. abt. 1854
Granville C., b. abt. 1856
Ellis M., b. abt. 1861

- - - - -

BRINDLY

Brindly, HENRY (csl - E22)(map, Sect. L)	b. (abt. 1805) d. March 28, 1865

Aged 60

Notes:
--Bur. plot of William Crosby, q.v.

- - - - -

BROWER

Brower, ABRAM D. b. 1820 (bapt. Aug., 21, 1820)
(gmnj) (csl - E61) d. November 12, 1864
(map, plot owner, Sect. I) *Co.H, 26th NJ inf*
(nps)(pension to widow, Margaret Ann)

wife, MARGARET ANN b. 1828
(Personett) d. 1901

INFANT of Abram Brower b.
(map, Section I) d.

daughter, CATHERINE b. (abt. 1848)
(map, Section I) d. November 22, 1868
 Aged 20

grandson, EDW. WALLACE b. 1889
(son of John Edwin Brower d. 1889
and Phebe Catherine Sprigg)
(map, Section I)

Brower, HARRIET ANN b.
(map, Section I) d. May 14, 1901

Notes:
Served: Civil War. Co. H, 26th NJ Inf. Pvt. (nps)
Gov't headstone provided; sighted in 2009
He died as a result of wounds suffered in the war. The 26th Regiment "the Flower of Essex Co." boasted that it learned to drill on the battlefield. 123 men of the 26th fell dead or wounded in the siege of Fredericksburg.
--Abram David Brower was the son of David Abram Brower and Margaret Fielding. He married Margaret Ann Personett, July 4, 1844 at Millburn, NJ. She was the daugher of John Personett, q.v., and Fannie Harrison. Margaret married #2, Romanzo Gage, q.v.

--1850 Census, p.228B, Orange: Abram D. Brower, age 30, hatter; Margaret, age 22; Fanny, age 5; Catherine, age 2; Lydia Personett, age 20

--1860 Census:p.377B, Orange 3rd Ward, NJ:Abram Brower, age 40, hatter, b. NJ; Margaret M. age 32; Fanny, age 15; Catherine age 12; Abram W., age 9; Ada L.,age 7; Lydia P. age 3; Mary E., age 1 Also at address, Lydia Personett a. 30; George W. Brown,a.13,hatter apprentice (son?); Charles Personett,brother-in law a 21,hatter; George Tucker a. 19, hatter apprentice,b.Conn.; Gorham Devereux,a. 39, mason, (Near George Personett and his wife Caroline)

--1870 Census: p.350, 2nd Ward Orange, NJ: Margaret Brower age 42, seamstress;; Lydia age 13; John age 5; Also at house:, Thomas Casey age 30 felt hat worker, b. NY; Hannah age 24 b. Ireland; James age 9 months; "Thomanzo" Gage (q.v.) age 46, felt hat worker.

--1880 Census, p.225.1, 3Wd, Harrison, Hudson Co., NJ: "Romulus" Gage, age 50, married, b. CT, parents b. CT, hatter; Margaret Gage, wife, age 52, b. NJ, parents b. NJ; Edward 'Gage" (stepson, John Edwin Brower) age 15, b. NJ

Children of Abram D. Brower and Margaret A. Personett:
Fannie, b. abt 1845; m. William Haycock
Ella, b. 1846; d. 1846
Catherine, b. abt 1848; d. 1868
Abram D., b. abt. 1851; m. Mary .....
Ada L., b. abt 1853; m. Charles S. Cadmus
Lydia P., b. abt. 1857; m. #1, Wellington F. Potter
    m. #2, Frederick W. Foster; m. #3, George W. Weeks
Mary Em, b. abt 1859; m. Edward Ouderkirk
Almira, b. abt 1862
John Edwin, b. Feb. 28, 1865, m. Phebe Catherine Sprigg

- - - - -

BROWN

Brown, Amzi*	b. (abt. 1821)
	d.
wife, MARY ELIZABETH (gmnj)(csl - E89)	b. (August 1, 1836)
	d. December 1, 1862
	Aged 26.4.0

Notes:
--Amzi Brown was b. abt 1821 at Orange. He was son of Kelitah Brown (q.v.) and Maria Canfield.
--?Amzi m. #2, January 5, 1865, Aramenta Cresman at East Brunswick, Middlesex Co., NJ.

--1850 Census, p.198, Orange Twp: Kelita Brown, age 64, shoemaker; Maria age 52; Amzi, age 27, shoemaker; all b. New Jersey

- - - - -

BROWNE

Browne, ANNA P.
(gmnj)(csl - E75)
(map, plot owner, Sect. G)
b.
d. (no dates)
Aged 75

Browne, ARTHUR
(gmnj)(csl - E77)
(map, Sect. G)
b. (abt. 1834?)
d. August 6, 1865
Aged 34 years

Suddenly

Browne, CATHERINE
(gmnj)(csl-E76)(map,Sect.G)
b. (abt. 1832?)
d. (no dates)
Aged 34 years

A native of France

Browne, CHILDREN of WM.
(map, Section G)
b.
d.

Browne, CHILD
(map, Section G)
b.
d. (in Anna P. Browne grave)

Browne, CHILDREN of T.
(map, Section G)
b.
d.

Brown, MISS
(map, Section G)
b.
d.

Notes:
--See: Christopher Harrold; see: Frances L. Morgan

--1850 Census, p.110, 8Wd, New York City: Arthur Browne age 28 b. Ireland, tailor?; 'Cath' age 25, b. France; William, age 8 months b. NY
--1860 Census, p.338, 8Wd, New York City: Arthur Browne, age 34, b. Ireland, tailor?; 'Ctharne' age 28 b. 'Ireland'; William L., age 10, b. 'Ireland'; Arthur age 9, b. 'Ireland'; 'Slena A' age 7 b. 'Ireland'; Amelia C., age 1 month, b. NY
--1880 Census, p.151.2, Orange: Arthur 'Brown' age 27, b. New York, father b. England, mother b. France; hatter; Ellen K., wife, age 28 b. Vermont, father b. Canada, mother b. Ireland; Frances, daughter, age 2 b. NJ

Children of Arthur Browne and Catherine .....:
William L., q.v., b. abt. 1850; d. 1900
Arthur, q.v., b. abt 1851; m. Ellen K. .....
Selena A.. b. abt. 1853
Amelia C. b. 1860

- - - - -

Brown(e), ARTHUR   b. (abt. 1851)
(map, ch.property,Section N) d. October 4, 1908
(removed to (St.John's? Cem.) *Aged 56*

wife, Mary Ellen*   b. (abt. 1852)
                              d. (aft. 1920)

Notes:
--son of Arthur Browne, q.v.
--1860 Census, p.338, 8Wd, New York City: Arthur Browne, age 34, b. Ireland, tailor; 'Ctharne', age 28 b. 'Ireland'; William L., age 10 b. 'Ireland'; Arthur, age 9 b. 'Ireland'; 'Slena A.' age 7 b. Ireland; Amelia C., age 1 month, b. NY
--1880 Census, p.151.2, Orange, Essex Co., NJ: Arthur Brown, age 27 b. NY, father b. England, mother b. France, hatter; Ellen K., wife, age 28 b. VT, father b. Canada, mother b. Ireland; Frances, dau., age 2, b. NJ
--1900 Census, p.9A, 3Wd, Orange, Essex Co., NJ: (near corner of Scotland Rd. and Main Street)Arthur Browne, b. Jan 1851,m.25 yr, b."NY,parents NY", hat finisher; Ellen b. May 1854 NY, 3 born-3 living, b. "NY, father b. Ireland, mother b. France" (birthplace data is reversed); Selina b. May 1882 NJ; Eva, b. March 1893 NJ; John Morgan, b. Oct. 1874, son-in-law, m.5 yrs. b. NY, father NY, mother NJ, hat flanger; Frances Morgan, dau., b. Sept. 1877 NJ; John D.

Morgan, grandson, b. Dec. 1897; Irving Morgan, grandson, b. Aug. 1899

--1900 Census, p.9A, 3Wd, Orange, Essex Co., NJ: Arthur Browne, b. Jan 1851,m.25 yr, b."NY,parents NY", hat finisher; Ellen b. May 1854 NY, 3 born-3 living, b. "NY, father b. Ireland, mother b. France" (birth data is reversed); Selina b. May 1882 NJ; Eva, b. March 1893 NJ; John Morgan, b. Oct. 1874, son-in-law, m.5 yrs. b. NY, father NY, mother NJ, hat flanger; Frances Morgan, dau., b. Sept. 1877 NJ; John D. Morgan, grandson, b. Dec. 1897; Irving Morgan, grandson, b. Aug. 1899

Children of Arthur Browne and Ellen K. ......:
Frances, b. abt. Sept. 1877; m. John Morgan
Selina Mary, b. abt. May 1882; m. ... Flynn; m. ... Leonard
Eva, b. abt. March 1893; m. ..... Carvell

- - - - -

Brown, James* (map, plot owner, Sect.N)	b. (abt. 1830) d.
wife, Maria*	b. (abt. 1831) d.
son, JOHN EDWARD (gmnj)(csl-EC6)(map,Sect. N)	b. November 6, 1854 d. November 8, 1861
daughter, MARY (gmnj)(csl-EC6)(map,Sect. N)	b. July 23, 1860 d. December 28, 1860

Notes:
--The children above are also recorded as buried at the adjacent Old Burying Ground of the First Presbyterian Church

--1860 Census: p.411, 2Wd., Orange, NJ: James Brown age 30, hatter, b. Ireland; Maria age 29 b. Ireland; John E. age 5, b. NY; James age 4 b. NY; Mary age one month b NJ.

Children of James Brown and Maria .....:
John Edward, b. 1854; d. 1861
James, b. abt 1856
Maria, b. 1860; d. 1860

- - - - -

Brown, KELITAH
(map, Section F)
b. (December 23, 1776)
d. (December 23, 1867)

wife, AMANDA
(Maria Canfield?)
(gmnj)(shaw)(csl - E96)
b. April 4, 1792
d. January 13, 1859
Aged 67

daughter, MARY
(csl - E95)(gmnj)(map,Sect. F)
b. (abt. 1822)
d. March 17, 1838

*In
Memory of
Mary Brown
who died March 17th, 1838
In the 17th year
of her age*

son, CHARLES C.
(map, plot owner, Sect. F)
b. (abt. 1815?)
d. May 10, 1882

Brown, MARIA
(map, Section F)
b.
d. January 14, 1859

Note:
--See: John Vermilye
--Kelitah Brown married, October 4, 1812, Maria Canfield. She was daughter of Ebenezer Canfield and Rhoda Baldwin. Her parents are buried in the Old Burying Ground.

--1830 Census, p.426A, Orange Twp: Kelitah Brown
--1840 Census, p.258A, Orange Twp: Kelitah Brown
--1850 Census: p.198, Orange Twp., NJ: Kelitah Brown, age 64, shoemaker, b. NJ; Maria age 52, b. NJ; Amzi age 29, shoemaker, b. NJ
--1850 Census, p.336, West Ward, Newark, NJ: Harriet Vermilyea age 33 b. NJ; John age 14 b. NJ; Ellen 12 b. NJ;
Anna 11 b. NY; William 9 b. NJ; Harriet 3, b. N; Ira E. Brown, age 20 b. NJ, carpenter; 5 boarders
--1850 Census, p.450, North Mulberry Wd, Philadelphia PA: C. C. Alvord age 38 b. MA, carpenter; Sarah 37 b. NJ; Mary 13 b. PA; Emily 10 b. PA; Henry 8 PA; Ellen Hale, age 25 b NJ; Ruth Hale age 50 b. NJ

--1860 Census, p.336, 1Wd, Orange: Ira E. Brown, age 39 b. NJ, carpenter; Mary E. age 38 NJ; Anna L. age 3, b. NJ; 'Kalila' Brown, age 75, b. NJ, shoemaker

--1880 Census, p.509.4, East Orange, NJ: Ira E. Brown, age 49, carpenter; Mary E., age 48; Charles C., age 62, brother, single, stonemason; Nicholas W. Rutan, age 26, son-in-law, painter; Anna L. Rutan, age 23, daughter; George M. Brown, age 15, son, drugstore clerk; Ella A. Brown, age 12, daughter; Daniel H. Brown, age 10, son; Ada B. Rutan,a ge 4, granddaughter

Children of Kelitah Brown and Maria Canfield:
George,
Sarah Ann, b. July 15, 1813;
    m. Christopher Columbus Alvord
Charles, b. abt 1815; d. May 10, 1882(?)
Harriet, b. June 3, 1816; d.July 26, 1858;
    m. John Vermilye, q.v.
Amzi, q.v., b. abt. 1821; m. Mary Elizabeth .....
Mary, b. abt. 1822, d. 1838
Ira E., b. abt. 1830, m. Mary E. .....
Caroline
John

- - - - -

Brown, THOMAS   b. (abt. 1818)
(gmnj) (csl-E28)   d. January 9, 1857
                                    Aged 39

"A native of Hexam, England"

Notes:
--?Thomas Brown "chr. March 2, 1817, Stonecroft With Hexham - RC, Hexham, Northumberland, England; son of Joan (sic) Brown and Maria Robson"

--?1850 Census, p.169, Bloomfield, Essex Co., NJ: Thomas Brown, age 35, b. England, teacher; Margaret age 25 b. England; William C. age 14, b. NY; James, age 7, b. NJ; Margaret A. age 2, b. NJ; Mary J. age 9 months, b. NJ

- - - - -

Brown, Thomas E.*   b. (abt. August 1834)

(map, plot owner, Sect. J)   d. December 5, 1916?
                                          Aged 81.3.15

wife, ANNA G.(Featherstone?)
(map, Section J)   b. (abt. April 1836)
                                          d. September 10, 1911
                                          Aged 75.5.4

Brown, THOMAS W.   b. (abt. 1813)
(map, Section J)   d. February 1, 1864
                                          Aged 51

Brown, CHILD   b.
(map, Section J)   d.

Notes:
--See: Thomas F. Featherstone
--See: ..... Bennett
--1860 Census, p.385, 3Wd, Orange, NJ: Thomas E. Brown, age 25 b. Ireland, hatter; Anna G., age 24, b. Ireland; Francis, son, age 4 b. NJ; Grace, age 3, b. NJ; Helena, age 1, b. NJ
--1900 Census, p.5A, 1Wd, Orange, NJ: Thomas E. Brown, b. Aug. 1834, Ireland, m.45 years, hatter; Anna G. b. April 1836 Ireland; Grace E. b. June 1859 NJ; Henry Featherstone, b. July 1837 Ireland, bro.-in-law; 2 boarders
--1910 Census, p.5B, 3Wd, East Orange, NJ: Thomas E. Brown, age 75, b. Ireland; Anna G., age 75 b. Ireland, 8 born 5 living; Grace E., dau. age 50 b. NJ, dressmaker; Mary Bennet, age 47, dau., widow b. NJ, 12 born 8 living, private nurse; 1 boarder

Children of Thomas E. Brown and Anna G. Featherstone:
Francis, b. abt. 1854
Grace E., b. abt. 1857
Helen, b. abt. 1859
Mary Anna, b. abt. 1863; d.1882; m. ..... Bennett, q.v.

- - - - -

Brown, WILLIAM L.   b. (abt. 1850?)
(map, Sect. G)   d. March 19, 1900
(map says "wrong space")

wife, Sarah F.*　　　　　　　　b. (abt. February 1856)
　　　　　　　　　　　　　　　d.

Notes:
--?Son of Arthur Browne, q.v.
--?1860 Census, p.338, 8Wd, New York City: Arthur Browne, age 34, b. Ireland, tailor?; 'Ctharne' age 28 b. 'Ireland'; William L., age 10, b. 'Ireland'; Arthur age 9, b. 'Ireland'; 'Slena A' age 7 b. 'Ireland'; Amelia C., age 1 month, b. NY
--?1870 Census, p.370, 3Wd Orange NJ: William Brown, boarder, age 20 b. NJ, works at felt hat factory
--?1880 Census, p.157.2, Orange, NJ: William L. Brown, age 28, b. NY, father b. Ire., mother b. France; Sarah F., age 26, b. Ire.; Grace C., age 6 NJ; Willie, age 4 NJ; Agnes, age 1 NJ
--?1900 Census, p.4B, 1Wd, Orange, NJ: Sarah F. Brown, widow, b. Feb. 1856 Ireland; Sarah A., b. Sept. 1885 NJ; George W., b. July 1887 NJ

Children of William L. Brown, and Sarah F. ......:
Grace C., b. abt. 1874
William L., b. abt. 1876; m. Mary F. .....
Agnes, b. abt. 1879
Sarah A., b. abt. Sept. 1885
George W., b. abt. July 1887

- - - - -

Brown, WILLIAM T.*　　　　　b.
(gmnj)(csl-E53)　　　　　　　　d. (January 30, 1864)
(nps) (map, Section G)　　　　　*Co.E, 71st NY Inf.*

Notes:
Served: Civil War; Co. E, 71st Reg't., NY Inf,, Pvt. (nps)
Gov't headstone provided: 'd. January 30, 1864'
('gov't. stone seems to have been moved' 2009)
(Co. E. was recruited at Orange, NJ)

--?1850 Census, p.136&137 East Ward, Newark, NJ: J. D. Brown, age 40 b. Scotland, physician; Margaret age 38 b. Scotland; James L., age 16, b. NY, trunkmaker; Jessie B., dau., age 15, b. NY; W. T., son, age 10, b. NY; John, age 7, b. NY; Catherine, age 6, b. NY; Margaret, age 3, b. NY; Agnes B., age 1, b. NJ

--?1860 Census, p.189, San Andreas PO, Twp.5, Calaveras Co.,CA: James D. Brown, age 48, b. Scotland, physician; no other family members listed
--?1870 Census, p.52&53, Bridgeport, Fairfield Co., CT: James D. Brown, age '68', b. Scotland, physician & surgeon; Marguerite, age 55, b. Scotland; Marguerite, age 18, b. "Scotland"; 1 servant

- - - - -

BRUEN

Bruen, JOHN C.   b. (July 20, 1783)
(gmnj)(shaw)(csl-E200)(Sect.A)   d. February 15, 1826
(NJ Will #11714G, 1826)

> *John C. Bruen*
> *Died Feb. 15th 1826*
> *In the 45th Year*
> *of his age*

wife, HANNAH (Harrison)   b. July 30, 1781
(gmnj)(csl - E201)(map, Sect. A)   d. March 1, 1848

> *Hannah*
> *wife of*
> *John C. Bruen*
> *Born July 30th 1781*
> *Died March 18th, 1848*
> *In the 67th year of her age*

Notes:
--John Bruen m., August 30, 1806, Hannah Harrison, daughter of Simeon Harrison,q.v., and Hannah Crane. (*Harrison Gen.*,p.46)(m. by Rev. Asa Hillyer, Presb. Ch., Orange)
--John F. Bruen was b. July 20, 1783 at Newark, son of Eleazer Bruen and Rebeckah Ellis.(IGI)

- - - - -

BUCHANAN

Buchanan, MARY   b. (abt. 1781)
(gmnj)(shaw)(csl - E99)   d. January 29, 1848

(map, Section F)
(Will #13689G, 1848)   On Alexander Bell (q.v.) stone

Mary Buchanan
Died Jan. 29th, 1848
Age 67 years

Notes:
--See: map, Section F, plot of John Bell

- - - - -

BURNSIDE

Burnside,
ANDREW TEN EYCK   b. (July 9, 1778)
(gmnj)(csl - E195)   d. June 1816
                             In 39th year

wife, SARAH (Crane)   b. (June 6, 1778)
(gmnj)(csl - E195)   d. May 22, ... (1824)
(map, Section A)   *In 47th year*

son, CORNELIUS DAVIS   b. (abt. 1816)
(gmnj)(csl-E195)(map,Sect. A) d. August 1833

Cornelius Davis
Son of
Andrew & Sarah
Burnside
Died Aug. 1833
In the 17th year of his age
Thy Brother shall rise again

daughter, ARIAN   b. October 18, 1805
(gmnj)(shaw)(csl - E199)
(map, Section A)   d. July 19, 1874
(NJ Will #18119G, 1874)   *Aged 66*

son, GEORGE   b. (abt. 1811)
(gmnj)(shaw)(csl - E194)   d. February 26, 1861
(map, Section A)   *Aged 50*

son, JAMES W.
(gmnj)(shaw)(csl - E193)
(map, Section A)

b. (abt 1813)
d. April 23, 1871
Aged 58

Notes:
--Andrew TenEyck Burnside was born July 9, 1778, Albany, NY, son of Thomas Burnside, Sr. and Arian/Arientje TenEyck who were married November 7, 1773 at Albany.(Roots.web.com)
--Andries Burnside was baptised August 12, 1778 at the Dutch Church, Albany, New York, son of Thomas Burnside and Arien TenEyck.(IGI)
--Sarah was daughter of Col. Isaac Crane(q.v.) and Joanna Ogden.
--1850 Census: p.233, Orange Twp., NJ: Frances Burnside age 34 b. NJ; Charlotte age 18, b.NJ; Arian, daughter, age 16, b. NJ; George age 40, b. NJ, (bro-in-law) seaman.
--1850 Census, p.160, East Ward, Newark: "Jowel" (Joel) W. Condit, age 50 merchant, real estate value $25,000; Margaret 46; Mary H. 24; Caleb H. age 20, student; Margaretta, age 18; Sarah H. age 16; Ann E. age 14; Alice E. age 7; all b. NJ; Arian Burnsides, age 40 b. NJ; 3 other persons, hired help?
--1870 Census: p.187, East Orange, NJ: James Burnside age 50, hatter, b. NJ. At residence of Stephen Allen a 40, hatter and his wife Martha A. a 40.

Children of Andrew Ten Eyck Burnside and Sarah Crane:
Thomas, q.v., b. 1802; m. Frances Bruen
Arian, b. 1805; d.1874
George, b. 1811; d. February 26, 1861
James W., b. 1813; d. 1871
Cornelius Davis, b. 1816; d. 1833

- - - - -

Burnside, Francis*
(map, plot owner, Sect. A)

b.
d.

- - - - -

Burnside, THOMAS
(gmnj)(csl - E195)(map,Sect.A)
(NJ Will #12488G)

b. July 20, 1802
d. September 25, 1833
In 32nd year

wife, FRANCES S. (Bruen)
(csl - E195)

b. March 7, 1807
d. January 16, 1883

(NJ Will #20849G, 1883)

daughter, SARAH b. February 15, 1830
(csl - E195)(map, Sect. A) d. May 12, 1835
In 6th year

Notes:
--?Thomas was son of Andrew Burnside,q.v., and Sarah Crane.
--Thomas Burnside married Frances S. Bruen, April 14, 1829, Essex Co., NJ (IGI)

--1850 Census: p.233, Orange Twp., NJ: Frances Burnside age 34 b. NJ; Charlotte age 18, b.NJ; Arian, daughter, age 16, b. NJ; George age 40, b. NJ, seaman.
--1860 Census: p.423, 2Wd, Orange, NJ: Frances Burnside age 52 b. NJ; Charlotte age 27, b.NJ; Francis C. Cantin age 28, lawyer, b. NY; Arian age 25 b. NJ; Charles K. age 2, b. NJ; George Burnside age 49, (Brother-in-law) b. NJ, mariner.
--1870 Census: p.481, West Orange, NJ: Frances Burnside age 55, b. NJ; Charlotte Burnside, age 30; Francis C. Cantine, a.33, lawyer, b. NY; Arian B.(Burnside) Cantine, age 28; Charles K. Cantine age 12 and Thomas Cantine, age 9 and Frank Cantine, age 1.
--1880 Census: p.260B, West Orange, NJ: Francis C. Cautine, age 47, b. NY, lawyer; Arian, wife, age 44, b. NJ;Charles K. Cautine, son, age 22, dry goods; Thomas B. Cautine,son, age 19, b. NY, at home; Francis M. Cautine, son, age 13, b. NY;Frances Burnside, mother, age 67, b. NJ; Charlotte Burnside, sister, age 47, b. NJ; Mary Davis, age 36, b. Scotland,widow, domestic;Elizabeth Davis, age 16, b. Scotland, domestic.
--1910 Census, p.7A, Banister, Halifax Co. VA: Francis C. Cantine age 78, m.53 yr, b. NY, own income; 'Oraian' B, age 76 b. NJ; Thomas B. age 49 b. NJ, labor on home farm; Charlotte C. Burnside, age 79 b. NJ; 1 servant

Children of Thomas Burnside and Frances Bruen:
Charlotte C. , b. abt. 1831; d. after 1910 unm.
Arian, b. abt. 1835, m. Oct. 22, 1856, Francis Carr Cantine

- - - - -

CANNING

Canning, CHILD of J. b.

(map, Section H)   d.

Notes:
--See: map, Section H, plot of Isaac Baldwin

- - - - -

CARPENTER

Carpenter, HENRY   b.
(gmnj)(CSL - E13)   d. (January 25, 1877)
(map, ch. property,Sect. M)   U.S. Navy
(? NJ Will #19308G, 1878)

CHILD of H. Carpenter   b.
(map, ch.property,Sect. M)   d. April 12, 1872

Notes:
Served: Civil War, United States Navy
Gov't headstone provided; observed in 2009
--?1870 Census, p.470, West Orange: Henry C. Carpenter age 30, b. England, hatter; Alice, age 26, b.Ireland
--?Alice Carpenter b. August 26, 1869, West Orange; daughter of Henry Carpenter and Alice .....

- - - - -

CHEETHAM

Cheetham, GEORGE   b.
(map, plot owner, Sect. M)   d. April 20, 1859

wife, MARY A.   b.
(map, Section M)   d. April 11, 1861

Notes:
--?1860 Census, p.368, 3Wd, Orange, NJ: Robert Cheatham, age 45, b. England, hatter; Mary A., age 43 b. NJ; ALice, age 5, b. NJ; James, age 3, b. NJ; John, age 24, b. NJ
--?1870 Census, p.351, Piscataway, Middlesex Co., NJ: John Vorhees, age 76, b. NJ, farmer; Julietta Vorhees, age 38 b. NJ; Peter Low, age 21, b. NJ, farm labor; Alice 'Cheater' age 16, b. NY, domestic; James 'Cheater' age 14, b. NJ, farm labor

CLARK

Clark, MILTON PALMER
(map, Section A)

b.
d. January 27, 1896

Notes:
--See: Henry Proctor

- - - - -

CLARKE

Clarke, JAMES HENRY
(gmnj)(map,plot owner)
(map, plot owner, Sect. H)

b. March 1, 1836
d. December 17, 1916
Aged 81.9.16

wife, CATHARINE E.
(map, Sect. H)

b. (abt. 1837)
d. June 17, 1889
Aged 52

Clark, INFANT of Jas.
(map, Section H)

b.
d. January 26, 1865

Clark, INFANT of Jas.
(map, Section H)

b.
d. November 10, 1859

Notes:
--1860 Census: p.369, 3Wd, Orange, NJ: James Clark age 24, hatter, b. Ireland; Catherine age 23 b. Ireland
--1870 Census, p.409, 3Wd Orange: James Clark, age 34 b. Ireland, grocer; Catherine age 33 b. Ireland; Alexander age 9 b. NJ; Catherine E. age 8 b. NJ; Edward T. Jones age 29 b. Wales, coachman; 'Sarahphine' Howard age 25, b. Bavaria, works at felt hat factory.
--1880 Census, p.163.2, Orange: James Clark age 47 b. Ireland, works at hat factory; Catherine age 46, b. Ireland; Alexander age 18 b. NJ, works at hat factory; Catherine age 16 b. NJ, dressmaker; Frances R. age 9 b. NJ; Mary Ann, age 3, b. NJ
--1900 Census, p.7A&B, 3Wd, Orange: George Mittleston b. Feb. 1868, m.6 yr, b. NJ, father b. Germany, mother b. NY,
fire chief at telephone co.; Frances R. b. Oct. 1871 NJ; Douglas C., b. Jan. 1895 NJ; "L. Henry" Clark b. Mar 1836 Ireland, father-in-law,

gardener; Catherine C. Clark, b. Feb. 1865, sister-in-law, b. NJ, dressmaker; Mary Ann Clark b. Feb. 1878 NJ, sister-in-law, telephone operator
--1900 Census, p.11A, 4Wd, Orange: Alexander Clarke, b. November 1860,m.13 yrs., b. NJ, parents b. Ireland, foreman at hat factory; Ida, b. Feb. 1865 NJ, parents b. NJ, 0 born 0 living
--1910 census, p.6A, 3Wd, Orange: James H. Clark age 74, b. Ireland, widower; Rose Middleston age 33, b. NJ; George Middleston age 34; Douglas Middleston, age 15 b. NJ; (census page faded)

Children of James H. Clarke and Catherine .....:
Alexander, b. November 1860; m. Ida M. .....
Catherine E., b. February 1865
Frances Rose, b. October 1871; m. George 'Mittleston'
Mary Ann, b. February 1878

- - - - -

CLAY

Clay, George* (map, plot owner, Section O)	b. (abt. 1820) d.
1st wife, SARAH (map, Section O)	b. d.
2nd wife, MRS.(Elizabeth) (map, Section O)	b. (abt. 1823) d. September 3, 1862
Clay, JOSEPH L. (map, Section O)	b. d. February 10, 1879

Notes:
--1850 Census, p.234, Orange Twp. NJ: Elizabeth Smith, age 49 b. NJ; George, age 27 b. NJ, shoemaker; Joseph, age 23, b. NJ, shoemaker; Moses, age 20, b. NJ, shoemaker; George Clay, age 30 b. NY, shoemaker; Elizabeth Clay, age 28, b. PA; Pierson Bond, age 23, b. NJ, shoemaker; Elias Sindler, age 30, b. NJ, shoemaker; Josiah Kilburn, age 37, b. NJ, shoemaker; Elizabeth Smith, age 26, b. NJ; Thomas J. SMith, age 3 b. NJ; Joseph W., Smith, age 1, b. NJ; Mary A. Dorr, age 14, b. Ireland

--1860 Census, p.370, 3Wd, Orange, NJ: George Clay,age 40 b. NY, shoemaker; Elizabeth, age 37, b.PA; Sarah A., age 15, b. PA; George, age 8, b. NJ; James, age 5, b.NJ; Eliza J., age 2, b. NJ

?Children of George Clay and Sarah .....:
Sarah A., b. abt. 1845

Children of George Clay and Elizabeth .....:
George, b. abt. 1852
James, b. abt. 1855
Eliza J., b. abt. 1858
?Joseph L.

- - - - -

CLEGG

Clegg, Kershaw (map, plot owner,Sect. N)	b. (abt. November 1847) d.
wife, Annie (Wood)	b. (abt. 1852) d.
CHILD of Kershaw (map, Section N)	b. d.
CHILD of Kershaw (map, Section N)	b. d.
CHILD of Kershaw (map, Section N)	b. d.

Notes:
--Kershaw was son of William Clegg, q.v.
--Kershaw had a flower and seed business on Valley Road opposite St. Mark's Church.
--1880 Census, p.265D, West Orange, NJ: Kershaw Clegg, age 32, b. England, farm laborer; Anna, wife, age 29 b. NJ; Caroline, dau., age 2 b. NJ; William, son, age 6 mos. b. NJ; Wm. McCormick, age 18 b. NJ, farm laborer
--1900 Census, West Orange, NJ: Kershaw Clegg, age b. Nov. 1847, England; Annie, age 48; Carrie, age 22; William, age 20; Fanny, age 18; Laura, age 16; Addie, age 14; Ernest, age 12; Edward, age 9; William, (father) age 77

Children of Kershaw Clegg and Annie ......:
Carrie, b. abt. 1878
William, b. abt. 1880
Fanny, b. November 22, 1881
Laura, b. abt. 1864
Addie, b. abt. 1866
Ernest, b. abt. 1868

- - - - -

Clegg, Samuel   b. (abt. December 1857)
(map, plot owner, Sect. N)   d. (aft. 1920)

wife, Margaret A.   b. (abt. 1848
                                  d. (bef. 1910)

CHILD   b.
(map, Section N)   d.
CHILD   b.
(map Section N)   d.
CHILD   b.
(map, Section N)   d. November 21, 1881

Notess:
--Samuel was son of William Clegg, q.v.
--1870 Census, p.170 East Orange, NJ: William Clegg, age 46; Caroline, age 44; Ann, age 17; Samuel, age 13; James, age 5; 2 other persons
--1880 Census, p.264B, West Orange, NJ: William Clegg, age 55, b. England, housepainter; Caroline, wife, age 53 b. England; Samuel, married son, age 25 b. England, coachman; Margaret, dau-in-law, age 32 b. NJ, father b. Scotland, mother b. England; John, son, age 18, b. England, florist; James, son, age 14, b. NJ; Lillie Clegg, age 1, b. NJ, granddaughter
--1900 Census, p.7B, 3Wd, Orange, NJ: Samuel Clegg, d. Dec. 1837, m.22 yr. b. England, immig. 1863, provisions dealer; Margaret A. b. June 1847, 7 born 3 living; b. NJ, parents b. England; Lillian P., b. NJ March 1879, bookkeeper in prov. store; Jas. F. b. March 1882 NJ, clerk in prov. store; Margaret S., b. March 1886 NJ, at school
--1910 Census, p.4A, 3Wd, Orange, NJ: Samuel "Celgg", age 52 b. England, merchant/butcher store; Lillian, age 31, b. NJ; James, age 28 b. NJ, store clerk; Margaret, age 24, b. NJ, store clerk

--1920 Census, p.18B, Raritan, Monmouth Co., NJ: Samuel Clegg, age 62, b. England, widower; Lillie P., age 40, b. NJ, single dau.; Margaret, age 33, b. NJ, single, dau.

Children of Samuel Clegg and Margaret A. ......:
Lillian P., b. abt. March 1879
James F., b. abt. March 1882
Margaret S., b. abt. March 1886

- - - - -

Clegg, WILLIAM
(map, plot owner, Sect. N)
b. (abt. June 1822)
d. December 11, 1901

WIFE of Wm. Clegg(Caroline)
(map, Section N)
b. (abt. 1826)
d. (aft. 1880)

Smith, VIRGINIA L.
(map, Section N)
b. (abt. 1918)
d. May 17, 1919
Aged 1

Smith, CHARLES L.
(map, Section N)
b. (abt. 1918)
d. September 29, 1918

Notes:
--January 26, 1863: Arv. New York from Liverpool, S.S. Harvest Queen: William Clegg, age 38 painter; Caroline, age 35; Daniel, age 16, miner; Kershaw, age 14, spinner; Hannah, age 7; Samuel, age 5; John William, age 1; all b. England (listed adj. to the family of James Kershaw)
--1870 Census, p.170, East Orange, NJ: William Clegg, age 46; Caroline, age 44; Anna, age 17; Samuel, age 13; William, age 8; James, age 5; 2 other persons
--1880 Census, p.264B, West Orange, NJ: William Clegg, age 55, b. England, house painter,Caroline, wife, age 53 b. England; Samuel, son, age 25 b. England, coachman; Margaret, dau-in-law, age 32, b. NY; John Clegg, son, age 18 b. England, florist; James, son, age 14, b. NJ; Lillie, age 1, b. NJ, granddaughter
--1900 Census, West Orange, NJ; William Clegg, age 77, b. England; at res. of son, Kershaw Clegg

Children of William Clegg and Caroline .....:
Daniel, b. abt. 1847
Kershaw, b. abt. 1849

Hannah, b. abt. 1856
Samuel, b. abt. 1858
John William, b. abt. 1862
James, b. abt. 1865

- - - - -

CLEVELAND

Cleveland, SAMUEL C.
(gmnj)(shaw)(csl - E69)
(map, plot owner, Sect. H)

b. (March 12, 1801)
d. October 25, 1851
Aged 50

wife, Sarah M.* (Kaneck)

b. (February 24, 1805)
d.

son, HENRY VAIL
(csl - E69)(map, Sect.H)

b. November 9, 1831
d. October 23, 1850

Notes:
--Samuel Caldwell Cleveland was born March 12, 1801, Guilford, Connecticut, son of George Cleveland and Catey Caldwell.
--Samuel m. July 9, 1828 at Philadelphia, Sarah M. Kaneck, b. February 24, 1805. (Rootsweb.com)
-- There was a William Cleveland (brother?), Warden, of **St. Mark's** Church in 1884. (Shaw p. 809)

--1850 Census: p.202, Orange Twp., NJ: Samuel C. Cleveland age 49, accountant, b. Connecticut; Sarah M. age 46, b. Penna; Henry V. age 18, shoemaker b. NY; Henrietta O. age 16, b. NY; Sarah K. age 14, b. Penna; DeLancey age 11, b. Penna; Hobart age 8, b. NJ.
--1860 Census: p.344, 1Wd, Orange, NJ: Sarah M. Cleveland age 56 b Pennsylvania; Sarah K. age 23 b. Penna; Delancy age 21, bookkeeper, b. Penna; Hobart age 18, clerk, b. NJ; Isabella Branch, ,age 13 b. Washington, DC.
--1870 Census, p.222, East Orange: Wm. B. Munn, age 52, b. NJ, hatter; Henrietta, age 50, b. NJ; Frank, age 25, b. NJ, clerk at store; Florence, age 22, b. NJ; Richard McDaniel age 27 b. NY, builder mason; Mary McDaniel age 25, b. MD; Sarah Cleveland, age 65, b. PA; Sarah Cleveland, age 26, b. PA
--1880 census, p.480.1, Rahway, Union Co. NJ: Sarah Cleveland age 76, b. 'NJ', widow, boarder

Children of Samuel C. Cleveland and Sarah M. Kaneck:
Henry Vail, b. 1831 NY; d. 1850
Henrietta O., b. abt 1834, NY; m. William B. Munn
Sarah K. b. abt 1836, PA
DeLancey, b. abt. 1839, PA; m. Fanny M. ......
Hobart, b. abt 1842 NJ; m. Nellie .....

- - - - -

COCHRAN

Cochran, MRS.   b.
(map, Section H)   d. March 6, 1877

Notes:
--Bur. map, Section H, plot of Isaac Baldwin, q.v.

- - - - -

COLE

Cole, SALINA   b.
(map, Section O)   d.

Notes:
--Map says: "Section O, Row 5: Negro Burial Ground"

- - - - -

Cole, MRS. Stephen   b.
(map, Section A)   d.

Notes:
--See: John Markwith

- - - - -

COLLINS

Collins, EDWARD   b.
(map, grave owner, Sect. F)   d. June 27, 1853

Collins, GEORGE   b.

(map, Section F)   d. May 19, 1856

Collins, MARY   b.
(map, Section F)   d. October 13, 1858

Notes:

--?1850 Census, p.156, East Wd, Newark, NJ: Edward G. Collins, age 35, tailor; Mary B., age 32; Charles, age 8; Alfred, age 7; Thomas, age 5; Caroline L., age 0; Margaret J. Luse, age 32

- - - - -

COLLINSON

Collinson, HENRY   b.
(map,ch. property, Sect. H)   d.

Collinson, CHILD of Henry   b.
(map, ch. property, Sect. H)   d.

Notes:

- - - - -

CONDIT

Condit, DAVID   b. (November 25, 1768)
(map, Section E)   d. (July 18, 1851)

wife, SARAH (Chandler)   b. (abt. 1780)
(map, Section E)   d. (aft. 1850)

daughter, SARAH   b. February 3, 1809
(gmnj)(shaw)(map,Sect. E)   d. February 15, 1884

daughter, FANNIE   b. (abt. 1812)
(map, Section E)   d.

son, HORACE   b. (November 19, 1801)
(map)   d. October 24, 1855

son, David Chandler*   b. (1814)

d. (d. April 7, 1814)
Aged 0.3.7
(Bur. Old Ground, Orange)

Notes:
--bur. map, Section E, Vault of Horace Condit, q.v.
--David Condit, b. November 25, 1768 son of Col. David Condit and Joanna Williams. He m. Sarah Chandler of Elizabethtown. David d. July 18, 1851. David was a blacksmith and lived at Centre Street, Orange.(*Condit Gen.*, p.26)

--1850 Census, p.227, Orange Twp: David Condit, age 81 b. NJ; Sarah, age 70; Sarah F. age 40; Fanny, age 38; Martha F. age 12; all b. New Jersey
--1860 Census, p.391, 3Wd, Orange: Sarah F. Condit age 50; Fanny age 48; Martha F. age 20, school teacher; all b. NJ
--1870 Census, p.375, 3Wd, Orange: Sarah T. Condit age 61, b. NJ, $10,000 real estate value; Fannie Condit, age 59, $10,000 real estate value; 3 boarders
--1880 Census: p.173.1, Orange, NJ: Sarah T. Condit, single, age 71; Fanny Condit, age 69, single

Children of David Condit and Sarah Chandler:
Stephen Van Rensselaer, b. March 22, 1800;
    m. Mary A. Groome
Horace b. November 19, 1801 d. October 24, 1855, unm.
George W. b. July 30. 1803; m. 1827, Julia C. Dickerson;
    m. 1840, Sarah A. Ogden
Susan b. August 5, 1805 d. January 4, 1828
Sarah b. February 3, 1809 d. February 15, 1884, unm.
Fanny b. April 28, 1811; d. aft. 1880; unm.
Mary B. b. November 10, 1812; m. Orlando Quimby
David C. b. January 1814 d. April 7, 1814

- - - - -

Condit, DAVID W.   b. (September 26, 1801)
(gmnj) (shaw)(csl - E27)   d. May 11, 1884
(NJ Will #21255G, 1884)   *In 83rd year*

wife, CORNELIA (Perry)   b. (March 31, 1806)
(csl - E26)   d. August 27, 1874
     Aged 68

daughter, ROSENA   b. (abt. 1835)
                               d. April 9, 1876
                               Aged 41

Notes:
--David W. Condit was b. September 26, 1801, son of Japhia Condit and Dorcas Dodd.
--He married Cornelia Perry July 8, 1829 at Orange, New Jersey. David was a member of the First Presbyterian Church of Orange. He was a carpenter and a farmer. He died at the old homestead. (*Condit Gen.*, p.56)
--Cornelia Perry was born March 31, 1806. (IGI)

--1850 Census, p.243, Orange: David W. Condit, age 49, farmer; Cornelia age 44; 'Ronna' age 16; John age 12; all b. New Jersey
--1860 Census, p.394, 3Wd, Orange: David Condit age 58 farmer; Cornelia 54; Rosanna 26; John age 21; all b. NJ
--1860 Census, p.394, 3Wd, Orange: Lewis Condit age 30, farmer; Harriet, age 33; Charles age 3; all b. NJ
--1870 Census, p.461, West Orange: David W. Condit, age 68, farmer; Cornelia age 63; Rosena, age 36, dressmaker
--1880 Census: p. 274.2, West Orange, NJ: John P. Condit, age 40, farmer; Martha A. age 40, b. NJ; Elmer, age 7, b. NJ Stewart, age 5, b. NJ; David, age 3, b. NJ; Bentley, age 1, b. NJ; David W. Condit, age 78, father, farmer, b. NJ, widower.

Children of David W. Condit and Cornelia Perry:
Lewis Condit, b. June 6, 1830, m. Harriet E. Pierson
Rosena Condit, b. November 29, 1834; d. 1876; unm.
John P. Condit, b. November 2, 1838 m. Martha A. Baldwin

- - - - -

Condit, George W.*   b. (abt. 1826
(map, Section E)   d. (July 29, 1883)

wife, Charlotte* (Ford)   b. (abt. May 5, 1831)
                                d. (February 1903)

son, CHARLES   b.
(map)   d. May 5, 1855

son, CHARLES b. (abt. 1848)
(map) d. April 16, 1850

daughter, LUCY b. (abt. October 12, 1851
(map) d. August 24, 1855

?son, JOHN H. b.
(map) d. February 28, 1856

?Condit, ADA b.
(map) d.

?Jones, CHARLOTTE b.
(map) d. February 6, 1900

Notes:
(?)Served: Civil War, Co. M, 2nd NJ Calvary (nps)
--Members of this family bur. in plot of Henry D. Condit,q.v.
--George W. Condit was son of Henry Day Condit, q.v. and Rachel King

--1850 Census, p.235, Orange Twp., NJ: George W. Condit, age 23, b. NJ; Charlotte, age 23, b. NY
--1860 Census, p.372, 3Wd, Orange NJ: George W. Condit, age 36, shoemaker; Charlotte, age 29 b. NY; Christopher, age 2; Augusta, age 8; Ann A. Haggerty, b. NY
--1870 Census, p.335, 2Wd, Orange, NJ: George W. Condit, age 34, b. NJ, works boot/shoe factory; Charlotte, age 32, b. NY; Christopher, age 12 b. NJ; George, age 8, b. NJ; Henry, age 4, b. NJ; Augusta, age 18, b.NJ, works felt hat factory
--1880 Census, p.128.3, Orange NJ: George W. Condit, age 52, works in hat shop, Charlotte, age 42, b. NY, parents b. Ireland; Christopher, age 21; George, age 15; Henry, age 13

Children of George W. Condit and Charlotte Ford:
Charles, d. April 16, 1850
Augusta, b. abt. 1852
Charles, d. May 5, 1855
Christopher, b. abt 1858
George Ford, b. abt. 1862
Henry, b. abt. 1866
son, d. June 5, 1883

- - - - -

Condit, HENRY D.
(map, plot owner, Sect. E)
b. (abt. 1809)
d. October 31, 1850

wife, Rachel* (King)
b. (abt. 1810-1816)
d. (aft. 1880)

Condit, CHARLES
(map, Section E)
b.
d. April 16, 1850

Condit, CHARLES
(map, Section E)
b.
d. May 5, 1855

Condit, ANN E.
(map, Section E)
b.
d. June 27, 1854

daughter, MARY E.
(m. Charles Duryea)
(map, Section E)
b. (abt. June 10, 1847)
d. (abt. June 24, 1883)

Condit, GEORGE F.
(map, Section E)
b.
d. June 18, 1907

Condit, SON of G. Condit
(map, Section E)
b.
d. June 5, 1883

Condit, ADA
(map, Section E)
b.
d.

Condit, LUCY
(map, Section E)
b.
d. August 24, 1855

Condit, JOHN H.
(map, Section E)
b.
d. February 28, 1856

Jones, CHARLOTTE
(map, Section E)
b.
d. February 6, 1900

Notes:
--Henry Day Condit was son of Uzal Condit and Phebe Wade
--Rachel was dau. of Gideon King

--1850 Census, p.231, Orange Twp., NJ: Henry D. Condit, age 41, shoemaker; Rachel, age 40; Elizabeth, age 20; Charles D., age 14; Mary C., age 3; all b. NJ
--1870 Census, p.14, 7Wd, Newark, NJ: Rachael Condit, age 48; Charles Duryea, age 26, work at hat factory; Mary E. Duryea, age 22; James Duryea, age 1; all b. NJ
--1880 Census, p.44B, Newark, NJ: Rachel Condit, widow, age 63, b. NJ; Charles W. Duryee, son-in-law, age 37 b. NJ, hatter; Mary E. Duryee, dau., age 32, b. NJ, hat trimmer; James Duryee, grandson, age 11 b. NJ

Children of Henry Day Condit and Rachel King:
George W., q.v., b. abt. 1826, d. July 29, 1883;
    m. Charlotte Ford
Elizabeth, b. abt. 1830
Anna E., d. May 27, 1854
Charles, d. May 15, 1854
Mary E., b. June 10, 1847, d. June 1883; m.Charles Duryea

- - - - -

Condit, HENRY S. (map, Section K) (NJ Will #27825G, 1899)	b. (July 19, 1819) d. June 17, 1899 *Aged 79*
first wife, SARAH E.(Robbins) (csl - E44)(map,Sect. K)	b. (abt. 1822) d. December 8, 1850 *Aged 28*
second wife, Matilda Perine* (Babb) (map, Section K)	b. (August 5, 1820) d. (August 11, 1892)
(?)daughter, _ _ _AH (stone found in 2009)	b. d. (December ....)

Notes:
--Henry S. Condit was son of William M. Condit and Maria Stryker
--He m. #1, April 13, 1854, Sarah Robbins, dau. of James P. Robbins, q.v.
--He m. #2, April 12, 1854, Matilda Perine Babb, daughter of William George Babb and Anna Earle

--1850 Census, p.235, Orange Twp: Henry S. Condit age 30, b. NJ, hatter; Sarah E. T. Condit, age 27 b. NY; James P. Robbins, age 55 b. NY; Matilda Robbins, age 40, b. NY; Robert P. Robbins, age 10 b. NJ; John J. Aymar age 52 b. NY, clerk; Sarah Aymar age 50, b. England; Eliza Babb, age 48, b. NY; Catherine Kelly, age 10, b. NJ
--1860 Census, p.406, 2Wd, Orange: Henry S. Condit age 41, b. NJ,hatter; 'Amelia' age 40, b. NY; William M. age 67, b. NJ, bar keeper
--1870 Census, p.243, Winchester, Scott Co., Illinois: Henry Condit age 50, b. NJ, hat & cap merchant; Matilda, age 49 b. NY
--1880 Census: p.154.4, Orange, NJ: Henry S. Condit, age 60, b. NJ, hatter; Matilda P. Condit, wife, age 59, b. NY

- - - - -

Condit, Horace*   b.
(map, plot owner, Sect. E)   d.

Notes:
--See: David Condit

- - - - -

Condit, Ichabod*   b. (December 8, 1787)
(NJ Will #13111G,1841)   d. (December 8, 1840)
     (Bur. Old Ground, Orange)

wife, Elizabeth* (Leonard)   b. (September 12, 1789)
     d. (November 11, 1825)
     (Age 36.1.29)
     (Bur. Old Ground, Orange)

second wife,   b. (February 5, 1810)
Phebe (Williams)   d. (August 20, 1873)

daughter, ELIZABETH ANN
(gmnj)   b. May 1, 1813
     d. August 27, 1874

son, Joseph*   b. (abt 1817)
     d. (August 17, 1819)
     (Aged 2.10.8)
     (Bur. Old Ground, Orange)

Note:
--Ichabod d. December 8, 1840 on the 43rd anniversary of his birth. His wife, Elizabeth d. November 11, 1825, age 36.1.29, and his son, Joseph Augustus d. August 17, 1819, age 2.10.8. All buried in the Old Ground.
--Ichabod Condit was b. December 8, 1787, son of Joseph Condit and Elizabeth Harrison. He m. #1, Elizabeth Leonard. He m. #2 Phebe Williams (dau. of Enos Crane William and Abia Munn). Phebe was b. February 5, 1810 and died August 20. 1873. Ichabod was a merchant and shoe dealer at Orange.(*Condit Gen.*, p.45)

--1860 Census, p.268, 3Wd., Newark: Caroline W. Waldron, age 29, widow; Julia C. 5; Annie E. 3; Phebe Condit age 52, widow; all b. NJ; 1 servant
--1880 Census, p.276.4, Kearney, Hudson Co. NJ: James W. Johnston,age 49 b. NY, butcher; Caroline W. age 49 b. NJ; William age 14 b. NJ; Mary age 10 b. NJ; Annie Waldron,a ge 23, stepdaughter, b. NJ

Children of Ichabod Condit and Elizabeth Leonard:
Elizabeth Ann Condit, b. May 1, 1813; d. Aug. 27, 1894
    m. Rev. James Alfred Williams, q.v.
Joseph A. Condit, b. abt 1815; d. 1819
Joseph A. Condit b. July 8, 1819; q.v.

Children of Ichabod Condit and Phebe Williams:
Caroline Williams Condit, b. November 16, 1830;
    m. Tunis A.Waldron; m. James Johnson

- - - - -

Condit, IRA
(gmnj)(shaw)(map,Sect.E)
(csl-E124 Family Vault)
(Will #18134G, 1874)

b. October 14, 1791
d. December 18, 1873
(small pox)

wife, REBECCA (Condit)
(gmnj)(shaw)(map)

b. September 28, 1798
d. December 12, 1873
(small pox)

son ALVIN MARCUS
(gmnj)(shaw)(map)
(Will #18132G, 1874)

b. January 31, 1820
d. December 12, 1873
(small pox)

daughter, Julia* b. at 1836
 d. (April 3, 1837)
 (Aged 1.3.0)
 (Bur. Old Ground, Orange)

daughter, HANNAH E. b.
(map, Section D) d. March 6, 1894

Notes:
--Ira was son of Joel Condit and Sarah Wheeler. He m. Rebecca Condit, b.September 28, 1798 d. December 12, 1873 daughter of Simon Condit and Hannah Pierson.
--Rebecca Condit was daughter of Simon Condit and Hannah Pierson.(*Williams Gen.*,p.54)
--Alvin m. Mary W. Crane of Newark, February 24, 1853. She was b. September 21, 1828 and died January 17, 1891. He was a farmer in West Orange where he died. Children were Louis A. and Frank.(*Condit Gen.*, p.77)

--1850 Census, p.238, Orange Twp: Ira Condit 58, farmer; Rebecca 50; Alvin M. 30, farmer; H. Elizabeth 28; Mary N. 25; Margaret M. 12; Julia J. 8; Sarah 49; Ruth 45; all b. NJ
--1860 Census, p.417, 2Wd, Orange: Ira Condit age 68, farmer; Rebecca 62; Hannah E. 34; Margaret M. 21, select school teacher; Julia J. 19; all b. NJ; 2 farm laborers
--1870 Census, p.479, West Orange: Ira Condit age 78 b. NJ, farmer; Rebecca, age 72 b. NJ; Mary C. 'William', age 4, b. NJ; John M. 'William', age 34, b. NJ,carpenter
--1870 Census: #378 West Orange, NJ: Alvin M. Condit age 50, farmer; Mary W. age 42; Louis A. age 15.

Children of Ira Condit and Rebecca Condit:
Alvin Marcus, b. January 3, 1820
Hannah E. b. October 24, 1821 d. unm. March 6, 1894
Mary W. b. October 31, 1823, d. unm. October 1854
Sarah b. December 11, 1825, d. August 13, 1843
Frances b. April 9, 1828, d. June 24, 1845
Margaret Matilda,b. August 12, 1833, d. Apr. 4,1837
Julia Ida b. December 27, 1835, D. April 3, 1837
Margaret Matilda,(II)b. January 12, 1838;
 m. John Newton Williams, of Daniel
Julia Ida, (II)b. August 11, 1841;
 m. Charles Payson Williams

(*Williams Gen.*,p.26)(*Condit Gen.*, p.31)

- - - - -

Condit, ISAAC B. (map, plot holder, Sect. E)	b. d. October 9, 1848
wife, Eliza* (Gray)	b. (abt. 1811) d.
Condit, PHEBE C. (map, Section E)	b. (abt. 1784) d. (aft. 1850)
Condit, OSCAR J. (map, Section E)	b. d.
Condit, ... (map, Section E)	b. d.
Wade, MARY J. (map, Section E)	b. d. May 14, 1856

Notes:
--See: Theodore Gray for other burials in this plot
--?Isaac Baldwin Condit was b. abt. 1821, son of Uzal Condit and Phebe Wade.(Uzal d. bef. 1850)
--Isaac Condit m. Eliza Gray, dau. of John Gray and Mary .....; Eliza was sister of Theodore Gray, q.v.

--1850 Census, p.235, 14Wd, NYC: 'May' Gray, age 60, b. NJ; Theodore Gray, age 24, b. NY; Eliza 'Conditt', age 39, b. NJ; Mary Gray, age 19, b. PA; Phebe A. Gray, age 14, b. NY; Joseph Conditt, age 4, b. NY; Harriott Conditt, age 7, b. NY
--1850 Census: p.464, Orange, NJ: Uzal W. Condit age 34; Martha E. age 32; William B. age 12; Mary E. age 10; Emeline P., age 8; Antonette, age 6; Phebe, age 66

Children of Isaac B. Condit and Eliza Gray:
Harriet, b. abt. 1843
Joseph (Oscar?), b. abt. 1846 (?served Civil War)

- - - - -

Condit, Joel Wheeler
Family Vault (erected 1843)

Condit, JOEL W.
(gmnj)(csl-123) b. July 2, 1795
(map,vault owner, Sect. D) d. September 11, 1860

(NJ Will #15349G, 1860)

wife, MARGARET (Harrison) b. May 10, 1800
(map, Section D) d. (aft. 1860)

Condit, CALEB HARRISON b. (August 3, 1828)
(map, Section D) d. January 16, 1881

Condit, FRANCIS b.
(map, Section D) d.

Condit, JULIA b.
(map, Section D) d.

Condit, SARAH b.
(map, Section D) d.

Notes:
--Tomb of Anna Condit was broken open.(gmnj)
--Joel Wheeler Condit, b. July 2, 1795 son of Joel Condit and Sarah Wheeler. Joel died September 11, 1860. He was one of the leading merchants of Newark, NJ.
--He married, February 10, 1823, Margaret Harrison daughter of Caleb Harrison, q.v., b. May 10, 1800.

--1840 Census, p.302, East Ward, Newark: Joel W. Condit
--1850 Census, p.160, East Ward, Newark: "Jowel" W. Condit, age 50 merchant, real estate value $25,000; Margaret 46; Mary H. 24; Caleb H. age 20, student; Margaretta, age 18; Sarah H. age 16; Ann E. age 14; Alice E. age 7; all b. NJ;
Arian Burnsides, age 40 b. NJ; 3 other persons, hired help?
--1860 Census, p.488, Newark, Essex Co. NJ: Joel W. Condit 60, acid and dye store, real estate value $125,000; personal $100,000; Margaret age 50, real estate value $30,000; Mary H. age 30; Margaret, age 26;

Estelle age 22; Alice age 17;all b. NJ; 1 coachman; 1 chambermaid; 1 waiter; 1 cook

Children of Joel Wheeler Condit and Margaret Harrison:
Mary H., b. abt 1824;
    m. Rev. Horace S. Bishop, Rector of
    Christ Episcopal Church in East Orange.
Charlotte M., b. abt 1826
Caleb Harrison, b. 3 August 1828
Margaret, b. March 11, 1831
Sarah Katherine, b. September 23, 1833
Estelle B., b. March 17, 1835;
    married Thomas Talmadge Kinney
Alice C., b. 1838; d. bef. 1843
Alice C., b. 9 February 1843
(*Williams Gen.*,p.26)(*Condit Gen.*, p.31)

- - - - -

Condit, John P.*	b. (November 2, 1838)
(map, Section L)	d. (aft 1920)
(tranferred from Lewis Condit, q.v.)	
wife, Martha A.*(Baldwin)	b. (August 5, 1839)
	d. (1900-1910)
son, RANDOLPH B.	b. (abt. 1871)
(csl - E19)(map, Sect. L)	d. July 5, 1878
	Aged 7
son, ROLAND	b. (abt. 1869)
(csl - E20)(map, Sect. L)	d. October 3, 1879
	Aged 10
daughter, ADA B.	b. (August 23, 1867)
(csl - E18)(map, Section L)	d. February 6, 1869
	Aged 1.5.14
son, BENTLEY B.	b. (December 7, 1878)
(csl - E21)	d. March 23, 1881
(map, Section L)	*Aged 2.3.16*
son, DAVID W.	b. (October 3, 1876)

(map, Section L)   d.

Condit, EMILY(?)   b.
(wife of David W. Condit)   d.
(map, Section L)

Condit, Miss ROSENA   b.
(map, Section L)   d.

Notes:
--John P. Condit was b. November 2, 1838, son of David W. Condit (q.v.) and Cornelia Perry.
He m. November 2, 1865, Martha A. Baldwin, b. August 5, 1839. John died "May 14, 1907" (after 1910). He was a farmer, residing on his father's land at West Orange.

--1850 Census, p.243, Orange: David W. Condit, age 49, farmer; Cornelia age 44; 'Ronna' age 16; John age 12; all b. New Jersey
--1860 Census, p.394, 3Wd, Orange: David Condit age 58 farmer; Cornelia 54; Rosanna 26; John age 21; all b. NJ
--1870 Census, p.461, West Orange: John Condit, age 31, farmer; Martha age 31; Roland, age 4 months; all b. NJ
--1880 Census: p.274B, West Orange, NJ:John P. Condit, age 40, farmer; Martha A. age 40; Elmer, age 7; Stewart, age 5; David, age 3; Bentley, age 1; David W. Condit, age 78, farmer.(q.v.)
--1900 Census, p.1A, West Orange: John P. Condit, b. Nov. 1838, m.34 yrs. farmer; Martha A. b. Aug. 1839, 7 born 3 living; Elmer b. Feb. 1873, single, carpenter; Stuart G. b. Aug. 1864, m.2 yr, dairyman; Edith, b. Dec. 1872, daughter-in-law; Marian b. August 1899; all b. New Jersey
--1910 Census, p.4B, 4Wd, Orange: John P. Condit, age 72, retired farmer, widower; Elmer 37, m. 7 yr, carpenter; Betsey I., age 35, daughter-in-law b. Maine, m.7 yr.; Lillian D. age 6 granddaughter; Ethel M. age 4, granddaughter; John E. age 3, grandson; all except Betsey b. NJ
--1920 Census, p.8B, 4Wd, West Orange: Elmer Condit 46, office work; Bessie 44; Lillian 15; Ethel 14; John 13; Carmelia 8; John age 81, widower, retired; all b. NJ; adjacent to Stewart Condit, age 45

Children of John P. Condit and Martha A. Baldwin:
Adda Condit, b. August 23, 1867
Roland Condit, b. September 12, 1869
Randolph Condit, b. July 31, 1871

Elmer Condit, b. 19 February 1873
Stuart Gomer Condit, b. August 12, 1874; m. Edith M. .....
David W. Condit, b. October 3, 1876
Bentley B. Condit, b. December 7, 1878
(Condit Gen., p.56, 113)

- - - - -

Condit, JOSEPH A. (map, plot owner, Sect. C) (gmnj)(csl - E142) (Will #20869G, 1883)	b. July 8, 1820 d. November 10, 1881(?)
wife, HARRIET NEWELL (Mooney)(map, Sect. C) (gmnj)(csl - E143)	b. June 17, 1818 d. February 24, 1880
dau.,HARRIET CLARA (csl - E145)(map,Sect. C)	b. (March 31, 1847) d. February 21, 1849 *Aged 1.10.21*
dau.,HARRIET CLARA (csl - E146)(map, Sect. C)	b. (September 30, 1849) d. February 27, 1851 *Aged 1.4.27*
son, ICHABOD (csl - E144)(map, Sect. C)	b. (September 16, 1843) d. February 26, 1870 *Aged 26.5.10*
son, HENRY NEWELL (csl - E147)(map, Sect. C)	b. (November 15, 1859) d. June 2, 1860 *Aged 0.6.17*

Notes:
--Joseph A. Condit was son of Ichabod Condit and Elizabeth Leonard. He m. Harriet N. Mooney. Joseph was a merchant and shoe dealer at Orange.(*Condit Gen.*,p.101)
--"The shoe manufacture was continued by his grandson, Joseph A. Condit, till 1861, when he failed in business by reason of heavy losses at the South." (*History of the Oranges*, p.275)
--Harriet was daughter of (?Henry Mooney and Fanny Sutfin, m. July 1811)

--1850 Census: #689, Orange Twp., NJ: Joseph A. Condit age 29, merchant; Harriet N. age 31; Sarah E. age 8; Ichabod age 6; Ann M. age 5; Harriet C. age 7 months.
--1860 Census, p.406, 2Wd, Orange: Joseph A. Condit age 39 merchant; Harriet M. 40; Sarah E. 18; Ichabod 16, student; Anna M. 15; Grace H. 8; Alice, 5; Joseph A. 3; all b. New Jersey
--1870 Census, p.357, 2Wd, Orange: Joseph A. Condit 50, works boot/shoe factory; Harriet 52; Sarah 28; Grace 18; Alice 15; Joseph A. 13; Mary J. 8; all b. NJ; Annie Wheeler, age 25, b. NJ; John Wheeler, age 1, b. Louisiana; 2 servants
--1880 Census, p.61.2 Orange: Jos. A. Condit 63, widower, shoe agent; Alice 25; Joseph A. 23, store clerk; Mary I. 18; Ann M. Wheeler, age 35, widow; John C. Wheeler, age 11, b. Louisiana; 1 servant

Children of Joseph A. Condit and Harriet Newell Mooney:
Sarah E. b. April 22, 1842
Ichabod b. September 16, 1844 d. February 26, 1870
Anna M. b. May 28, 1845; m. ..... Wheeler(?)
Harriet C. d. infancy
Harriet C. d. infancy
Grace H. b. February 12, 1852
Alice b. September 29, 1855
Joseph Augustus b. April 22, 1857
Henry N. d. infancy
Mary Isabelle b. October 3, 1861

- - - - -

Condit, Lewis* b.
(map, plot owner, Sect. L. d.
(transferred to John Condit,q.v.)

- - - - -

Condit, Morris Z. b. (March 12, 1807)
(map, plot owner, Sect. C) d. (before 1880)

wife, Abby A. (Lyon) b. (abt. 1820)
  d. (December 19,1886)

daughter, SELENA PHEBE b. (August 19, 1844)
(csl - E85)(map, Sect. C) d. September 16, 1845
  Aged 1.0.18

daughter, FRANCES ANN   b. (abt. 1837)
(csl-E86)(gmnj)(map Sect. C)   d. (November 24, 1852)
In 15th year

Notes:
--Morris Z. Condit was b. March 12, 1807, son of Jonathan Condit and Abigail Baldwin. He m. Abby Ann Lyon of Parsippany. (She) d. December 19, 1886 at Des Moines, Iowa.(*Condit Gen.*, p.74)

--1850 Census, p.245, Orange Twp: Morris Condit age 43, hatter; Abby A. age 38; Adelia age 16; Samuel W. 14; Frances A. age 11; Daniel M. age 8; all b. New Jersey
--1860 Census, p.136, Des Moines, Polk Co., Iowa: Morris Condit age 54, b. NJ, day labor; Abba age 43 b. NJ; Daniel M. age 16, b. NJ
--1870 Census, p.255, 5Wd, Des Moines, Polk Co. IA: Abbey A. Condit, age 49 b. New Jersey
--1880 Census, p.378.1, 5Wd, Des Moines, Polk Co. IA: Abbie A. Condit age 61, widow; Jane, age 27, daughter, single; James, age 21, son, single, laborer; all listed as "b. Ohio, parents b. Ohio" (adopted children?)

Children of Morris Z. Condit and Abby A. Lyon:
Adelia Morris, b. abt. 1834; d. May 6, 1882; unm.
Samuel Wilbur, b. abt. 1836; "lost at sea en route from
   British America to California"
Frances A., b. 1837 d. November 24, 1852
Daniel Morris, b. abt. 1842; d. July 26,1863; Civil War,
   Vicksburg Co.B, 23rd Iowa Infantry
Selina Phebe, b. 1844; d. 1845

- - - - -

CONDOR

Condor, MARY A.   b.
(map,ch property,Sect. H)   d. January 17, 1864

Notes:
--?1860 Census, p.387, 11 Wd., Newark, NJ: Adam Condor, age 36, b. Prussia, laborer; Mary, age 37, b. Prussia

- - - - -

COOPER

Cooper, HENRY C. b. October 28, 1820
(gmnj)(ch property, Sect. I) d. July 9, 1884
(nps)
wife, Catherine* b. (abt. 1831)
 d. (bef. 1870)

Notes:
--Served: Civil War, Co. E., 7th NJ Inf., Captain (nps)
--1860 Census: p.325, 1 Wd., Orange, NJ: Henry Cooper age 39, mason, b. Bavaria; Catherine age 29 b. Baden; Mary H. age 7, b. NJ; Josephine age 5; Maxmillian age 3; Hannah age 8 months.
--1870 Census: p.345, 2nd Ward, Orange, NJ: Henry Cooper, age 49, brick mason; b. Prussia; Mary age 17, works felt hat factory; Josephine age 14; Henry M. age 13, works hat shop; John age 8; Louis age 6, Joseph age 2.
--1880 Census, p.468.1, East Orange: Albert Poeller, age 31, b. Germany, hatter; Mary H. Poeller age 26, wife, b. NJ; Josephine Cooper, b. NJ, age 23, sister-in-law, works at hat
shop; Louis Cooper, age 16, b. NJ, brother-in-law, works for butcher (Henry Cooper not listed here)

Children of Henry Cooper and Catherine .....:
Mary H., b. abt 1853
Josephine, b. abt 1855
Henry Maximillion, b. abt 1857
Hannah, b. abt 1859
John, b. abt 1862
Louis, b. abt 1864
Joseph, b. abt 1868

- - - - -

Cooper, JOHN C. b.
(map, grave owned, Sect. I) d._ _ _ 18_ _

Cooper, JOSEPHINE b.
(map, grave owned, Sect. I) d. _ _ _ 18_ _

Notes:
--See: Henry C. Cooper

- - - - -

COTTRELL

Cottrell, THOMAS
(map, plot owner, Sect. K)
(removed to Rosedale? Cem.)

b. (abt. 1809)
d. bur. March 19, 1900
Aged 91

wife, JANE (PIERSON)
(map, Section K)
(removed to Rosedale? Cem.)

b. (abt. 1810)
d. May 19, 1891

Cottrell, HENRY
(map, Section K)
(removed to Rosedale? Cem.)

b.
d.

Cottrell, ... M.
(map, Section K)
(removed to Rosedale? Cem.)

b.
d. April 23, 1904

Notes:
--See: Zenas Pierson
--1850 Census, p.260, Paterson, Passaic Co. NJ: Thomas H. "Cotterell" age 42, newspaper bender; Jane, age 41; Elizabeth, age 20; Marie, age 14; Herbert, age 10; Phebe C., age 5; Wm., age 3; Mary J., age 1; all b. NJ
--1860 Census, p.773, 9Wd, Newark, NJ: Thomas H. "Cattrell" age 50 b. NJ, foreman of shop; Jane, age 50; Ann N., age 23, vest maker; Herbert, age 19, jeweler; Kate, age 15; William, age 12; Laura, age 11; Lucy, age 8; Moses E. Smith, age 29, carpenter; Elizabeth Smith, age 28; all b. NJ
--1870 Census, p.244&245, 3Wd, Newark, NJ: Thomas H. Cottrell, age 61, shoe fitter; Jane, age 60; Herbert 28; Catherine, age 24; William, age 22, hatter; Laura, age 19; Lucy, age 17; all b. NJ
--1880 Census, p.168.3, Newark, NJ: Jane "Cattrell" age 70, divorced, b. NJ; Kate, age 32 b. NJ; Lucy, age 23, b. NJ; William, age 29, b. NJ, hatter

Children of Thomas H. Cottrell and Jane Pierson:
Elizabeth, b. abt. 1830; m. Moses E. Smith
Ann Marie, b. abt. 1836
Herbert, b. abt. 1840; m. Ella J. .....
Phebe Catherine, b. abt. 1845

William, b. abt. 1847
Mary J., b. abt. 1848
Laura, b. abt. 1851
Lucy, b. abt. 1853

- - - - -

COURTNEY

Courtney, ADA
(map, ch.property,Sect. H)

b.
d. October 21, 1862

Notes:
-George Courtney m. Nov. 4, 1856, Orange, Susan Rellett
--1860 Census, p.357, 3Wd, Orange, NJ: George Courtney, age 25, b. Ireland, hatter; Susan, age 27, b. Ireland; Clara, age 3 b. NJ; Ida, age 1, b. NJ

- - - - -

COYNE

Coyne, Patrick*
(map, plot owner, Sect. L)
?NJ Will #28338G, 1900

b. (abt. 1836)
d. (abt. 1900)

(1st?)wife, MARY A.
(csl - E17)(map, Sect. L)
(partial stone found, 2009)

b. July 3, 1838
d. October 7, 1866

Notes:
Served: Civil War, Co. H, 26th NJ Inf., Pvt. (nps)
--Map: entries in this plot are illegible
--?1860 Census, p.360, 3Wd, Orange, NJ: Patrick Coyne, age 24, b. Ireland, mason; Mary, age 21, b. England; Charles F. age 4 months, b. NJ; Charles Presmica, age 51, b. England, hatter
--?1870 Census, p.360, 2Wd, Orange, NJ: Patrick Coyne, age 36, b. Ireland, mason builder; Mary A., age 32, b. Ireland; Charles F., age 10; Edward, age 7; Walter, age 4; Alexander, age 1;all children b. NJ John Youmans, age 19, apprentice mason, b. NJ; Catherine Fallen, age 21, b. Ireland 'at home'
--?1880 Census, p.124.4, Orange, NJ: Patrick Coyne, age 48, b. Ireland, brick mason; Mary, age 45, b. Ireland; Charles F., age 20, brick mason;

Edward F., age 18, florist; Walter, age 14; Alexander, age 11; all children b. NJ
--?1895 NJ State Census, Orange NJ: Patrick Coyne; Mary Coyne; Frederick Coyne

Child of Patrick Coyne and Mary A. .....:
Charles Ferdinand, b. abt. Feb. 1860; m. Catherine Baker
Edward F., b. abt. 1862
Walter, b. abt. 1866
Child of Patrick Coyne and Mary .....:
Alexander, b. abt. 1869
?Frederick

- - - - -

CRANE

Crane, ARAMINTA   b. (abt. 1843)
(map, Section M)   d. March 18, 1906

Notes:
--bur. plot of Aaron VanBuskirk, q.v.
--1900 Census, p.4A, Newark, NJ: Ar..nita Crane, age 58, widow, b. NJ, patient: Essex Co. Hosp. for Insane

- - - - -

Crane, HANNAH   b. (October 6, 1791)
(gmnj)(shaw)(csl - E160)   d. July 10, 1870
(map, Section C)   *Aged 78.9.4*

Notes:
--bur. map, Section C, plot of Samuel Williams, q.v.
--1850 Census: p.232, Orange Twp, NJ: Hannah Crane age 57 b. NJ; Phebe (sister?) Williams age 65 b. NJ. (Phebe was widow of Samuel Williams, q.v.)

- - - - -

Crane, Isaac*   b. (September 16 1746)
     d. (October 29, 1815)
     (Bur. Old Ground, Orange)

widow, JOANNA (Ogden) b. (September 16, 1746?)
(csl - E160) d. December 9, 1822
Aged 72

Notes:
--Same plot as Hannah Crane, q.v.
--Isaac Crane was born September 16, 1746, Williamsville, Orange Twp.,Essex Co., NJ, son of Lewis Crane and Mary Burr. (IGI)
--Isaac Crane m. Joanna Ogden, daughter of David Ogden.
--Isaac died October 29, 1815, age 69.1.13. (Will #10969G, 1816) He is buried in the Old Ground, Orange.

Children of Isaac Crane and Joanna Ogden:
Keturah, b. May 6, 1769; m.Caleb Harrison (q.v.)
Abigail, b. 13 February 1771
Hannah, b. August 4, 1773; d. May 4, 1813
Mary, b. October 17, 1775; d.September 1, 1794
Sarah, b. June 6, 1778
Isaac, b. June 10, 1781; d. October 1782
Phebe, b. October 17, 1783; d. November 1783
Phebe, b. February 21, 1785
Lewis, b. August 26, 1787
Charlotte, b. October 19, 1789

- - - - -

CRAWFORD

Crawford, MRS. b.
(map, Section I) d. October 18, 1869

Notes:
--map, Section I, plot illegible

- - - - -

CROGAN

Crogan, James b.
(map, plot owner, Sect. M) d.

Crogan, WILLIE b.
(map, Section M) d. January 30, 1876

Notes:
--?1870 Census, p.407, 3Wd, Orange, NJ: James Crogan, age 24, b. Ireland, works at felt hat factory; Margaret, age 22 b. NJ; Elizabeth, age 3 months, b. NJ
--?1880 Census, p.191A, Orange, NJ: James W. Crogan, age 34, b. Ireland, hat finisher; Margaret, age 32, b. Ireland; Fanncy C. Faster, other, single, b. NJ, music teacher

------

CROSBY

Crosby, WILLIAM (map, plot owner, Sect. L) (removed to Rosedale Cem.)	b. (abt. 1830) d. September 22, 1896
wife, Eliza*	b. (abt. November 1833) d. (bef. 1910?)
son, JOHN (map, Section L)	b. (abt. 1863 d. December 9, 1871
Crosby, GILBERT (map, Section L)	b. d. April _ _, 18_ _

Notes:
--1870 Census, p.328&329, 1 Wd Orange, NJ: William Crosby, age 40 b. Ireland, dealer in boots & shoes; Eliza, age 37 b. Ireland; Sarah J., age 14; William E., age 10; John, age 7; Edward, age 4; Margaret, age 1; all children b. NJ; William Lord, age 19, b. Ireland, painter; Gilbert Lord, age 14, b Ireland, apprentice shoemaker
--1880 Census, p.574D, Livingston, Essex Co., NJ: Wm. Crosby, age 50, b. Ireland, shoemaker; Eliza, wife, age 46, b. Ireland; Sarah J., dau., age 22 b. NJ; Wm. E. son, age 19 b. NJ, works in hat shop; Edw. son, age 14, b. NJ; Elizabeth, dau., age 7 b. NJ; Ella F. dau., age 4 b. NJ; also: at least 9 male workers in hat shop
--1900 Census, p.14B, 4Wd, Orange, NJ: Elisa J. Crosby, b. Nov. 1833 Ireland, widow, 8 born 5 living; Edward, b. Apr. 1866, hatter foreman; Elizabeth M. dau. b. Aug. 1872, bookkeeper; Helen F., b. Jan. 1876; all children b. NJ

Children of William Crosby and Eliza .....:

Sarah J., b. abt. 1856
William E., b. abt. 1860; d. aft. 1930; m. Martha .....
John, b. abt. 1863
Edward, b. April 2, 1866; unm. in 1910
Margaret, b. abt. 1869
Elizabeth M., b. abt. August 1872; unm. in 1910
Helen F. 'Ella', b. abt. January 1876

- - - - -

CROWELL

Crowell, FRANK E. b. November 25, 1848
(gmnj) d. October 27, 1891

wife, Anna R.* b. (abt. 1851)
  d.

Notes:
--Frank E. Crowell was son of Cyrus G. Crowell and Eveline E. .....

--1850 Census, p.230, Lombard Ward, Phildadelphia, PA: Cyrus Crowell age 27 b. NJ, merchant; 'Avlene' age 24 b. NJ; Louisa 4 PA; Frank, 2, b. NJ; 5 other persons
--1870 Census, p.35, Merchantville PO, Stockton Twp., Camden Co., NJ: Cyrus G. Crowell age 47 b. NJ, farmer; Eveline E. age 45, b. Delaware; Louis Irene age 24 b. NJ; Frank E. age 21, b. PA; James W., age 19, b. PA; Charles L. age 13, b. PA; 3 farm laborers
--1880 Census: p.343A, Union, Union Co.,NJ:Frank E. Crowell, age 31, b. PA, farmer, parents b. NJ; wife, Anna R. age 29, b. LA, father b. NJ, mother b. PA;James W. Crowell, brother, age 28, b. PA, farmer;Mary A. Crowell, cousin, age 25, b. NJ

- - - - -

Crowell, JOHN b.
(map, Section D) d.

Notes:
--bur. map, Section D, plot of Charles Hand, q.v.

- - - - -

CUNNINGHAM

Cunningham, MRS. MARY b. (abt. 1851)
(map, ch. property,Sect. N) d. March 10, 1895
Aged 44

Notes:
--?1880 Census, p.245.4, West Orange, NJ: C. Cunningham, age 34, b. Scotland, laborer; Mary, age 29, b. Ireland; Anna, age 1, b. NJ; Cornelius, age 1 month, b. April 1880, NJ

- - - - -

CUSACK

Cusack, PATRICK b. (abt. 1840)
(map, Section M) d. February 28, 1878
(nps) d. (May 28, 1882?)

wife, Rosa b. (abt. January 1842)
  d. (aft. 1920)

Notes:
--Served: Civil War, Co. C, 7th Reg't NJ, Pvt. (nps)
Gov't headstone provided; 'd. May 28, 1882'
--Pension: to widow, Rose; appl. Oct. 1891
--bur.map, Section M, plot of Matilda Cusack, q.v.
--1870 Census, p.340, 2Wd, Orange: Patrick Cusack, age 31, b. Ire., labor; Rose, age 29 b. Ireland; Fannie, age 5, b. Canada; Theressa, age 4 b. Canada; Annie Farrell, age 13 b. PA; John Farrell, age 10 b. PA., James Farrell, age 4, b. NJ
--1880 Census, p.540A, East Orange, NJ: Patrick Cusack, age 45, b. Ireland, labor; Rose, age 42 b. Ireland; Fanny, age 15, b. NJ, hat trimmer; Tressa, age 14 NJ; Rosa age 6 NJ; Patrick age 4 b. NJ; Ellen, age 2 b. NJ
--1895 NJ State Census, p.34, 2Wd. Orange, NJ: Rose Cusack; Rose; Patrick, Nellie
--1900 Census, p.17B, 2Wd, Orange: Rose "Cussich" age 58 b. Ire., grocer dealer; Patrick, b. Aug. 1877 NJ; Rose b. Oct. 1876 NJ; Nellie b. Dec. 1879 NJ; Fannie Flynn b. Feb. 1867 Canada, widow, hat trimmer; Ella Flynn b. Oct. 1892 NJ; Alice Flynn, b. Dec. 1894 NJ; Thomas Flynn, b. Sept. 1895

--1910 Census, p.15A, 2Wd, Orange: Rose Cusack, age 72, widow, b. Ire. immig. 1850; Fannie Flynn, age 44 widow b. Canada, hat trimmer; Rose Cusack Jr., age 34, b. NJ, hat trimmer; Patrick Cusack, age 32 b. NJ, hat finisher; Ellen Cusack, age 30 b. NJ, hat trimmer; Ellen Flynn, age 18, granddau., b. NJ, father b. NJ, telephone operator; Alice Flynn, age 16 ganddau., age 16, b. NJ, telephone operator; Thomas Flynn, age 14, grandson, b. NJ

--1920 Census, p.26A, 2Wd, Orange: Rose "Cerrick", age 83, widow, b. Ire; Rose, age 42, dau., dress maker; Patrick, son, age 40, hatter; Helen, dau., age 38, hat trimmer; Fannie Flynn, age 52, dau., widow; Ella Flynn, age 27, tel. operator; Alice Flynn, age 26, tel. operator; Thomas Flynn, age 24, machinist at electric factory

Children of Patrick Cusack and Rose .....:
Fannie, b. abt. Feb. 1867; m. ..... Flynn
Theressa, b. abt. 1866; d. bef. 1880?
Rosa, b. abt. Oct. 1876
Patrick, b. September 24, 1875
Ellen, b. abt. Dec. 1879

- - - -

Cusack, RICHARD S.   b. (abt. 1834)
(gmnj)(map, Sect. M)   d. December 9, 1901
(nps)   *Aged 68*
            Co.H, 39th NJ Inf.

wife, MATILDA (Hull)   b. (December 16, 1834)
(map, plot owner, Sect. M)   d. September 3, 1883
            Aged 48.4.18

Cusick, CLARISSA   b. (abt. 1863)
(map, Section M)   d. December 26, 1895
            Aged 32

Notes:
--Served: Civil War; Co.H, 39th Inf. Pvt. (nps)
--Served:(?) also, Civil War; Co. C., 7th NJ Inf., Pvt. (nps)
--Richard m. May 1, 1856, Matilda, daughter of Peter V. Hull, q.v. and Harriet Walker.

--1850 Census, p.244, Orange Twp: Peter V. Hull, age 43, farmer; Harriet, age 35; Matilda, age 15; George A. age 13; Charles H. age 12;

Sarah I. age 10; Alexander age 8; David M. age 6; Mary L. age 5; Charlotte age 3; all b. New Jersey
--1860 Census: p.387, 3Wd, Orange, NJ: Richard S. Cusack age 25, carpenter, b. Ireland; Matilda age 25; George B. age 3; Alvah age 3 months. (Adj. to Harriet Hull, widow of Peter V. Hull (q.v.)
--1870 Census: p.413, 3rd Ward, Orange, NJ: Richard S. Cusack age 37, carpenter, b. Ireland; Matilda age 35; George B. 13; Alva E. age 10; Viola age 4; Grant A. age 2
--1880 Census, p.183.1, Orange, NJ: Valley St.: Richard Cusick age 46, b. Ireland, carpenter; Matilda age 45 b. NJ, parents b. 'Ireland'; George B. age 23,b. NJ, hat maker; Alvin E. age 20, b. NJ, carpenter; Viola age 14, b. NJ; Grant A., age 12 b. NJ; Eva J., age 7, b. NJ
--1900 Census, p.2A, 1Wd, Kearny, Hudson Co., NJ; NJ Home for Disabled Soldiers: Richard S. Cusack, age 64, b. Ireland, inmate

Children of Richard S. Cusack and Matilda Hull:
George B., b. abt. 1857; m. Elizabeth .....
Alvah Edison, b. March 7, 1860; m. Elizabeth Murphy
Viola, b. abt 1866; m. John Harry Bowman
Grant A., b. abt 1868; m. Margaret .....
Eva J. b. abt. 1873

- - - - -

DANGLER

Dangler, CHILD of B. (map, Section H)	b. d. 1882
Dangler, CHILD of B. (map, Section H)	b. d. 1882

Notes:
--bur. map, Section H, plot of Isaac Baldwin

- - - - -

DANIEL

Daniel, ROBERT GEORGE (map, church property)	b. d. September 24, 1863

Notes:

DANIELS

Daniels, WILLIAM b. (abt. 1790)
(map, plot owner, Sect. L) d. October 24, 1866
(gmnj)(shaw)(csl - E29) *Aged 76*
(NJ Will #16293G,1866)

wife, EMELINE b. (abt. 1808)
(map, Section L) d. (aft. 1880)

Notes:
--1850 Census, p.275, South Ward, Newark, NJ: WIlliam Daniels, age 59, b. CT, letter carrier; Emeline, age 42, b. NJ; 'Hellen Smith', age 16, b. NY
--1860 Census, p.796, 9Wd, Newark: William Daniels, age 69, b. CT, letter carrier; Emeline, age 54, b. NJ
--1870 Census, p. 279, 9 Wd, Newark: Emeline Daniels, age 62, b. NJ, widow
--1880 Census, p.224.1, Newark: Emeline Daniels age 70, b. NJ, widow

- - - - -

DAVIS

CHILD of Dr. Davis b.
(map, Section N) d. 1880

Notes:
--bur. map, Section N, Osborne plot)

- - - - -

Davis, MRS. b.
(map, Section O) d.

Notes:
--Map says: "Section O, Row 5: Negro Burial Ground"

- - - - -

DEAN

Dean, CHARLES
(map, plot owner, Sect. J)
b. (abt. 1798)
d. November 23, 1872

wife, LYDIA (Tompkins)
(map, Section J)
b. (abt. 1801)
d. (bef. 1870)

Notes:
--1850 Census, p.240 Orange Twp., NJ: Charles Dean, age 52, shoemaker; Lydia, age 50; Peter, age 28, hatter; Rachel E., age 25; Mary A., age 23; Phebe, age 14; all b. NJ
--1860 Census, p.384, 3Wd.Orange NJ: Charles Dean, age 62 b. NJ, butcher; Lydia, age 59, b. NJ; Mary A., age 32, b. NJ; Phebe, age 24 b. NY?
--1870 Census, p.466, Charles Dean, age 72, b. NJ, shoemaker; Edward 'Stockford' age 42, hat manufacturer, b. England; Anna, age 44 b. NJ; Martha E., age 17, b. NJ; Joseph, age 15, b. NJ; Thomas, age 7 b. NJ; Charles Dean, age 72, b. NJ, shoemaker (near Peter Dean)
--1900 Census, p.8B, West Orange NJ: Emmaline R. Ward, b. Jan. 1825 NJ, widow; Phoebe Stevens b. Jan.1836 NJ, sister, widow; Anna G. Stevens b. June 1763 niece, b. NJ, seamstress; Harry C. Stevens, b. Sept. 1875, nephew, b. NJ
(near Jane A. Dean)

Children of Charles Dean and Lydia Tompkins:
Peter, b. abt. 1822;d. bef. 1900; m. Jane Augusta Canham
Rachel Emeline, b. abt. Jan.1925; m. 1858, George Ward?
Mary Anna, b. abt. 1827; m. Edward Stopford, q.v.
Phebe, b.abt. Jan.1836; m. ..... Matthews?
    m. Henry Stevens,q.v.

- - - - -

Dean, ISAAC M.
(gmnj)(csl - E50)
(map, plot owner, Sect. J)
b. (August 3, 1810)
d. April 27, 1867
Aged 56.8.24

widow, MARY JANE
(Beach)
(gmnj)(csl - E50)
(map, Section J)
b. (February 3, 1814)
d. May 4, 1872
Aged 58.3.1

CHILD of I. M. Dean   b.
(map, Section J)   d.

Notes:
--1850 Census, p.10&11, North Ward, Newark, Essex Co., NJ: Isaac M. Dean, age 40, b. NJ, carpenter; Mary, age 36 NJ; David, age 14, b. NJ; Sarah, age 10 b. NJ; William, age 5, b. NJ
--1860 Census, p.151, 11Wd, Brooklyn, Kings Co.NY: Isaac M. Dean, age 47 b. NJ, sash&blind maker; Mary age 40 b. NJ; William, age 15, b. NJ; David, age 24, b. NJ, lawyer; Benjamin 'Mifred' age 25, b. NY, salesman; Sarah 'Mifred' age 20, b. NJ
--1870 Census, p.86, 20Wd, Brooklyn, Kings Co. NY: Mary Dean, age 56, b. NJ; William Dean, age 25, b. NJ, house carpenter

Children of Isaac M. Dean and Mary Jane Beach:
David, b. abt. 1836; m. Susan M. .....
Sarah Frances, b.abt 1840; m. Benjamin Prince Mulford, q.v.
William, b. abt 1845

- - - - -

DeGROAT

Degroat, AMZI   b. (abt. 1851)
(map, Section O)   d. October 24, 1882

wife, Mahalia*   b. (abt. 1859)
    d.

Notes:
--Map: says "Section O, Negro Burial Ground"
--1850 Census, p.132, Pompton, Passaic Co., NJ: David 'Degrote', age 59,mulatto, b. NJ, laborer; Tyney (Christina?), age 57; Joseph, age 30, labor; Ann, age 25; Peter, age 17; Martha, age 15; David, age 4; all b. 'NJ'
--1850 Census, p.221, 2Wd, Orange, NJ: David Degroot, age 60, mulatto, b. NY, laborer; Christina, age 58, mulatto, b. NY
(same house as Charles and Martha Blanchard)(adj. to Daniel and Cath M. Milligan)
--1860 Census, p.188, Livingston, NJ: Joseph 'Degroat' age 39, mulatto, b. NJ, 'colier'; Sarah E., age 21, b. NY; David, age 14, b. NJ; Amzi, age 9 b. NJ; Martha 3, b. NJ; Mary S., age 1, b. NJ

--1870 Census, p.404, 3Wd, Orange, NJ: Joseph 'DeGroot', age 51, mulatto, b. NJ, laborer: Sarah E., age 33, wife, b. NY; Amzi, age 18, b. NJ; Hannah A., age 9, b. NJ; Josiah, age 7, b. NJ; Ellen, age 4, b. NJ; Samuel, age 3, b. NJ; Sarah C., age 5 months, b. NJ
--1880 Census, p.256A, West Orange, NJ: Samuel P. Milligan, age 57, mulatto, b. NY, parents b. NY, wheelwright; John W. Milligan, son, age 19, mulatto, b. NJ, parents b. NY; Amzi 'DeGwat', married, nephew, age 28, mulatto, b. NJ, parents b. NY; Mahalia 'DeGwat', married niece, age 21, mulatto, b. NJ, parents b. NY; Elsie A. 'DeGwat', grandniece, age 1, b. NJ, parents b. NJ
--1900 Census, p.10A, 7Wd, Newark, NJ: 'Auezi DeGroat', b. April 1860, black, b. NY, parents b. NY, m.20 years, 0 born 0 living; Christiana, b. Jan. 1858, black, b. NY, parents b. NY

Children of Amzi DeGroat and Mahalia .....:
Elsie A., b. abt. 1879

- - - - -

DeHART

DeHart, ADELAIDE
(map, ch. property, Sect. I)

b. (abt. September 1898)
d. September 28, 1898
Aged 6 days

Notes:

- - - - -

DIGHT
(see DYKES)

- - - - -

DOBRIDGE

Dobridge, HENRY A.
(gmnj)(shaw)(csl - E120)
(map,plot owner,Sect.E)
(NJ Will #17837G, 1873)

b. September 6, 1800
d. October 10, 1873
d. October 14, 1872(?)

Dobridge, JULIA J.
(gmnj)(csl - E119)

b. June 22, 1805
d. March 17, 1882

(map, Sect. E)   d. March 21, 1882
(Will #20895G, 1883)

Dobridge, SELENA F.   b. May 20, 1811
(gmnj)(map, Sect. E)   d. July 6, 1891

Notes:
--1840 Census, p.262, Orange Twp., NJ: Robert Dobridge
--1850 July 18: Arv. Philadelphia from Rum Cay, Bahamas, S. S. Fairy (brig): Dr. Dobridge, age 50, destination U.S.
--1850 Census: p.239, Orange Twp., NJ: Henry A. Dobridge age 50, surgeon, b. West Indies: Sarah A. age 46; Martha M. Ross (Rose) age 43; John S. Dobridge age 42; Selina F. age 39; John Ross age 19, clerk; Elizabeth age 20; Henry age 17; Martha age 13; Sarah W. age 12; all b. West Indies
--1860 Census, p.230, 15Wd, Philadelphia, PA; Henry Dobridge, age 60, b. West Indies, physician; Eliza Dobridge, age 40, b. NJ
--1860 Census: p.368, 3Wd., Orange, NJ: Sarah Dobridge age 56, b. West Indies; Julia J. age 52 b. West Indies; Selina F. age 49 b. West Indies.
--1870 Census: p.390, 3rd Ward, Orange, NJ: Henry A. Dobridge age 69, physician, b. West Indies; Sarah A. age 66, school teacher, b. West Indies; Julia J. age 62 b. West Indies; Selina F., age 59 b. West Indies.
--1880 Census: p.169.2, Orange, NJ: Sarah A. Dobridge, single, age 75, b. British West Indies, parents b. England;
Julia J. Dobridge, single, age 72, b. BWI; 'Selma' F. Dobridge, sister, age 69, b. BWI.

Children of Robert Dobridge and Martha .....:
Henry A., b. abt. 1800
Sarah A., b. abt. 1804
Martha A., b. abt. 1807; ?m. John Rose, q.v.
Julia J., b. abt. 1808
Selena F., b. abt 1811

- - - - -

Dobridge, ROBERT, Esq.   b. (abt. 1765)
(gmnj)(csl - 121)(map)   d. February 28, 1845
(map, plot owner, Sect. E)

In
memory of
Robert Dobridge

He closed his
active probationary life of
eighty years
on Feb. 28th A.D. 1845
in the communion of the Church
cheered by the Christian faith

wife, MARTHA b. (July 20, 1767).
(gmnj)(shaw)(csl-E122) d. January 20, 1835
(map, Section E) *Aged 67.6.0*

Sacred
to the memory of
Martha
wife of
Robert Dobridge, Esq
a native of England
who after a long & tedious
illness, closed a life of Religion
the 20th of January 1833
aged 65 years.6 months

- - - - -

DOE

Doe, CHILD of W. b.
(map, Section H) d.

Doe, CHILD of W. b.
(map, Section H) d.

Notes:
--bur. map, Section H, plot of Isaac Baldwin, q.v.

- - - - -

DOUGHERTY

Dougherty, MISS b.
(map, ch. property, Sect. M) d. January 28, 1869

Notes:

DUCKER

Ducker, CHILD of ..... b.
(map, Section H) d.

DUER

Duer, JOHN H. b.
(map, Section H) d. March 28, 1869

Notes:
(?)Served: Civil War, Co. G, 7th NJ Inf., Pvt. (nps)
(?)Served: Civil War, Co. F, 39th NJ Inf., Pvt. (nps)

DYKES

Dykes, MARY b. (abt. 1807)
(on stone of Alex. Bell, q.v.) d. January 19, 1858
(map, plot owner, Section F)

Dykes, PETER b.
(on stone of Alex. Bell, q.v.) d.
(map, Section F)

Dykes, MARY b.
(map, Section F) d. February 18, 1872

Dykes, JOHN b.
(map, Section F) d. July 20, 1860

Dykes, WILLIAM b.
(map, Section F) d. July 31, 1863

Dykes, Basil b. (abt. 1840)
(csl - E98) d. May 6, 1864
(nps) *Co. G., 2nd NJ Inf.*

Killed in action

Notes:
Served: Civil War: "mustered in May 28, 1861; re-enlisted Gov't headstone provided 'd. May 6, 1864' February 26, 1864; killed in action at (Battle of the) Wilderness, VA., May 6, 1864; buried at National Cemetery, Fredericksburg, VA; Div.C, Section A; Grave #196" "originally buried at Locust Grove, Spotsylvania, VA"

--?1839-1840 NYC Directory: Basil Dykes, baker
--?1840 Census: p.368, 14th Ward, New York, NY: Basil Dykes
--1850 Census, p.99, North Ward, Newark, NJ: Mary Dykes, age 43, b. Scotland; William, age 22 b. NY, baker; Theodore, age 15, b. NY, iron worker; Basil age 10 b. NY; Mary age 12 b. NY
--1860 Census, p.416, 11Wd, Newark: William Dykes, age 30 b. NY, hat body worker; Mary, age 20 b. NY; male, age 27 (Theodore?); male, age 21 (Basil?), painter; (adj. to Elias Baldwin family)
--1870 Census, p.461, 11Wd, Newark, NJ: William Dykes, age 38 b. NY, works hat mfg.; Mary, age 27, b. NY (adj. to Elias Baldwin and family)

Children of ..... Dykes and Mary .....:
William, b. abt. 1828; m. Mary .....
Theodore, b. abt. 1835
Mary, b. abt. 1838
Basil, b. abt. 1840; d. May 6, 1864

- - - - -

EARL

Earl, Agustus* (map, plot owner, Sect. L)	b. (abt. 1823) d.
wife, MARIA (Nafie) (map, Sect. L)	b. (abt. 1837) d. November 1866 *Aged 29*
Earl, HATTIE (map, Sect. L)	b. (abt. 1853) d. 1867 *Aged 14*
dau., AMANDA (Meeker) (map, Section L)	b. d.

'Farrer', THEODORE A. b. (abt. 1847)
(map, Section L) d. March 13, 1895

'Farrer', WILLIAM b.
(map, Section L) d. February 1883

Notes:
--?Augustin Earl: m. #1, bef. 1848, 'Miranda .....
--?Augustine E. Earl m. #2, Feb. 18, 1854, Caroline C. 'Ferris'
--?Augustine E. Earl m. #3, Sept. 6, 1857, Sarah L. Roswell
--1850 Census, p.100&101, Livingston, Essex Co. NJ: Moses S. Earl, age 62, farmer; Mary, age 60; Mary M., age 23; Julia L., age 21; Rebecca W., age 17; Augustin E. Earl, age 27, farmer; 'Miranda' age 24; 'Manery' A., age 2; Emma L., age 0; Edward Galazar, age 13, b. NY
--1860 Census, p.392, 3Wd, Orange, NJ: Augustine E. Earl, age 37 shoemaker; Sarah, age 21; 'Mineria' age 13; Emma, age 8; Emma, age 8; Anna, age 1
--1870 Census, p.460&461, West. Orange, NJ: Henry H. Moore, age 29, b. Prussia, works at shoe shop; Emma L. age 20 b. NJ; Joseph H., age 2 b. NJ; Amelia, age 54, b. Prussia; Augustine Earl, age 48, b. NJ, shoemaker; Rebecca Earl, age 9, b. NJ

Children of Augustine E. Earl and Maria .....:
Minerva? A., b. abt 1848
Emma L., b. abt. 1850; m. Henry H. Moore
Children of Augustine E. Earl and Caroline C. Ferris:
?Hattie, b. abt. 1853
Children of Augustine E. Earl and Sarah L. Roswell:
Anna, b. abt. 1859
?Rebecca, b. abt. 1861

- - - - -

EDWARDS

Edwards, CHILD of Jacob b.
(map, Section H) d. 1872

Notes:
--bur. map, Section H, plot of Isaac Baldwin,q.v.

- - - - -

Edwards, A. EDWARD b. (September 3, 1873)
(csl - E70) d. December 27, 1873
Aged 0.3.24

- - - - -

Edwards, DAVID b. (abt. 1801)
(gmnj)(csl - E191) d. May 19, 1845
(map, Sect. B, plot owner) *Aged 44*
(NJ Will #13431G, 1845)

The Grave of
David Edwards
He died in the
Christian faith
May 19th, A.D. 1845
Aged XLIV years

wife, RHODA (Dean) b. December 12, 1803
(csl - 192)(map, Sect. B) d. August 16, 1875

Notes:
--David Edwards married Rhoda Dean, December 24, 1836, Essex Co., NJ (IGI)

--1850 Census: p.223, Orange Twp., NJ: Rhoda Edwards age 46 b. NJ; Richard O'Leary age 48 hatter b. Ireland; Ann O'Leary age 33 b. Ireland.
--1860 Census: p.356, 3Wd. Orange, NJ: Rhoda Edwards age 56, keeps boarding house; One boarder was Charles H. Hull age 23, carpenter (q.v.)
--1870 Census, p.387, 3Wd, Orange: Rhoda Edwards, age 66, b. NJ

- - - - -

Edwards, Joseph b.
(map, plot owner, Sect. M) d.

wife, Charlotte (Condit) b.
  d.

LeClerc, PHEBE C. b.
(map, Sect. M) bur. May 24, 1928
 Aged 83(?)

LeClerc, GRANDCHILD b.
of Eugene LeClerc d.
(map, Section M)

Sprigg, ANNA MARIA b. (abt. 1894)
(map, Section M) d. February 25, 1910
 Aged 16

Notes:
--1880 Census, p.247D, West Orange, NJ: Joseph Edwards, age 60, shoemaker; Charlotte, widow, age 64, Hannah, dau.single, age 33, seamstress; David, son, age 26, carpenter; all b. NJ
--1880 Census, p.273D, West Orange, NJ: Eugene LeClerc, age 36, b. NJU, parents b. France, carpenter; Phebe, wife, age 35, b. NJ, Hannah P., age 15; Joseph W., age 13, Charlotte M., age 10; Theodore M. age 6
--1900 Census, p.1B&2A, West Orange, NJ: Hannah Vincent, b. Apr. 1847 widow; 'Jean' Vincent, dau., b. Sept. 1891; Joseph Edwards, age 80, b. Oct. 1819, father, widower; David T. Edwards, brother, age 46, b. Sept. 1855, widower; Phebe C. LeClerc, age 55, b. July 1844, widow; all b. NJ

- - - - -

Edwards, THADDEUS S. b. (abt. 1843)
(map, plot owner, Sect. L) d. January 14, 1878
(gmnj) (csl - E24)(nps) *Co. C., 17th Conn. Inf.*

Edwards, MARY(Hartness) b.
(wife of 'T.E.' Edwards) d. April 1, 1879
(map, Section L)

son, CHARLES H. b. (abt. 1875)
(map, Section L) d. October 17, 1905
 Aged 30

Bonnell, CHILD of T. b.
(map, Section L) d. April 15, 1878

Higginson, T.   b.
(map, Section L)   d. November 7, 1881

Notes:
--Served: Civil War: Co. C. 17th Connecticut Inf., Pvt.
Gov't headstone provided: 'd. January 14, 1878'
--Thaddeus m. 1874, Our Lady of the Valley Church, Orange, NJ, Maria A. Hartness
--1850 Census, p.90, Danbury, Fairfield Co., CT: Charles Edwards age 35, hatter; "Margetta" age 29; Thadeus 7; Emily F. 5; Lewis P. 2; John C. 75; Lydia 67; all b. CT; 4 boarders
--1860 Census, p.569, Bethel, Fairfield Co., CT: Chas. Edwards age 44, hat maker; Mariet age 39; Thaddius S. age 16; Emily F. 13; Inez I. age 10; Charles H. age 8; Willie H., age 5; Marietta age 3; Blanche E. age 5 months; all b. CT
--1870 Census, p.246, Millburn, Essex Co., NJ: Charles Edwards age 55, b. CT, hatter; 'Margetta', age 50 b. CT; Thaddeus, age 27, hatter; Emily F. 24; Chas. H. Edwards, age 17, hatter; Marietta Edwards age 13; Blanche Edwards, age 10; James H. Walters, age 22, marketman; Julia Inez Walters, age 20; all b. CT
--1880 Census, p. 152.4&153, Orange, NJ: Catherine Bonnell, age 33, widow, b. VT; Joseph Bonnell, age 6, son, b. NJ; Theodore Bonnell, age 5, son, b. NJ; Charles W. Edwards, age 4, nephew, b. NJ; William Hartness, age 23, brother, b. VT, works at hat factory; James Hartness, age 20, b. VT. works at hat factory

Child of Thaddeus Edwards and Mary Hartness:
Charles W., b. abt. 1876

- - - - -

EVANS

Evans, JOSEPH H.   b. (abt. 1834)
(map, ch. property, Sect. N)   d. September 29, 1902
                                           Aged 68

Evans, MRS. ELIZABETH   b. (abt. 1836)
(map, ch. property, Sect. N)   d. September 13, 1908
                                           Aged 70

Notes:
--?1880 Census, p.273.3, West Orange, NJ: Joseph Evans, age 46, b. Scotland, hotel keeper; Sarah E., age 42, b. NJ

--1900 Census, p.3A, West Orange, NJ: Joseph Evans, b. Jan. 1837, m. 40 yrs., b. Scotland, Justice of the Peace; Elizabeth b. Sept. 1840, NJ

- - - - -

F........ (?)

F......, Harriet(?)   b.
(map, ch. property, Sect. I)   d.

Notes:

- - - - -

FAIRCHILD

Fairchild, Samuel Augustus   b. (June 28, 1820)
(map, plot owner, Sect. L)   d. (aft. 1880, Virginia)

wife, Charity C.*(Wright)   b.
    d. (February 27, 1847, NJ)

wife, Caroline S. (Lyon)   b. (abt. 1826)
    d. (abt. 1866, Virginia)

dau., EMMA CAROLINE   b. (abt. 1852)
(map, Section L)   d. (April 15, 1862)
(removed to Rosedale? Cem.)

Fairchild, ANNA   b.
(map, Section L)   d.

Lyon, ABBY   b.
(map, Section L)   d. February 28, 1859

CHILD of Stokes   b.
(map, Section L)   d.

Notes:
--See: Henry B. Stokes
--Samuel was son of John Fairchild and Lucy Kitchell
--Samuel m.#1, 1841, Charity Wright; m. #2, 1850, Caroline S. Lyon

--?1850 Census, p.276, Springfield, Essex Co.NJ: Samuel Fairchild, age '26' b. NJ, carpenter; Moses Smith,age 31, b. NJ, carpenter; William A. Edward, age 20 b. NJ, carpenter; boarders at res. 1of Anna Drake, widow
--?1850 Census, p.271, Springfield, Essex Co. NJ: Samuel Fairchild, age 36, b. NJ, carpenter; at res. of Elijah Middlebrook, hatter, and his wife, Anne E., age 25 (adj. to Stephen A. Kitchell, age 38, blacksmith)
--1860 Census, p.421, 2Wd, Orange, NJ: Samuel Fairchild, age 40, carpenter; Caroline, age 34; Emma C., age 8; Laura, age 6; Susan, age 3; Samuel, age 4 mos. all b. NJ
--1870 Census, p.327, Chancellor, Spotsylvania Co. VA: Saml Fairchild, age 50 b. NJ, farmer; Laura, age 17; Susan, age 13; Saml L., age 10; Charlotte 7
--1880 Census, p.365A, Spotsylvania Co., VA: Lyman Fairchild, age 20 b. NJ, farming; Sharlott S., sister, age 18, b. NJ; Samuel A., father, widower, age 60 b. NJ, carpenter; Walter R. nephew, age 2 b. NJ; Alfred, nephew, age 1, b. NJ

Children of Samuel Augustus Fairchild and Caroline S. Lyon:
Emma Caroline, bapt. Aug.29,1851, St. Mark's Church;
    d. April 15, 1862
Laura Frances, bapt.August 23, 1853, St. Mark's Church;
    m. abt. 1875, Jilson W. Jett
Susan Phebe, bapt. August 28, 1856, St. Mark's Church;
    m. #1, unknown
    m. # 2, Charles M. Jett (brother of Jilson W. Jett)
Samuel Lyman, bapt. January 29, 1860, St. Mark's Church;
    d. Apr. 14, 1927, Butte, MT; m.abt. 1881, Hannah ....
Charlotte S., b. September 29, 1862;
    m.#1, unknown;
    m. #2 William C. Gordon

- - - - -

FARLEY

Farley, JOHN   b.
(map, grave owned,Sect. I)   d.

Notes:

- - - - -

FEATHERSTONE

Featherstone, THOMAS F. (map, Section J)	b. d. (1894?)
Featherstone, MRS. (map, Section J)	b. d.
Featherstone, WILLIAM (map, Section J)	b. d.

Notes:
--See: Thomas E. Brown
--?1870 Census, p.400, 3Wd, Orange, NJ: William P. 'Fetherston', age 64, b. Ireland, tailor; Ellen, age 64 b. Ireland; Eliza, age 34 b. Ireland; Thomas, age 32, b. Ireland, printer; Rebecca, age 24, b. NY; Edward F., age 1 b. NY; Ellanora, age 29, b. Ireland

- - - - -

FERGUSON

Ferguson, CHILD of Chas. (map, Section H)	b. d.

Notes:
--bur. map, Section H, plot of Isaac Baldwin, q.v.

- - - - -

FIELD

Field, Hezekiah*	b. d.
widow, PHEBE (Coe) (gmnj)(shaw)(csl - E181) (map, Section B)	b. (July 30, 1745) d. January 2, 1845 *Aged 99.5.3*

Phebe Field
widow of
Hezekiah Field
Died

> *Jan. 2nd, 1845*
> *Aged 99 years 5 mo*
> *& 3 days"*

son, JAMES b. (June 6, 1778)
(gmnj)(shaw)(csl-E181) d. August 21, 1863
(map, Section B)

> *James Field*
> *Died*
> *Aug 21st 1863*
> *Aged 85 years*
> *2 months*
> *& 15 days*

Field, Lydia* (Lindsely) b. (December 12, 1798)
wife of James, b. 1778 d. (after 1860)

Coe, SUSANNAH b. (April 6, 1734)
(shaw)(map, Sect. B) d. November 10, 1839.
(sister of Phebe) *Aged 105.7.4*

> *Susannah Coe*
> *Died*
> *Nov.r 10th, 1839*
> *Aged 105 years*
> *7 mo.*
> *& 4 days*

Notes:
--?Served: Revolutionary War
--Hezekiah Field was son of Benjamin Field.
--Hezekiah Field married a cousin, Phebe Coe December 27, 1776 at Newtown, Queens, NY; daughter of Robert Coe and Mary Field.
--Susannah Coe was an unmarried sister of Phebe Coe.
--James Field m. Lydia Lindsley, daughter of Daniel Lindsley and Hannah Williams.
--James W. Field, Esq. (b.abt.1830), Vestryman, of **St. Mark's** Church in 1882. He was son of James Field, q. v., and Lydia Lindsley.
--James W. Field m. Josephine Kissam; October 15, 1856, Trinity Church, New York City

--1887 May 20: *NY Times:* "died, Josephine K., wife of James W. Field. Relatives and friends are respectfully invited to attend her funeral at **St. Mark's** Church, Orange, on Friday, May 20. carriages will be at the Orange Station on arrival of the train."

--1850 Census: p.241, Orange Twp., NJ: James Field a.70, b. NY, no occup; Lydia (nee Lindsley) age 51, b. NY
--1850 Census, p.133, East Ward, NewarK; James 'Fields' age 19, b. NJ, clerk, boarder
--1860 Census, p.397, 3Wd, Orange: Jas. W. Field age 29 b. NJ, lawyer; Josephine R. age 30 b. NY; Joseph R. age 2 b. NJ; Lizzie E. age 4 months, b. NJ; James Field age 63, b. NY; Lydia Field, age 63 b. NY; 2 servants
--1870 Census, p.477&478, West Orange: James 'Fields' age 39 b. NJ, lawyer; Josephine K. age 38 b. NY; Joseph K. age 12 b. NJ; Lizzie E. age 10 b. NJ; 3 servants
--1880 Census, p.272.1&272.2, West Orange: James W. Field, age '43', b. NJ, lawyer; Josephine, age '40' b. NY, parents b. NY; Joseph K. age 22 b. NJ, lawyer; Lizzie E., age 20 b. NJ; 2 servants

Child of James Field and Lydia Lindsley:
James Wheeler Field, b. September 1, 1831; d. 1898;
    m. Josephine Kissam (see: "Stained Glass Windows"

- - - - -

FREEMAN

Freeman, ZENAS
(map,plot owner, Sect. E)

b. (abt. 1815)
d. (aft. 1880)

wife, MARY A. (Condit)
(gmnj)(shaw)(csl - 107)
(map, Section E)

b. (abt. 1819)
d. June 4, 1866
Aged 47

son,CHARLES AUGUSTUS
(csl - 106)(map, Sect. E)

b. (November 15, 1846)
d. March 28, 1866
Aged 18.4.13

CHILD of Zenas
(map, Sect. E)

b.
d.

Notes:

--See: Enos Condit Tompkins
--?Zenas Freeman married, January 4, 1842 at Essex Co., NJ, Mary A. Condit.(IGI)

--1850 Census: p.230, Orange Twp., NJ: 'Linas Fruman' (Zenas Freeman) age 35, shoemaker; Mary A. age 30; Rhoda C. age 7; Charles A. age 3; Mary 'Fruman' age 59; all b. NJ; 1 servant b. Germany
--1860 Census: p.362, 3Wd. Orange, NJ: Zenas Freeman age 43, shoemaker; Mary A. age 40; Caroline R. age 17, school teacher; Charles A. age 13; all b. NJ
--1870 Census: p.369, 3rd Ward, Orange, NJ: Joseph C. Tomkins age 48, constable; Mary A. (nee Bush) age 48; Horace B. age 26, carpenter; Elizabeth, age 17; Rhoda, age 76; Zenas Freeman, age 55, works at boot/shoe factory; all b. NJ (Joseph C. Tomkins was son of Luther Crowell Tompkins, q.v., and Rhoda Condit)
--1880 Census, p.161.1, Orange: Samuel M. Freeman,a ge 59, retail grocer; Elma (nee Smith) age 52; Minnie, age 13; Augustus Bloodgood, age 35, son-in-law, mason; Endora Bloodgood, age 26, dau., dressmaker; Zenas Freeman, age 67, brother, boot/shoe maker; all b. NJ; 2 boarders

Children of Zenas Freeman and Mary A. Condit:
Rhoda Caroline, b. abt 1843; m. Enos C. Tompkins
Charles Augustus, b. 1846; d. 1866

- - - - -

FUREY

Furey, ANDREW J. b. (abt. 1833)
(map, Section H) bur. March 10, 1905
Aged 72

Notes:
--bur. map, Section H, Plot of Daniel Webb, q.v.

- - - - -

FURGUSON

Furguson, ELLEN b. July 6, 1877
(csl - E65) d. January 19, 1878

Furguson, MARGARET b. September 10, 1886
(csl - E65) d. September 3, 1887

Notes:
--?1870 Census, p.395, 3Wd. Orange: Robert Furgoson,a ge 38, b. Scotland, gardener; Jane age 38 b. Ireland; Robert G. age 7 b. NJ; Jane age 6 b. NJ; James age 3 b. NJ; William, age 11, b. NJ; Maria L., age 2, b. NJ
--?1880 Census, p.257.3, West Orange: Charles Ferguson age 34 b. Ireland, laborer; Jane, age 32, b. Scotland; James age 18 b. Scotland; Anna, age 10 b. Scotland; Samuel age 9 b. Scotland; Charles, age 7, b. NJ; Charles age 7 b. Scotland; John age 5, b. NJ; Elizabeth age 1, b. NJ;
--?1900 Census, p. 4B, 5 Wd. Orange: Charles H. Ferguson b. April 1850, m.32 yr. b. Ireland, laborer; Jane b. January 1850 Scotland, 12 born 4 living; William, b. Nov. 1881 NJ, teamster

- - - - -

GAGE

Gage, ROMANZO b. (April 30, 1830)
(gmnj)(map, Section I) d. (May 24, 1882)

Notes:
Served: Civil War; Co. H, 26th NJ Inf., Pvt.
Gov't headstone provided: 'd. May 24, 1882'; sighted in 2009
--bur. map, Section I, plot of Abram Brower, q.v.
--Romanzo Gage was b. April 30,1830, Danbury, Connecticut; son of Elias Palmer Gage and Mary Oakley
--Romanzo Gage of Danbury m. March 2, 1851, Mary Nealy of Orange, NJ"
--?Romanzo Gage m. before 1860, Rachel .....
--Romanzo Gage m. before 1880, Margaret Personett Brower, widow of Abram D. Brower, q.v.
--1850 Census: p.229, Orange Twp., NJ: Elizabeth "Sime" age 60, b. Nova Scotia; Nathaniel "Sime" age 64, b. Nova Scotia, hatter; "Reminge Gaige" age 22, b. "NY" hatter; Mary "Killet" age 20, b. Ireland
--1860 Census, p.324, Danbury, Fairfield Co., CT: "Romango" Gage, age 30 b. CT, hatter; Rachel age 27 b. NJ; "Romango: age 8 b. CT
--1870 Census: p.350, 2nd Ward Orange, NJ: Margaret Brower age 42, seamstress;; Lydia age 13; John age 5; Also at house:, Thomas Casey age 30 felt hat worker, b. NY; Hannah age 24 b. Ireland; James age 9 months; "Thomanzo" Gage, age 46, felt hat worker.

--1880 Census, p.225.1, 3Wd, Harrison, Hudson Co., NJ: "Romulus" Gage, age 50, b. CT, parents b. CT, hatter; Margaret, (Brower?) age 52, b. NJ, parents b. NJ; Edward, (stepson?) age 15, b. NJ

- - - - -

GARDNER

Gardner, WILLIAM 'W.G.' (map, plot owner, Sect. G)	b. (abt. 1847) d. February 16, 1895 *Aged 48*
Gardner, MARY A. (map, Section G)	b. d. August 1, 1858
Gardner, JULIA (map, Section G)	b. d.
CHILD (map, Section G)	b. d.
CHILD (map, Section G)	b. d.

Notes:
--?1850 Census, p.431&432, 5 Wd. Newark, NJ: William G. Gardner. age 39, feed & flour merchant; Elizabeth, age 35; Pheletta C., age 16; Mary Ann, age 15; Catharine A., age 10; Emirah T. age 18; Frances E., age 1; Sarah R. age 1; Hannah M., age 1; all b. NJ
--?1850 Census, p.432&433, 5 Wd. Newark, NJ: Julia Gardner, age 34; George A., age 5; Burt, age 1, all b. NJ

- - - - -

GARDNER

Gardner, MOSES HEADLEY (map, Sect. B, plot owner)	b. (August 1, 1815) d. (October 5, 1892)
first wife, SARAH A. (Baldwin) (map, Section B)	b. d. (bef. 1850)
second wife, ABIGAIL A.	b. (abt. June 12, 1831)

(Edwards) d. January 26, 1856
(gmnj)(map, Sect. B) *Aged 21.7.14 (24.7.14?)*

third wife, Mary Alecia* b. (May 30, 1827)
(Williams) d. (November 26, 1913)

(?)CLARISSEY, 'wife' of Moses Gardner
(map, Section B) b.
  d.

Gardner, CHILD of George b. (abt. 1869)
(map, Sect. B) (Ellen F. Gardner) d. February 18, 1872

Notes:
--Moses Headley Gardner was born August 1, 1815, son of Jesse Gardner and Lydia Condit.
--Moses died October 5, 1892 (*Condit Genealogy*)
--He m. #1 Sarah Baldwin, November 6, 1837; she may have been a dau. of Jonathan Baldwin and Susannah Williams.
--He m. #2, bef. 1850, Abigail Almira Edwards; she may have been a dau. of David Edwards and Rhoda Dean.
--He m. #3, July 29. 1857, Mary A. Williams, widow of John M. Condit; dau. of Nathanial Williams and Ruth Ludlow

--1850 Census, p.207, Orange Twp: "Mons" Gardner, age 32, shoemaker; Abigail,age 19; George, age 4; all b. NJ
--1860 Census: p.324, 1Wd, Orange, NJ: Moses Gardner, age 48, leather cutter; Mary A. age 33; George Gardner, age 14; Sarah O. Condit age 11; Aaron H. Gardner age 9; John M. Condit age 8; Charlotte Condit age 29, tailoress; Eva Condit age 1.
--1870 Census, p.204, East Orange: Moses Gardner age 54, works boots & shoes; Mary, age 42; Henry (Aaron) age 20; apprentice carpenter; Frank, age 21, (Condit)carpenter; John M. (Condit) age 19, bar keeper; Lewis Baldwin, age 76, farmer; (Lewis Broadwell Baldwin, 1795-1880, son of Jonathan Baldwin and Susannah Williams)
--1880 Census: p.484.3, East Orange, NJ:Moses H. Gardner, age 64, b. NJ, works in shoe factory; Mary A. , wife, age 53, b. NJ; Frank E. Condit,stepson, age 31, carpenter; John M. Condit, stepson, age 28, painter
--1900 Census, p.108, 2Wd East Orange, Essex Co., NJ; Mary A. Gardner b. May 1827, age 73, widow; Frank Condit b. Nov. 1848, single; John Munson, son b. Dec. 1851, m. 15 yrs; Mary H., dau-in-law,

b. Jan 1865 NY; Percy H., grandson b. Jan 1889; Hazel, granddaughter b. Jan 1896
--1910 Census, p.8B, 2Wd, East Orange, NJ: Mary A. Gardner, age 83, widow, 2 born 2 living; Frank E. Condit, age 61, son, single, carpenter; John M. Condit, age 58 married son, decorator; Mary H., age 40 b. NY, dau-in-law, 3 born 2 living; Percy H., age 21, grandson, chemist at lab; Hazel, age 14, granddaughter

Child of Moses Headley Gardner and Sarah A. Baldwin:
George T., b. abt. June 1845; Served: Co. H, 26th NJ Inf., Drummer
    m. Sarah M. Personett, q.v.

Child of Moses Headley Gardner and Abigail A. Edwards:
Henry Aaron, b. abt. 1851; (m. Jennie Loree?)

- - - - -

GARRABRANT

Garrabrant, MUNSON (gmnj)(plot owner, Sect. M) (nps)	b. (abt. 1835) d. (November 19, 1884) *Co.H., 26th NJ Inf*
wife, JANE (Wallace) (map, Section M)	b. (abt. March 1841) d. January 25, 1920
son, WILLIAM M. (map, Section M)	b. (abt. 1868) d. December 7, 1880
Wallace, MARY (map, Section M)	b. d.
Wallace, WILLIAM (map, Section M)	b. d.

Notes:
Served: Civil War;, Co. H, 25th New Jersey Inf., Pvt.(nps)
Served: (?) also, Co. B, 26th NJ Inf., Cpl. (nps)
Gov't headstone provided: 'd. November 19, 1884'
--Munson Garrabrant b. Essex Co., NJ, son of Jacob Garrabrant and Jane .....
--Munson Garrabrant married, September 8, 1858 at Orange Twp., Jane Wallace.

--1850 Census, p.172, Bloomfield, Essex Co., NJ: Jacob G. "Garabrant" age 43, shoemaker; Jane age 40; Munson age 15; 6 younger children; all b. New Jersey
--1860 Census: p.370, 3Wd, Orange, NJ: Munson "Garabrant", age 25, carpenter, b. NJ; Jane age 18 b. Ireland; Edward W. age 10 months, b. NJ.
--1870 Census: p.394, 3rd Ward, Orange, NJ. Munson Garrabrant, age 35, carpenter, b. NJ; Jane age 30 b. Ireland; Edward age 11; George age 9; Margaret age 8; Emma age 6; Samuel age 6; William age 2; Margaret Wallace age 50, dressmaker b. Ireland; William Wallace age 16, b. NJ
--1880 Census, p.167.1, Orange: "Menson" Garrabrant, age 45 b. NJ, carpenter; Jane, age 40 b. Ireland; Edward W. age 20, works hat factory; George H., age 19, works hat factory; Margaret J. age 17, dressmaking; Mary E. age 15, twin;
Samuel, age 15, twin; William M. age 12; all children b. New Jersey
--?1900 Census, p.14A, West Orange: Frederick Merwin, b. May 1857 NJ; Lena b. Mar 1860 NJ; 6 children; Jane Garrabrant b. March 1841, widow, mother-in-law, m.40 yrs., 5 born 5 living; all b. NJ

Children of Munson Garrabrant and Jane Wallace:
Edward W., b. abt 1859
Lena, b. March 1860; m. Frederick Merwin
George H., b. abt. 1861
Margaret J., b. abt. 1862
Mary Emma, twin,b. abt. 1864
Samuel, twin, b. abt. 1864
William M. , b. abt. 1868; d. 1880

- - - - -

GILL

Gill, W. H.   b. (abt. 1856)
(map, grave owned,Sect. I)   d. April 14, 1860

Notes:

- - - - -

GILMAN

Gilman, Zebulon*   b. (abt. 1785)

                                    d. (aft. 1860)

wife, MARIA   b. (abt. 1788)
(gmnj)(csl - E51)   d. October 20, 1862
                                    Aged 74

Notes:
--1850 Census: p.222&223, Orange Twp., NJ: "Tibriton: Gilman, age 58, farmer, b. New Hampshire; Maria age 55 b. Massachusetts; boarders: Robert Blinkiron, age 24, b. England, teacher; William Onderdonk, age 32 b. NY, grocer;
Julia (nee Julia Morris Bleecker) age 26 b. NY; Sarah Onderdonk age 3 b. NY; William Onderdonk, age 1, b. NJ; 2 servants
--1860 Census: p. 427 & 428, 2nd Ward Orange, NJ.: Zebulon Gilman, age 75 b. 'Massachusetts'; Maria age 75, b. 'New Hampshire'; Isabell Dever, age 16, seamstress, b. Ireland

- - - - -

Gilman, MRS. ALECIA(?)   b.
(map, Sect.J)   d. ?(November 11, 1903)
(removed to Rosedale Cem.)

Notes:
--bur. map, Section J, plot of George N. Boyd, q.v.

- - - - -

GIST

Gist, Robert F.*   b. (abt. 1823)
(map, plot owner, Sect. J)   d. (aft. 1910)

wife, MARY A.   b. (abt. 1825)
(map, Sect. J)   d. August 30, 1854

daughter, MARY A.   b. (December 29, 1846)
(csl - E57)(map, Sect. J)   d. August 29, 1854
                                    Aged 7.8.0

daughter, MARGARET S.   b. (May 1, 1849)
(gmnj) (csl - E57)   d. September 1, 1854
(map, Sect. J)   *Aged 5.4.0*

SON of Robert Gist   b.
(map, Sect. J)   d.

Notes:
--1850 Census, p.254, 4Wd, New York City: Robert "Gest" age 27 b. England, hatter; Mary A., age 25, b. England; Mary A. age 3, b. NY; Margaret, age 1, b. NY
--1860 Census, p.428, 2Wd, Orange: Robert T. "Guest" age 33, b. England, hatter; Mary A., age 30 b. England; Robert F., age 9, b. NY
--1870 Census, p.355, 2Wd, Orange: Robert "Gest" age 47 b. England, works at felt hat factory; Mary, age 40, b. Ireland; Robert, age 18, b. NY; John age 9, b. NJ
--1880 Census: p.125A, Orange, NJ: Robert Gist, age 57, b. England; Mary Ann, wife, age 52, b. Ireland; Robert F. son, age 26, b. NY, works in hat shop; John Gist, son, age 19, b. NJ, works in hat shop.
--1900 Census, p.10A, 5Wd, Orange City: Robert Gist b. Feb. 1852, m.3 yr, b. NY, parents b. England, hat manufacturer; Elenore, b. January 1873 NJ, father b. NJ, mother b. Ireland; Margaret b. Jan. 1898 NJ; Robert b. Feb. 1899, NJ
--1910 Census, p.5B, 5Wd, Orange: Robert Gist, age 58, widower, hat manufacturer; Margaret age 12 b. NJ; Robert, age 10 b. NJ; 1 housekeeper
--1910 Census, p.7B, 5Wd, Orange: John Gist age 49 m. 5 yr, b. NJ, father England, mother Ireland, hat manufacturer; Alice age 41 b. NJ, parents b. England; Marine age 3 b. NJ; John age 1 yr 5 mos. b. NJ; Elizabeth Sutcliff, age 32, sister-in-law, single, b. NJ, parents b. England

Children of Robert Gist and Mary Ann .....
Mary A., b. 1846; d.1854
Margaret, b. 1849; d. 1854
Robert F., b. abt 1851; m. Elenore .....
John W., b. abt 1861; m. Alice Sutcliff

- - - - -

GONZALES

Gonzales, FRANK L.   b. (May 12, 1870)
(csl - E9)   d. October 17, 1870
(map, ch. property, Sect. M) *Aged 0.5.5*

son of E.B. and V.A.

Notes:
--1870 Census: p.180, East Orange, NJ: Emanuel Gonzales age 40, retail grocer, b. Penna; Victoria age 30 b. Vermont. (Will of Emanuel #19087G, 1877)
--1880 Census p.467C East Orange: Mary C. Pierson age 76 widow b. NJ parents b. NJ; Phebe A. Pierson dau. div. age 49 b. NJ; Ernest F. Pierson son married age 24 b. NJ works on farm; Mary J. Pierson 'dau' married age 24 b. NJ; Walton H. Baldwin grandnephew age 21 b. NJ works on farm; George McClennan other single age 28 b. NJ parents NJ; Victoria Gonzales other married age 39 b. VT parents b. VT; Entz Gonzales other single female age 9 b. NJ father b. PA mother b. VT; Lester "Woodard' father age 78 b. VT parents VT; Hannah 'Woodard' wife age 78 b. VT parents b. RI
--1895 NJ State Census, p.50, 2Wd, Orange: Victoria A. Gonzales; David L. Pierson; Entz Pierson; (census page damaged)
--1900 Census p.3B 2Wd East Orange: "Rid. I." Pierson age 34 b. Feb. 1866 m.11 yrs. b. NJ parents b. NJ 'printer'(?); "Ersty G." Pierson wife age 28 b. Sept. 1871 0 born 0 living b. NJ father b. 'NY' mother b. 'NH'
--1910 Census, p.6B, 2Wd, East Orange: David L. Pierson, age 45, m.20 yr. b. NJ, parents NJ, newspaper reporter; 'Entz gurzales' Pierson, age 37 b. NJ, father NJ, mother VT, 0 born 0 living; Anna E. Sully, age 34, friend, single, b. England, trained nurse for private families

Children of Emanuel Gonzales and Victoria A. Woodard:
Frank, b. 1870; d.1870
Entz, b. September 1871; m. David L. Pierson

- - - - -

GORDON

Gordon, ROBERT b. (abt. 1875)
(gmnj)(map, Section H) d. May 15, 1899
Aged 24

Notes:
--bur: map, Section H, plot of Alexander Willis, q.v.

- - - - -

GRAHAM

Graham, SAMUEL
(map, plot owner, Sect. N)
b. (abt. 1804)
d. June 25, 1883

wife, MARY
(map, Section N)
b. (abt. 1803)
d. December 12, 1878

DAUGHTER, of S. Graham
(map, Section N)
b.
d.

CHILD
(map, Section N)
b.
d.

Notes:
--1860 Census, p.377, 3Wd, Orange NJ: Samuel Graham, age 56, b. Ireland, laborer; Mary, age 57, b. Ireland; Georgianna, age 18 b. England, hat trimmer; Sarah, age 11, b. England
--1870 Census, p.376, 3Wd, Orange, NJ: Samuel Graham, age 64, b. Ireland, agent for Samuel Hurlbut; Mary A., age 65; Sarah, age 21, b. England
--1880 Census, p.142.3 Orange, NJ: Mary Malone, age 48 b. Ireland, single; Samuel 'Grahan' age 74, widower, b. Ireland, collecting agent

Children of Samuel Graham and Mary A. .....
Georgianna, b. abt. 1842; m. John Lightholder
Sarah, b. abt. 1849

- - - - -

GRANT

Grant, ANNE E.
(map, Section O)
b.
d. October 14, 1882

Grant, ARAMINTHA
(map, Section O)
b.
d. March 14, 1872

Notes:
--Map says: "Section O, Row 5: Negro Burial Ground"
--See: James Grant?
--?1850 Census, p. 239, Orange Twp., NJ: James Grant, age 50, hatter; Ann, age 29, Mary, age 23; Anna, age 20; all b. England (adj. to Samuel Blanchard, age 30, black; see Blanchard)

--?1860 Census, p.393, 3Wd, Orange, NJ: John Weston, age 33, b. England, contractor; Mary, age 32, b. England; 4 Weston children; 6 boarders; Ann Grant, age 58, b. England
--?1870 Census, p.469, West Orange, NJ: John Weston, age 46, b. Engl., gardener; Mary, age 44 b. Engl.; 4 Weston children b. NJ; Ann Grant, age 68, b. England, no occup.
--?1880 Census: p.256.1, West Orange, NJ: Mary E. Teachman, age 38, white, widow, b. CT; Ida Teachman, dau.,age 13, b. NJ, father b. NJ; Ann Grant, mother, widow, age 78 b. England (same page as Amzi DeGroat, q.v.)

- - - - -

Grant, JAMES
(map, plot owner, Sect.H)

b.
d. April 1, 1857

Notes:
--See?: Ann Grant, Section O
--See, map, Section H: also bur. in this plot: 'wife of Levi Talbert, q.v.; 'child of ..... Ducker'q.v. and 'child of C. H. Johnson'q.v.
--?1850 Census, p. 239, Orange Twp., NJ: James Grant, age 50, hatter; Ann, age 29, Mary, age 23; Anna, age 20; all b. England (adj. to Samuel Blanchard, age 30, black; see Blanchard)

- - - - -

GRAY

Gray, THEODORE H.
(map, Section E)

b. (December 21, 1826)
d. April 12, 1867
Aged 40.3.22

widow, MATILDA T.
(Thirston/Thurston?)
(gmnj)(csl-E104)(map,Sect.E)

b. (November 27, 1829)
d. June 10, 1880
Aged 50.6.13

son, THOMAS PORTER
(gmnj)(csl-108)(map,Sect.E)

b. (abt. 1851)
d. May 24, 1872
In 21st year

daughter, MARY ELLA
(csl - E109)(map, Sect. E)

b. (abt. 1856)
d. March 17, 1864
Aged 8

Gray, JOHN (map, Section E)	b. d. April 29, 1850
Gray, MARY (map, Section E)	b. (abt. 1790) d. May 3, 1859
Gray, MISS (map, Section E)	b. d. March 16, 1864 *Aged 11 years*
Gray, MARY (map, Section E)	b. d. February 16, 1850

Notes:
--See: map, Section E, plot of Isaac B. Condit
--?Theodore H. Gray was son of John Gray and Mary Gray
--Theodore was brother of Eliza Gray who m. Isaac B. Condit, q.v.

--1850 Census, p.235, 14Wd, New York New York: Mary Gray, age 60 b. NJ; Theodore Gray, age 26 b. NY, printer; Eliza Conditt age 39 b. NJ; Mary Gray,age 19 b. PA; Phebe A. Gray, age 14, b. NY; Joseph Conditt, age 4, b. NY; Harriet Conditt, age 7, b. NY
--?1850 Census, p.296, 11Wd, New York City, NY: Matilda Thurston, age 20 b. NY. boarder
--1860 Census, p.0, 22Wd, Dist. 1, New York, New York: Catherine Thirston, age 55, b. NJ, book & paper dealer; Theodore H. Gray, age 35, b. NY, printer; Mathilda Gray age 30 b. NY; T. P. Gray, age 8 b. NY; Ella Gray, age 4, b. NY
--?1880 Census, p.241.3, Staten Island, Richmond Co.NY: A. Furguson, age 35, b. Scotland, engraver; Anna D. Furguson age 24 b. NY; Florence Furguson age 1 daughter, b. NY; Matilda Gray, age 51, widow, boarder, b. NY

Children of Theodore H. Gray and Matilda 'Thirston?':
Thomas Porter, b. 1851; d. 1872
Mary Ella, b. 1856; d. 1864

- - - - -

GREEN

Green, AARON	b. (abt. 1820)

(gmnj)	d. (April 23, 1890)
(map, plot owner,Section J)	*Co. D. 13 NJ Inf.*
wife, RUTILLA	b. (abt. 1820)
(map, Section J)	d.
Green, LAFAYETTE	b.
(map, Sect. J)(child)	d. April 14, 1860
Green, LIZZIE	b.
(map, Section J)	d. February 1, 1872

Notes:
Served: Civil War; Co. D, 13th NJ Inf., Pvt. (nps)
Gov't headstone provided: ' d. April 23, 1890'
--Aaron was son of Gilbert Green and Belinda Harrison

--1850 Census: p.222, Orange Twp., NJ: Aaron Green age 31, shoemaker; Rutilla age 30, William H. age 7; Warren W. age 4; Martha age 1; all b. New Jersey
--1860 Census, p.215, 7Wd, Newark: Aaron Green, age 40, shoemaker; Rotilla age 41; William age 17; Martha J. age 11; Charlotte E. age 9; 'Wainee', male, age 50(?) (Warren W., age 15); all b. New Jersey
--1870 Census, p.148, 7 Wd, Newark: Aaron Green age 51, works at shoe factory; Rutilla age 50; Martha J. age 21, works at cotton (hat?) factory; Charlotte age 19, works at cotton (hat?) factory; all b. New Jersey
--1900 Census, p.9A, 1Wd, Kearny, Hudson Co. NJ: William H. Green b. July 1843 NJ, insurance agent; Cornelia b. Nov. 1853, NJ, parents b. NJ; Annie E. b. Sept. 1876 NJ, lamp tester; Esther M. b. April 1880, NJ, 'winder'; Rutilla S. b. Oct. 1888, NJ, at school

Children of Aaron Green and Rutilla .....:
William H.,q.v. b. July 1843; m. ?Lizzie .....;
      m. Cornelia Amelia .....
Warren W., b. abt 1846
Martha J., b. abt 1849
Charlotte, b. abt. 1851

- - - - -

Green, ANN S.	b.
daughter, of W.P.Green	d. May 1868

(map, Section N)

Notes:
--bur. map, Section N, plot of Samuel Graham, q.v.

- - - - -

Green, William H.* b. (July 1843)
 d.

?first wife, LIZZIE b. June 11, 1843
(csl - E48)(map, Sect. J) d. February 16, 1872
(removed to Rosedale Cemetery)

Notes:
--?William H. Green was son of Aaron Green, q.v.

--1850 Census: p.222, Orange Twp., NJ: Aaron Green age 31, shoemaker; Rutilla age 30, William H. age 7; Warren W. age 4; Martha age 1; all b. New Jersey
--1860 Census, p.215, 7Wd, Newark: Aaron Green, age 40, shoemaker; Rotilla age 41; William age 17; Martha J. age 11; Charlotte E. age 9; 'Wainee', male, age 50(?) (Warren W., age 15); all b. New Jersey
--?1870 Census
--?1880 Census, p.230.3, Harrison, Hudson Co.NJ: Wm. H. Green, age 36, b. NJ, parents NJ, bell hanger; Cornelia A., age 25, b. NJ, father NJ, mother CT; Emily A. age 5, b. NJ; Annie E., age 3, b. NJ; Ella A., age 1 b. NJ
--?1900 Census, p.9A, 1Wd, Kearny, Hudson Co. NJ: William H. Green b. July 1843 NJ., m. '4' yrs., insurance agent; Cornelia b. Nov. 1853 NJ; Annie E. b. Sept. 1876 NJ, lamp tester; Esther M. b. April 1880, winder; Rutilla S. b. Oct. 1888, at school; all b. NJ
--?1910 Census, p.4B, 1Wd, Kearny, Hudson Co. NJ: William H. Green age 66, m. '45 yr' b. NJ; "Con A." age 56 b. NJ, 3 born 3 living; 'Ester' age 20, b. NJ, winder at cotton mill
--?1920 Census, p.8A, 3Wd, Kearny, Hudson Co., NJ: 'Delman' McAllister age 53 b. Scotland, clerk at thread co.; Anna age 42 b. NJ; Mary age 22 b. NJ, stenographer at thread co.; William H. Green, age 76, father-in-law, b. NJ,
retired; Amelia C. Green age 64, mother-in-law, b. NJ; Ester M. Green age 39, sister-in-law, b. NJ, stenographer at Colgates.
--?1930 Census, p.2B, Kearny, Hudson Co. NJ: Duncan McAllister age 63 b. Scotland; Annie E. age 53 b. NJ; Mary J. age 33; William Green,

age 86, father-in-law, b. NJ; "Camelia A." Green, age 76, mother-in-law b. NJ

Children of William H. Green and Cornelia Amelia ....:
Emily A., b. abt. 1875
Annie E., b. abt. 1877; m. Duncan McAllister
Ella A., b. abt. 1879
Esther M., b. abt. 1880
Rutilla S., b. abt. 1888

- - - - -

HAND

Hand, Charles
(map, plot owner, Sect. D)
b.
d.

Hand, CHILDREN of Chas.
(map, Section D)
b.
d.

Hand, MATTIE F.
(map, Section D)
b.
d. June 16, 1863

Hand, ALBERT
(map, Section D)
b.
d. April 10, 1883

Note:
--?Charles Hand, b. abt. 1814, Orange, NJ; son of Elias Hand and Gwin Williams
--?1880 Census, p.581D, Millburn, Essex Co.NJ: Charles J. Hand, age 31, b. NJ, parents b. Ireland, carpenter; Mary (Kelly), wife, age 29, b.Ireland; John, age 7;James, age 4; Mary, age 1

- - - - -

HANSON

Hanson, H.
(map, Section H)
b.
d. December 21, 1876

Notes:
--bur. map, Section H, plot of Isaac Baldwin, q.v.

--?1870 Census, p.356, 2Wd. Orange, NJ: Henry Hanson, age 48 b. Prussia, carpenter; 'Erica' age 38 b. Prussia; Ida, age 13 b. Prussia; Henry, age 10 b. Prussia; Bernard, age 6 b. Prussia; Charles, age 2, b. NJ
--?1880 Census, p.276B, West Orange, NJ: 'Ida' Hanson, widow, age 47 b. Hostein; Henry, age 19, b. NJ; 'Benjamin' age 14 b. NJ; Charles, age 11, b. NJ; Jenny, age 5 b. NJ; Martha C., age 3 b. NJ
--?1900 Census, p.11B, 2Wd, Orange, NJ: Augustus Reeves, age 48, b. NJ, supt. coal yard; Ida age 43, b. Germany; Charles B. 16, b. NJ; Emily T. age 6, NJ; Ida Hanson, age 67, widow, mother-in-law b. Germany; Charles Hanson, age 31, bro.-in-law, b. NJ; Martha Hanson, sis-in-law, age 22 b. NJ

?Children of Henry Hanson and Ida Hanson:
Ida, b. abt. 1857; m. Augustus W. Reeves, q.v.
Henry, b. abt. 1860; m. ? Minnie .....
Bernard, b. abt. 1864
Charles, b. March 16, 1868; m. ?Edith D. .....
Jenny, b. abt. 1875
Martha C., b. January 11, 1877

- - - - -

HARRISON

Harrison, CALEB b. April 17, 1777
(gmnj)(shaw) d. September 10, 1854
(map, Section A, plot owner)
(NJ Will #1453G, 1854)

Caleb Harrison
Born April 17, 1771
Died Sept. 10,1851
in the 84th year
of his age

wife, KETURAH (Crane) b. May 6, 1769
(gmnj)(csl - E196)(map,Sect. A) d. April 9, 1855

Keturah
wife of Caleb Harrison
Born May 6th, 1769

> *Died April 9th 1855*
> *in the 86th year*
> *of her age*

son, SIMEON   b. April 26, 1792
(csl - E196)(map,Sect. A)   d. September 30, 1799
                                Aged 7.5.4

> *Simeon*
> *Son of*
> *Caleb Harrison*
> *Born April 26, 1792*
> *Died Sept 30, 1799*
> *in the 8th year*
> *of his age*

daughter, MARY   b. September 24, 1793
(csl - E196)(map,Sect. A)   d. September 24, 1815

> *Mary*
> *Daughter of*
> *Caleb Harrison*
> *Born Sept 24 1793*
> *Died Sept. 24, 1815*
> *aged 22 years*

daughter, PHEBE   b. March 17, 1802
(map, Section A)   d. February 22, 1892
(?NJ Will #24514G, 1892)

Notes:
--Caleb Harrison was son of Simeon Harrison, q.v., and Hannah Crane.
--Caleb Harrison m. Keturah Crane, February 15, 1792 at Caldwell, NJ. (IGI)
--Caleb Harrison was a founder of **St. Mark's** Church in 1827.(Shaw, p.807)
--Keturah Crane was daughter of Isaac Crane q.v. and Joanna Ogden. (*Harrison Gen.*, p.64)

--1850 Census, p.240, Orange Twp: Caleb "Hamson" age 79, farmer; "Katura" age 80; Phebe, age 48; Simeon age 46, farmer; Abby M. age '15'; all b. NJ; 7 labor

--1860 Census, p.383, 3Wd, Orange: Simeon Harrison, age 56, farmer; Phebe age 58; Abby age 25; all b. NJ; 2 farm laborers; 3 servants
--1870 Census, p.466, West Orange: Simeon Harrison,a ge 66, b. NJ, farmer, real estate value $125,000; Phebe (sister), age 68, b. NJ; Saml. C. Rollinson age 39, b. NY, merchant; Abby M. Rollinson, (dau. of Simeon) age 35, b. NJ
--1880 Census: p.272 A, West Orange, NJ: Phebe Harrison, aunt, single, age 78, b. NJ, at home; at residence of Samuel O. Rollinson(q.v.)

Children of Caleb Harrison and Keturah Crane:
Simeon, b. abt. 1792; d. 1799
Mary, b. abt. 1793; d. 1815
Margaret, b. May 10, 1800; d. April 17,1865;
    married Joel Wheeler Condit q.v.
Phebe, b. abt. 1802; d. 1892, unm.
Simeon Harrison (q.v.)b. Feb.1804; d. March 10, 1872; m.   Abby Maria Condit
Hannah Harrison b.1805; d. 1879; m. Wm.Whittingham (q.v.)

- - - - -

Harrison, HENRY   b. (abt. 1813)
(map, plot owner, Sect. G) d. June 5, 1853
                           Aged 40

Harrison, WILLIAM H.   b.
(map, Section G)   d. May 6, 1855

Harrison, ... C.   b.
(map, Section G)   d. November 5, 1855

Notes:
--?Henry W. Harrison, m. May 9, 1838, Mary S. Pierson

--?1850 Census, p.94, North Wd, Newark, NJ: Henry W. Harrison, age 36, carpenter; Mary, age 36; Bethuel, age 11; Charles, age 10; Edward, age 8; Caroline, age 15; William, age 3; Mary, age 1; all b. NJ

- - - - -

Harrison, JOHN   b. May 29, 1776
(gmnj) (shaw)(csl - E196)   d. December 14, 1841
(map, Section A)

(NJ Will #1313G,1842)

> *John Harrison*
> *Born May 29, 1776*
> *Died Dec. 14, 1841*
> *in the 65th year*
> *of his age*

wife, ABIGAIL (Ogden) b. September 18, 1781
(csl - E196)(map, Sect. A) d. January 2, 1851

> *Abby*
> *wife of*
> *John Harrison*
> *Born Sept 18, 1781*
> *Died Jan 2, 1851*
> *in the 70th year*
> *of her age*

Notes:
--John Harrison was a founder of St. Mark's Church.
--John Harrison was son of Simeon Harrison and Hannah Crane. He married Abby Ogden January 14, 1799 at Essex Co., NJ.or April 24, 1799 at Caldwell, NJ.at Essex Co., NJ. (*Harrison Gen.*, p.46) (IGI)
--Abby/Abigail was daughter of John Ogden and Elizabeth Magie.

--1850 Census, p.233, Orange Twp: Jemima Baldwin, age 65; Caleb W. Baldwin, age 36, cabinet maker; Theresa Baldwin, age 20; Phebe Baldwin, age 1; Abby Harrison, age 58; all b. New Jersey

- - - - -

Harrison, NATHAN S.   b. (March 16, 1828)
(gmnj)(csl - E101)   d. June 1, 1849
(map, Section F)   *Aged 21.2.16*

> *This stone*
> *is Erected by the Members*
> *of*
> *Exchange Guard*
> *of Newark*
> *In memory of*
> *Nathan S. Harrison*

who died
June 1st 1849
Age 21 Years. 2 mo.
& 16 days

How short the race our friend has run
Cut down in all his bloom
The course but yesterday begun
Now finished in the tomb
This thus the Lord reveals his grace
Thy youthful love to gain
The soul that early seeks my face
Shall never seek in vain

Notes:
--bur. map, Section F, plot of James Petit, q.v.
--Nathan S. Harrison was the son of Amos A. Harrison and Sarah Badgely
--Amos A. Harrison was b. January 9, 1791, Orange, NJ; d. abt. 1852, St. Louis, Missouri. He m. #1, Cornelia Bainbridge; m. #2, October 20. 1812, Sarah Badgely.

--1840 Census: Clinton Twp., Essex Co., NJ: Amos A. Harrison
--1850 Census: p.478, 6Wd, St. Louis, Missouri: Mary Williams, age 32; Edwin Williams, age 7; Owen Williams age 4; Amos Harrison, age 61, spoke turner; Lewis Harrison, age 12; Charles Burgans, age 11; all b. New Jersey

Children of Amos A. Harrison and Sarah Badgely:
William. b. 1814; m. Mary Pierson
Martha C., b. 1816; d. 1899; m. Samuel Losey
Mary, b. 1818; m. Oscar B. Crane; m. Owen C. Williams
Catherine b. 1820; m. James Pettit, q.v.
Joanna b. 1821; m. George Hughes
Emily N. b. 1823; m. Moses Peck
Edward D. b. 1826
Nathan S. b. 1828; d. 1849
Frances E. b. 1830; d. 1857; m. Henry Ward
Benjamin b. 1834; b. bef. 1836
Benjamin, b. 1836
Lewis Condit b. 1838; d. 1919; m. Henrietta Toms

- - - - -

Harrison, SIMEON
(gmnj) (shaw)(csl - E196)
(NJ Will #11185G, 1819)

b. September 17, 1741
d. September 20, 1819

Simeon Harrison
Born Sept. 17, 1741
Died Sept 20 1819
in the 78th year
of his age

wife, HANNAH (Crane)
(csl - E196)

b. August 16, 1746
d. January 12, 1839

Hannah
wife of
Simeon Harrison
Born Aug 16, 1746
Died Jan 12, 1839
in the 93rd year
of her age

Notes:
--Simeon Harrison was son of Amos Harrison and Hannah Johnson.
--He m. Hannah Crane b. August 16, 1746, daughter of Caleb Crane.
--Simeon Harrison was on the Orange town council in 1862. (Shaw p.734)

Children of Simeon Harrison and Hannah Crane;
Caleb Harrison, q.v., b. 1770; d.1854
Phebe Harrison, b. 1774 m. Noah Matthews, q. v.
John Harrison,q.v., b. 29 March 1776 m. Abby Ogden
Hannah Harrison b. 1781 b. John F. Bruen, q.v.
Sarah Harrison b. 1783, d. 1841, m. Joseph Matthews
(*Harrison Gen.*,p.46)

- - - - -

Harrison, SIMEON
(csl - E197)
(map, Section A, plot owner)

b. February 17, 1804
d. May 26, 1872

wife ABBY MARIA (Condit)   b. (February 26, 1810)

Noah Matthews family plot
Photo: Vincent P. Dahmen

Bell family plot
Photo: Vincent P. Dahmen

Milne family plot
Photo: Vincent P. Dahmen

Unidentified plot
Photo: Vincent P. Dahmen

St. Mark's Church, south east side
Photo: Vincent P. Dahmen

St. Mark's Church, north east side
Photo: Vincent P. Dahmen

Corner Stone: "St. Mark Church" [sic]
Incorporated A.D. 1827; Erected A.D. 1828
Photo: Vincent P. Dahmen

Plaque for the chimes at St. Mark's Church
Photo: Vincent P. Dahmen

Window at St. Mark's Church (above)
in memory of Andrew Whittemore Ward
Photo: Vincent P. Dahmen

Oldest window at St. Mark's Church
in memory of Benj. Williams
Photo: Vincent P. Dahmen

Burnside plot in the year 2000
Photo: Carol P. Comfort

Burnside plot in the year 2008
Photo: Vincent P. Dahmen

(gmnj)(csl-E198)(map,Sect.A)   d. May 26, 1835

In/Memory of
Abby Maria Condit
wife of
Simeon Harrison
who died May 26th 1835
Aged 25 years & 28 days

Notes:
--His correct death date may be March 20,1872.
--In 1858 Simeon was elected as a representative of the Second Assembly District to the State Legislature.It was largely through his efforts that the new charter for Orange was obtained in 1860, and he was elected a member of the first Common Council under this charter. Simeon Harrison was on the West Orange Twp., Committee in 1863 and 1870. (Shaw p.806)
--Simeon was the fifth child of Caleb Harrison, q.v., and Keturah Crane.
--Abby Maria Condit, b. April 28, 1810 (or February 26, 1810). She was daughter of Stephen Condit and Mary E. Ogden.

--1850 Census, p.240, Orange Twp: Caleb "Hamson" age 79, farmer; "Katura" age 80; Phebe, age 48; Simeon age 46, farmer; Abby M. age '15'; all b. NJ; 7 labor
--1860 Census, p.383, 3Wd, Orange: Simeon Harrison, age 56, farmer; Phebe age 58; Abby age 25; all b. NJ; 2 farm laborers; 3 servants
--1870 Census, p.466, West Orange: Simeon Harrison,a ge 66, b. NJ, farmer, real estate value $125,000; Phebe (sister),
age 68, b. NJ; Saml. C. Rollinson age 39, b. NY, merchant; Abby M. Rollinson, (dau. of Simeon) age 35, b. NJ

Child of Simeon Harrison and Abby Maria Condit:
Abby Maria, m. Samuel O. Rollinson (q.v.)

- - - - -

Harrison, WILLIAM W.	b. (abt. 1822)
(gmnj)(csl - E79)	d. (March 3, 1868)
(map, Section G) (nps)	Co. G, 26th NJ Inf

wife,MARY G. (Joyner)	b. (abt 1829)
(map, Section G)	d. January 16, 1907

Aged 78

Harrison, CHILD of Wm. b.
(map, Section G) d.

Harrison, HARRIET A. b.
(map, Section G) d. August 22, 1859

Hodge, RHODA A. b.
(map, Section G) bur. May 8, 1913
Aged 0.6.28

Notes:
Served: Civil War; Co. H/G, 26th NJ Inf., Pvt. (nps)
Gov't headstone provided: d. May 3, 1865'
--William Wallace Harrison was born June 5, 1822 at Orange, NJ; son of Abram Harrison and Rhoda Tichenor OR son of Bethuel Vincent Harrison and Maria Sigler?
--? "Bethuel Vincent Harrison (13 May 1792-1829) m. 19 Dec. 1812 Maria Sigler at Stone House Plains Dutch Reformed Church. Their children included John, William Wallace, Charlotte, Phebe, Catherine, and Emily. The boys received $80 and the girls $40 from Moses' (Harrison) will.
--William Wallace Harrison m. Mary Georgiana Joyner, December 12, 1846, Orange, NJ
--Mary G. Joiner died in Orange NJ. Her surviving children: William W. Harrison of Columbus,OH; Mrs. R. G. Crane; Mrs. E. A. Ott; Mrs. William Clark, all daus. of Orange. 17 grandchildren and 9 great-grandchildren."

--1850 Census, p.393, Urbane, Champaign Co.Ohio: W. W. Harris age 25, b. NJ, hatter; Mary G. age 24 b. England; Alabama age 2, b. Ohio; Eliza F. age 1, b. Ohio
--1860 Census: p.419, 2Wd. Orange, NJ: Wm. W. Harrison age 38, hatter; Georgianna age 36, b. England; Elizabeth A. age 12 b. Ohio; Eliza F age 11 b. Ohio; Rhoda G. age 6 b Ohio; William W. age 2, b. NJ.
--1870 Census, p.344, 2Wd, Orange, NJ: Georgiana Harrison, age 41, b. England, seamstress; Alabama, age 22, b. OH, works felt hat factory; Eliza, age 20, b. OH, works felt hat factory; Georgiana age 16 b. OH; William, age 11, b. OH; Frederick, age 8, b. NJ
--1880 Census: p.96 D, Orange, NJ: Georgianna Harrison, widow, age 48, b. England, father b. France, mother b. England; Frederick J. Harrison, son, age 19, b. NJ, hatter apprentice.

--1900 Census, p.16A, West Orange: Georgeana Harrison, age 70, widow, b. England

Children of William Wallace Harrison and Mary Georgiana Joyner:
Elizabeth Alabama, b. abt 1848
Eliza F., b. abt 1849
Rhoda Georgiana, b. abt 1854
William W., b. abt 1858
Frederick J., b. abt. Oct. 1861; m. abt. 1885, Sarah .....

- - - - -

HARROLD

Harrold, CHRISTOPHER   b. (abt. 1820)
(gmnj)(map Section G)   d. (aft. 1880)
(nps)   *Co.D, #1 N.J. L.A.*

wife, ELIZABETH   b. (abt. 1820)
(map, Section G)   d. (aft. 1880)

Harrold, WILLIAM B.   b.
(map, Section G)   d. June 3, 1856

Notes:
Served: Civil War; Co. D. #1 NJ Light Artillery, Pvt. (nps)
--bur. map, Section G, plot of Ann P. Browne, q.v.

--1860 Census, p.389, 3Wd Orange: Christopher "Harden" age 33 b. NY, shoemaker; Elizabeth age 29, b. Ireland; Christopher age 9 b. NJ; Mary A., age 8 b. NJ; Arthur, age 1 b. NJ;
--1870 Census, p.383, 3Wd, Orange: Christopher "Hurld" age 50 b. Ireland, works boot/shoe factory; Eliza age 49 b. Ireland; Christopher age 20 b. NJ, works at felt hat factory; Mary A., age 18, b. NJ, apprentice to felt hatter
--1880 Census: p.151.2, Orange, NJ: James Savage age 35, b. NJ, parents b. Ireland, hatter; Mary Ann Savage, age 26, b. NJ; Ellen Savage age 6, b. NJ; Henry Savage age 1, b. NJ; Christopher Harrold, age 50, b.NY, father-in-law, works at shoe factory; Elizabeth Harrold, age 58, b. Ireland, mother-in-law

Children of Christopher Harrold and Elizabeth ..... :
Christopher, b. abt 1850

Mary Ann, b. abt, 1854, m. #1, James Savage
    m.#2, Benjamin Johnston
Arthur, b. abt 1859; d. before 1870?

- - - - -

HEALLY

Heally, JOHN
(map,ch property,Sect.H)
b.
d. April 18, 1882

Heally, CHILD of John
(map, ch. property, Sect. H)
b.
d. 1882

Heally, CHILD of John
(map, ch. property, Sect. H)
b.
d. 1882

Notes:

- - - - -

HEER

Heer, CHARLES M.
(map,plot owner, Sect. L)
b. (abt. 1828)
d. February 7, 1858

wife, Catherine*
b. (abt. 1823)
d. (aft. 1870)

Heer, CATHERINE
(map, Section L)
b.
d. November 20, 1854

Notes:
--See: John Boehner
--Charles M. Heer, age 22, son of Melchior Heer, m. Nov. 12, 1850 at Newark, Catherine Brady, age 27, dau. of Bernard Brady
--1850 Census, p.210, Orange Twp., NJ: Charles M. Heer, age 21, b. Switzerland, barber; Franklin Haniford, age 16, b. Maine, barber
--1860 Census, p.420, 2Wd, Orange, NJ: Catherine Heer, age 40, b. Ireland; Catherine, age 7, b. NJ; Emily age 3 b. NJ; Ellen, age 3, b. NJ
--1870 Census, p.468, West Orange, NJ: Catharine Heer, age 50 b. Ireland; Catharine, age 18, b. NJ, hat trimmer; Emily Heer, age 16, b. NJ, hat trimmer; Nellie, age 14, b. NJ

Children of Charles M. Heer and Catherine Brady:
Catherine, b. Jan. 28, 1852; m. John Boehner, q.v.
Emily, b. abt. 1857
Ellen "Nellie", b. abt. 1857

- - - - -

HENDERSON

Henderson, LYDIA
(map, Section A)

b. (abt. 1890
d. December 12, 1918
Aged 28.2.28

Notes:
--bur. map, Section A, plot of Caleb Townley, q.v.
--?dau. of William Rainard Henderson and Clara Louise Williams
--1880 Census, p.277D, West Orange, Essex Co., NJ; Wm. H. Henderson, age 38, works hat mfg; Louise E. age 33; Wm. R. age 19, works hat mfg.; Emily T. 17, hat trimmer; Carrie, age 14; Theodore, age 11; Jennie age 9; Lilly, age 5; all b. NJ
--1900 Census, p.14A, Verona, Essex Co., NJ: William R. Henderson b. Jul 1870, m.17 yr., b. NJ, father NJ, mother Germany, hatter; Clara L., b. Dec. 1857 NJ; Albert S., b. Feb. 1884 NJ

- - - - -

HENNESSEY

Hennessey, LOUISA
(map, Section G)

b.
d. April 21, 1859

Notes:
--bur. map, Section G, plot of Morris Condit, q.v.

- - - - -

HEPFNER

Hepfner, AUGUST
(map, Section L)

b. (abt. 1835)
d. December 18, 1894

wife, Anna* (Wethling) b. (abt. 1842)
(map, Section L) d.

Notes:
--bur. map, Section L: plot of Henry Weidemeyer, q.v.
--Anna was daughter of Henry Wethling and Anna Canehel.
Her mother Anna Canehel m. #1, Henry Wethling; m. #2, Henry
Weidemeyer, q.v.
--Anna m. #1 George Wendell; #2 August Hepfner
(?George Wendel m. 1864, Newark, Margaret Butterfass)

--?1860 Census; p.265, 11Wd, New York, New York: August Hefner
age 25 b. Baden, laborer; Mary, age 22 b. Wurtemberg
--1860 Census, p.363, 3Wd, Orange: Henry 'Weidmyer' age 33 b.
Denmark, laborer; Anna M. age 48 b. Denmark; Anna age 19 b.
Denmark; Dora age 11 b. Denmark; Henry 9 b. Denmark; Charles age 4
months b. NJ
--1870 Census, p.397, 3Wd, Orange: Henry "Wedemeyer" age 40 b.
Denmark, laborer; Annie age 58 b. Prussia; Henry age 18 b. Prussia,
apprentice to felt hatter; Annie "Venner" age 30 b. Prussia, works at felt
hat factory; Theodore (m. abt. 1883, Hattie Maynard) "Venner" age 8, b.
NJ; Catharine Scheltfat, age 65, b. Prussia, no occupation
--1880 Census: p.165A, Orange, NJ: August Hepfner, age 45, b.
Germany, works in hat factory; Anna, wife, age 38 b. Sch.Holstein;
Theodore (Wendell), son, age 18, b. NJ, works in hat factory; Anna
Maria (Hepfner), daughter, age 5, b. NJ.

Child of August Hepfner and Anna Wethling:
Anna Maria, b. abt 1875

- - - - -

HERRON

Herron, ABEL b.
(map, plot owner Sect. I) d. 1869 (?)
  Aged 5_ years

Herron, MRS. b. (abt. 1816)
(map, Section I) d. March 29, 1868
  Aged 52 years

Notes:

--bur. map, Section I, plot illegible

- - - - -

HERTGEBE

Hertgebe, DOROTHEA
(csl - E73)

b. February 5, 1813
d. August 17, 1878

Notes:

- - - - -

HIERT

Hiert, Joseph*

b. (abt. 1804)
d. (aft. 1880)

Hiert, MRS. JOSEPH
(map,ch. property,Sect. H)

b. (abt. 1812)
d. August 12, 1878

Notes:
--1870 Census, p.204, East Orange, NJ: Joseph Hurt, age 66, saloon keeper, b. Baden; Dora, age 58, b. Baden; Augustus, age 18, b. Baden, laborer;
--1880 Census, p.503.4, East Orange, NJ: Joseph Hirt, age 76, widower, b. Germany; August Hirt, son, single, age 32, b. Germany, laborer

- - - - -

HIGGINSON

Higginson, T.
(map, Section L)

b.
d. November 7, 1881

Notes:

- - - - -

HIGGINBOTHAM

Higginbotham, JAMES
(map, Section I)

b.
d. February 28, 18 _6

Notes:
--bur. map, Section I, plot of 'illegible'
--?1860 Census, p.403&404, 2Wd. Orange, NJ: William Higginbotham, age 34, b. Scotland, hatter; Mary, age 34, b. Ireland; William, age 8 b. Ireland; Robert A., age 6, b. Ireland; John, age 3, b. Ireland; Sophia, age 1, b. NY
--?1870 Census, P.380, 3Wd. Orange NJ: Mary "Hegginbotten" age 45 b. Ire.; William, age 18 b. Ire. apprentice carpenter; Robert A., age 16 b. Ire., apprentice hatter; John J., age 13 b. Ire.; Annie S., age 11, b. England; George, age 9, b. Ire.
--?1880 Census, p.139.2, 3Wd, Orange, NJ: Mary Higginbotham, age 55, married, b. Ireland; R. Alexander, age 26, b. Ireland, works at hat factory; Anne Sophia, age 21, dau., b. Atlantic Ocean, works at hat forming; George B., age 19, b. NJ, works hat forming mill

?Children of William Higginbotham and Mary .....:
William, b. abt. 1852
Robert Alexander, b. abt. 1854
John J., b. abt. 1857; m. Mary H. .....
Anne Sophia, b. abt. 1859
George B., b. abt 1861

- - - - -

HITCHCOCK

Hitchcock, CHARLES b. (December 16, 1868)
(csl - E107) d. July 4, 1869
Aged 0.6.19

- - - - -

Hitchcock, JOEL b. (abt. December 11, 1831)
(gmnj)(csl - E68) d. October 11, 1853)
(map, Section I) *Aged 21.10.0*

"Of Derbyshire, England"

Notes:
--?Joel Hitchcock was baptised March 11, 1832 at Belper, Derbyshire, England, son of Thomas and Ann Hitchcock.(IGI)

--?1860 Census, Orange, NJ: David Hitchcock, age 20, b. NY, hatter; at res. of Joseph Bonnell
--?1870 Census, p.395,3Wd, Orange, NJ: David Hitchcock age 29 b. NJ, glass stainer; Carrie, age 24, b. NJ
--?1870 Census, p.395, 3Wd, Orange, NJ: A.(Anthony) W. Hitchcock, age 28 b. NJ, farmer; Eliza, age 30 b. NY; Richard W., age 1, b. NJ; Hannah Sexton,age 18 b. England, servant (same page as David Hitchcock
--?1880 Census, p.152D, Orange, NJ: David Hitchcock age 37 b. NY, father b. England, mother b. Scotland, glass stainer; Caroline, age 35, b. NJ, parents NJ; Mabel, age 6, b. NJ (near Letitia Suarez, widow, age 60 b. NY, father b. England, mother b. Scotland)
--?1900 Census, p.6B, Neptune, Monmouth Co. NJ: David "Hildecock" b. Aug. 1841 NY, parents England, glass blower; Caroline b. Dec. 1843 NJ; Mabel b. April 1876 NJ, factory hand

- - - - -

HOFFMAN

Hoffman, ... (map,ch. property,Sect. H)	b. d.

Notes:

- - - - -

HOLLUM

Hollum, AARON BENTLEY (map, Section F)	b. (abt. September 1825) d. February 7, 1916 *Aged 90*
wife, MARY E. (map, Section F)	b. (abt. August 1828) d. July 17, 1914 *Aged 85*
father, JACOB (map, Section F)	b. d. February 14, 1855
?mother, Rachel* (map?)	b. (abt. 1786) d. (aft. 1870)

son, JAMES b. (April 2, 1868)
(map, Section F) d. April 14, 1872

Hollum, SON of A.B. b.
(map, ch. property,Sect. H) d.

Notes:
--bur. map, Section F, plot of James Mills, q.v.
--Aaron was son of ..... Hollum and Rachel .....

--1850 Census, p.220, Orange Twp., NJ: Aaron B. Hollum, age 24, shoemaker, b. NJ; Mary E., age 19, b. NJ
--1860 Census, p.369, 3Wd, Orange, NJ: Aaron B. 'Hollarm' age 35, b. NJ, shoemaker; Mary E., age 30; Charles A.,age 9; 'Augusta', age 6; George, age 4; Ida, age 1; all b. NJ
--1870 Census, p.394, 3Wd, Orange, NJ: Aaron B. Hollum, age 45, works in felt hat factory; Mary E., age 40; Charles A., age 20, apprentice felt hatter; Augustus, age 18; George, age 15; Mary E., age 7; Frank, age 4; Rachel, age 84; all b. NJ
--1880 Census, p.167A, Orange, NJ: Aaron B. Hollum, age 54, b. NJ, father NJ, mother Scotland, works in hat factory; Mary E., wife, age 50 b. NJ, parents NJ; George E. age 24, works in hat factory; Mary E. age 16; Franklin age 14; William Perry, grand nephew, age 6, b. NJ; Mary Conway, age 19 b. NY, hat trimmer
--1900 Census, p.5B, 3Wd, Orange, NJ: "Arron B.' Hollum, b. Sept. 1825, m.50 yrs., hatter; Mary E., b. Aug. 1828, 6 born 3 living; Franklin, son, b. Apr. 1866, carpenter; Walter, b. Nov. 1876, grandson, carpenter; Lauretta b. Dec. 1888, granddau., Harry, b. April 1895, grandson; all b. NJ
--1910 Census, p.6A, 3Wd, Orange, NJ (page faded): "Erin B. Hollm..., age 85, retired; George, son, age 60, hatter; Franklin, age 44, works at .... house; Laura, age 20, granddaughter, typewriter at office; Harry,age 50,grandson

Children of Aaron Bentley Hollum and Mary E. ......:
Charles A., b. abt. 1850; m. Anna .....(Conway?)
Augustus, b. abt. 1852; m. Annie .....
George E., b. abt. 1856
Ida, b. abt. 1859; (d. bef. 1870?)
Mary E., b. August 1, 1863
Franklin, b. abt. April 1866; single in 1910
James, b. April 2, 1868; d. April 14, 1872

HOLMES

Holmes, BENJAMIN, Rev.	b. (December 16, 1797)
	d. (August 4, 1836)

*Beneath this stone
lies the remains of
Rev. Benj. Holmes
the founder of this church
Born November 10th, 1797
Died August 4th, 1836*

Plaque at St. Mark's Church
(behind the organ)

In loving memory of the Reverend Benjamin Holmes, rector of this church, who was born in New York December 16, 1797; and died at the parsonage, August 4th, 1836. From his youth meekness, gentleness, simplicity and godly sincerity marked him the child of God. Through his whole ministry, zeal in his mater's cause tempered by prudence, sustained by integrity and crowed with charity made him a pattern for his brethren and a pillar of the church, of his activities as a missionary, his faithfulness as a preacher, his devotion as a pastor, This church and that of St. Peter's at Morristown both which he founded are the enduring memorials. Their love for the man their admiration for the Christian their gratitude to the honest watchman of their souls the congregation of St. Mark's Church thus mournfully record.

wife, Jane Seaman*(Ogden)	b. (February 4, 1800)
	d. (1898)

Notes:
--Benjamin Holmes was the first Rector, **St. Mark's** Episcopal Church.
--He is buried under the chancel at **St. Mark's** Church.
--Benjamin was son of Benjamin Holmes and Phebe Jarvis.
--See: *Early History of St. Mark's Church* (this book)
--Benjamin Holmes was married October 19, 1829 at Orange by Rev. William R. Whittingham; (or, at St. Peter's Church, Morristown, NJ.) His bride was Jane Seaman Ogden. *Gen. Mag. of NJ, Volume 8)*
--Jane was daughter of Andrew Ogden and Mary Dixon. Jane died 1898 at Morristown, Morris Co., NJ; buried St. Peter's Church Yard, Morristown.

Children of Benjamin Holmes and Jane Seaman Ogden:
Mary Eleanor, b. abt 1834; d. April 18,. 1857
Benjamin, b. September 21, 1836

- - - - -

HOPKINS

Hopkins, CHILD of J. b.
(map, Section H) d. June 29, 1877

Notes:
--bur. map, Section H, plot of Isaac Baldwin, q.v.

- - - - -

HORN

Horn, ANTON b. (August, 1835)
(gmnj) d. March 6, 1901
(map, Section M) (nps) *Co. A., 54th NY Inf.*

wife, Mary* b. (abt. 1841)
  d. (before 1900)

Notes:
Served: Civil War Co. A, 54th NY Inf., Pvt. (nps)
--Gov't headstone supplied: d. 'March 5, 1901'
--bur. Section M, plot of John Horne, q.v.
--?Anton Alexander Horn, christened March 6, 1836, Langenau Bei Danzig, Westpreussen, Preussen, son of Salomon Horn and Maria Brand.)

--1870 Census: p.401, 3rd Ward Orange, NJ: Antoney Horn age 33, felt hat worker, b. Bavaria; Mary age 29 b. Ireland; Joseph age 5, b. Mass; John H. age 3 b. Mass.; Stephen b. December 1869 NJ
--1880 Census: p.159.1, Orange, NJ: Antone Horn, age 44, b. Bavaria, works in Hat Factory; Mary, wife, age 38, b. Ireland; Joseph, son, age 15, b. MA, works in hat factory; Henry J. son, age 13, b. MA.; Stephen, son, age 10, b. NJ; Antone, son, age 7, b. NJ; Marcella, dau., age 3, b. NJ; William, son, age 2 months, b. April, b. NJ

--1900 Census, p.14B, 5Wd, Orange City: Antoine Horn b. Aug 1835 PA, parents b. Germany, immig. 1861, widower, hatter sizing; Marcella b. Nov. 1866 NJ, inspector phone 'records?'; Anthony b. July 1872, NJ, Army; Peter W. b. April 1880 NJ, cook

Children of Anton Horn and Mary ....."
Joseph, b. abt 1865
Henry John. b. abt. 1867 or Nov. 1862; m. Mary .....,
    widow of ..... O'Dell
Stephen, b. abt. 1870
Antoney, b. July 9, 1872
Marcella, b. abt. November 19,1876; m. John A. Klem
Peter William, b. April 1880; unm. in 1920

- - - - -

Horne, John B.*	b. (abt. 1840)
(map, plot owner, Sect. M)	d. (aft. 1910)
first wife, SARAH JANE	b. (November 18, 1839)
(gmnj)(csl - E8)	d. July 2, 1869
(map, Section M)	*Aged 29.7.14*

Notes:
(?)Served: Civil War, Co. H, A, 7th NJ Inf., Pvt. (nps)
--1870 Census, p.333, 2Wd, Orange: John Horn, age 30, b. Bavaria, boarder,works at felt hat factory
--1870 Census, p.395, 3Wd, Orange: John Horn, age 30, b. Prussia, works at felt hat factory;at res. of Joseph Bonnell
--1880 Census: p.164C.3, Orange, NJ: John B. Horn, age 40, b. Germany, hat manufacturer; wife, Mary, age 39, b. PA, parents b. Ireland.
--1900 Census, p.395, 3Wd, Orange: John B. Horn, b. June 1840 Germany, m.25 yr.; hatter foreman,making caps; Mary b. Aug. 1849 Ireland; 0 born 0 living
--1910 Census, p.18B, 14Wd, Newark: John 'Horne' age 72 b. Germany, m. #2 for 43 yrs., own income; Mary, age 64, m. #2, 5 born 4 living, b. NY

- - - - -

HOWARD

Howard, JAMES
(map,ch. property, Sect. H)

b.
d. December 12, 1878

Notes:
--?1870 Census, p.470, West Orange, NJ: James Howard, age 36, b. CT, no occup.; Mary N., age 36, b. NJ; Bessie, age 14, b. CT; Joseph, age 12, b. NJ; 2 servants b. Ireland
--?1870 Census, p.466, West Orange, NJ: James K. Howard, age 43, b. NY, clerk; Eleanor S. age 40 b. NY; Clara H. Guins, age 14, b. NY; Thomas T. Guins, age 11, b. NY; Elenor N. Howard, age 3, b. NY; Mary Smith, age 24, b. Ireland, dom. servant; William C. Smith, age 20, b. NJ, coachman

-----

HUGHES

Hughes, JOHN
(map, ch.property, Sect. I)

b.
d.

Notes:
--bur. map, Section I, plot illegible

Hughes, WILLIAM
(map, ch.property, Sect. H)

b.
d. January 17, 1872

Notes:

HULL

Hull, CHARLES H.
(Death certificate)
(gmnj)(map, plot owner, Sect. K)
(nps)

b. April 9, 1838
d. November 28, 1902
Aged 64.1.9
Co. G, 26th NJ Vols.

CHARLES H. HULL
1838 - 1902

Co. G. 26th NJ VOLS.
LYDIA PERSONNETT (sic)
HIS WIFE
1830 - 1909

C. H. Hull
Co. G. 26th NJ Vols.
(separate government stone)

wife, LYDIA (Personett) b. abt. July 1830
(map, Section K) d. February 6, 1909
(Death certificate) *Aged 78*
(stone visible, Dec. 2000)

SON, of Chas. H. Hull b. (May 5, 1861)
(map, Section K) d. July 14, 1861

Notes:
Served: Civil War; Co.G, 26th NJ Inf., Pvt. (nps)
Served: ?also, Civil War; Co. F.,7th NJ Inf., Pvt. (nps)
--Gov't headstone provided; 'd. November 28, 1902'
--Charles H. Hull was son of Peter V. Hull, q.v. and Harriet Walker
--Lydia Personett was daughter of John Personett, q.v., and Fannie Harrison.

--1850 Census, p.244, Orange Twp: Peter V. Hull, age 43, farmer; Harriet 35; Matilda 15; George A. 13; Charles H., age 12; Sarah J. 10; Alexander 8; David W. 6; Mary L. age 5; Charlotte A., age 3; all b. New Jersey
--1850 Census, p.228B, Orange: Abram D. Brower, age 30, hatter; Margaret, age 22; Fanny, age 5; Catherine, age 2; Lydia Personett, age 20
--1860 Census: p.356, 3Wd., Orange, NJ: Charles H. Hull, age 23, carpenter. Boarder at house of Rhoda Edwards (q.v.)
--1860 Census:p.377B, Orange 3rd Ward, NJ:Abram Brower, age 40, hatter, b. NJ; Margaret M. age 32; Fanny, age 15; Catherine age 12; Abram M., age 9; Ada L.,age 7; Lydia P. age 3; Mary E., age 1 Also at address, Lydia Personett a. 30; George W. Brown(Brower?),a.13,hatter apprentice (son?); Charles Personett,brother-in law a 21,hatter; George Tucker a. 19, hatter apprentice,b.Conn.; Gorham Devereux,a. 39, mason, Near her brother,George Personett and his wife Caroline.

--1870 Census: p.400, 3rd Ward Orange, NJ: Charles H. Hull age 32, carpenter; Lydia age 40; Lyman F. age 8; Hattie L. age 6; Harriet age 55; Robert age 18, felt hat worker: all b. New Jersey
--1880 Census: p.156 D., Orange, NJ: Charles H. Hull, age 42, b. NJ, carpenter; Lydia wife, age 48, b. NJ; Lyman P. son, age 18, works in hat factory; Harriet F., dau., age 16, at school
--1900 Census, p.4B, 3Wd, Orange: Charles "Hall" b. April 1838 NJ, carpenter; Lydia b. July 1830, NJ, 5 born 2 living;
Lyman b. April 1862, single, son, b. NJ, hat finisher

Children of Charles H. Hull and Lydia Personett
Child, b. May 5, 1861; d. July 14, 1861
Lyman P., b. April 1862
Harriet F., b. 1864
Child b. aft. 1864

- - - - -

Hull, GEORGE A. (gmnj)(map,plot owner,Sect.M)	b. (abt. June 30, 1836) d. January 25, 1917 *Aged 80 yrs. 6 mos. 26 days*
first wife Adelaide J.*	b. (abt. 1841) d. (aft. 1880)
second wife Mary E. *	b. (abt. 1865) d.
CHILD of George Hull (map, Section M)	b. d. March 29, 1877
son, WALTER (map, Section M)	b. (abt. 1875) d. September 21, 1881
son, WILLIAM M. (map, Section M)	b. (abt. June 30, 1858) d. August 15, 1935 *Aged 77.1.16*
CHILD of W. Hull (map, Section M)	b. d.

Notes:
Served: Civil War, Co. C, 1st NJ Inf., Cpl. (nps)

--George was son of Peter V. Hull, q.v.
--George m. #1, Adelaide J. .....;
    m. #2, abt. 1909, Mary E. .....

--1850 Census, p.244, Orange Twp: Peter V. Hull, age 43, farmer; Harriet 35; Matilda 15; George A. 13; Charles H., age 12; Sarah J. 10; Alexander 8; David W. 6; Mary L. age 5; Charlotte A., age 3; all b. New Jersey
--1860 Census p.53 1Wd Newark: George "Hall" age 23 b. NJ works sash & blinds; Adelaide J. age 19 b. NY; Wm. M. age 2 b. NJ
--1870 Census p.35 1Wd. Brooklyn Kings Co. NY: Geo. A. "Hall", age 33 b. NJ millwright; Adelaide J. age 29 b. NY; Wm. 'H' age 12 b. NJ; Frank E. age 9 b. NJ; Joseph A. age 7 b. NJ; Sarah age 11 months b. NY
--1880 Census p.404.3&404.4 Newark Essex Co. NJ: George A. "Hall" age 44 b. NJ parents b. NJ book agent; Adelaide age 41 b. NY father b. England; mother b. NJ; William M. age 20 b. NJ father NJ mother NY apprentice carpenter; Frank E. age 18 b. NJ 'lamp liter'; Joseph A. age 16 b. NJ 'lamp liter'; Sarah J. age 10 b. NJ; Peter E. age 7 b. NY; Walter J. age 5 b. Pennsylvania; Laura A. age 3 b. Pennsylvania
--1900 Census: not found
(?)George A. Hull, Hull Mine, Leadville, Colorado)
--1904, Sept. 14: (NY Times) "Thought Dead 19 Years"
"Orange, NJ: Sept. 13 - George A. Hull, who recently returned to Orange after nineteen years' absence, during which time his family thought him dead, has asked the authorities of Orange for an adjustment of taxes on property on the east side of Prince Street. During his absence taxes and assessments have accrued on this property amounting to $1,134.40, in addition to interest and costs. Mr. Hull has asked for a reduction in the valuation of $500 a year on account of being a veteran of the First New Jersey Volunteers, and of an allowance on interest and costs, to enable him to clean off the liens. When Mr. Hull went away he owned property in Orange, East Orange, and South Orange. HIs wife sold some of the land, believing him to be dead, and collected rents from the houses. Since his return Hull has given new deeds for this property."
--1910 Census p. 21B 1Wd East Orange: George A. Hull age 72 m. #2 for 1 year b. NJ parents NJ no occupation listed; Mary E. Hull age 45 wife; m. "#1" for 1 year b. NJ parents NJ
--?1920 Census, p.5B, Verona, Essex Co., NY: Mary B. 'Beecher' age 51, widow, keeps boarding house; Charles H. Beecher, age 10; Clara L. Henderson, age 61; Wm. R. Henderson,age 60, hatter; Henry Roberson,age 57, bookkeeper; Sara Roberson,age 40, school teacher; Sara Roberson,age 12; all b. NJ

--?1930 Census, p.6A, Lynbrook, Nassau Co., NY: Charles E. Williams, age 59, widower, b. NY, parents b. NJ, commercial travel-hat bands; Clara S. Henderson,age 73, widow, sister, b. NJ; Emma A. Williams, age 68, single, sister, b. NJ; Mary F. Hull, age 62, widow, sister, b. NJ

Children of George A. Hull and Adelaide J. .....:
William M.,b.June 1858;m. abt.1881, Mary F. Duhart/Duffar
Frank E. b. abt. 1862
Joseph A. b. August 1863; m. abt. 1881 Lilly Stephens
Sarah J. b. abt. 1870
Peter E. b. December 1872
Walter J. b. abt. 1875; d. Sept. 1881
Laura A. b. abt. 1877

- - - - -

Hull, JOSEPH A.   b. (abt. August 10, 1863)
(map, Section M)   d. April 2, 1916
(plot of George Hull)   *Aged 52.7.23*

wife, LILLIAN (Stephens)   b. (abt. April 7, 1869)
(map, Section M)   d. June 4, 1930
         Aged 61.1.28

daughter, LILLIAN FISHER TANFIELD
(gmnj)   b. October 16, 1900
(map, Section M)   d. March 30, 1934
         Aged 33.5.14

Notes:
--bur. plot of George Hull, q.v.
--Joseph was son of George A. Hull, q.v., and Adelaide .....

--1870 Census p.35 1Wd. Brooklyn Kings Co. NY: Geo. A. Hull age 33 b. NJ millwright; Adelaide J. age 29 b. NY; Wm. 'H' age 12 b. NJ; Frank E. age 9 b. NJ; Joseph A. age 7 b. NJ; Sarah age 11 months b. NY
--1880 Census p.404.3&404.4 Newark Essex Co. NJ: George A. "Hall" age 44 b. NJ parents b. NJ book agent; Adelaide age 41 b. NY father b. England; mother b. NJ; William M. age 20 b. NJ father NJ mother NY apprentice carpenter; Frank E. age 18 b. NJ 'lamp liter'; Joseph A. age 16 b. NJ 'lamp liter'; Joseph A. age 16 b. NJ; Sarah J. age 10 b. NJ; Peter E. age 7 b. NY; Walter J. age 5 b. Pennsylvania; Laura A. age 3 b. Pennsylvania

--1900 Census, p.3A, 5Wd, Newark, Essex Co., NJ: Joseph Hull, b. August 1862, m. 19 yr., b. NJ, parents b. NJ, brakeman; Lilly, b. April 1870, 1 born 1 living, b. NY, father b. England, mother b. France; Adelaide b. Sept. 1898 NJ; Mamie Stephens, sister, b. Feb. 1880 NY, father b. England, mother b. France, collar shaper

--1910 Census, p.8B, 3Wd, Orange, Essex Co., NJ: Joseph Hull, age 46, m.18 yrs. b. NJ, parents b. NJ, motorman on street railway; Lillie, age 39, b. NY, parents b. England, 3 born 3 living; dressmaker; Adelene, age 10, b. NJ; Lillian, age 8, b. NJ; George, age 5, b. NJ

--1920 Census, p.4A, 3Wd, West Orange, Essex Co., NJ: Lily Hull, age 45, b. "Florida, father b. England, mother b. Sweden", widow, works at Edison; Lily Hull, dau., b. NJ, father NJ, mother Fl, assembler at Edison; George, age 15, son, b. NJ, drill press at Edison; Adliade Rogers, age 21, dau., married, b. NJ; Donald Rogers, age 4 yrs. 7 mos., b. NJ, grandson, father b. NJ

--1930 Census, p.4A, Orange, Essex Co., NJ: Lillie Hull, age 58, widow, m. at age 28; George Hull, age 25, single, son, (Donald Rogers, grandson) tester at radio factory; Donald Hull, age 14, son; Lillian Fisher, age 29, single, boarder, clerk at real estate office;

Children of Joseph A. Hull and Lillian Stephens:
Adelaide, b. September 1898
Lillian Fisher, b. 1900; d. 1934; m. ..... Tanfield?
George, b. abt 1905

- - - - -

Hull, Peter V.*   b. (abt. 1805)
(NJ Will #14077G,1851)   d. (abt. 1851)

wife, HARRIET (Walker)   b. April 12, 1815
(gmnj)(map, Section K)   d. January 5, 1891
(NJ Will #24050G, 1891)

son, PETER R.   b. (abt. October 11, 1851)
(map, Sect.M, Cusack plot)   d. October 23, 1874
(stone found 2009)

Peter R. Hull
Died
October 23D, 1874
Age 23 years and 12 days
Gone But Not Forgotten
Erected by his Mother

H. Hull

Notes:
--1850 Census, p.244, Orange Twp: Peter V. Hull, age 43, farmer; Harriet 35; Matilda 15; George A. 13; Charles H., age 12; Sarah J. 10; Alexander 8; David W. 6; Mary L. age 5; Charlotte A., age 3; all b. New Jersey
--1860 Census: p.387B, 3Wd Orange:Harriet Hull age 45, b. NJ; Sarah J. age 20, hat trimmer; Alexander 18; David M. 16; Mary L. age 15; Edward 9; Peter R. 8. Adj. to Richard and Matilda (Hull) Cusack
--1870 Census, p.400, 3wd Orange: Charles H. Hull, age 32, carpenter; Lydia, age 40; Lyman, F. age 8; Hattie L. age 6; Harriet, age 55; Robert age 18, hatter apprentice
--1880 Census, p.156D, Orange, NJ: Harriet Hull, widow, age 65, b. NJ, parents b. NJ; adj. to son, Charles H. Hull

Children of Peter V. Hull and Harriet Walker:
Matilda, b. December 16, 1834; m. Richard S. Cusack(q.v.)
George A., q.v. b. abt. 1836; d. 1917; m. Adelaide J. .....
Charles H., q.v. b. abt. 1838; m. Lydia Personett
Sarah J., b. abt. 1840
Alexander, b. abt. 1842; m. Amanda .....
David M. b. abt. 1844; m. Mary L. .....
Mary Lavinia, b. abt. 1845; m. Byron W. Quimby, q.v.
Charlotte A., b. abt 1847
Edward, b. abt. 1851
Peter Robert, b. abt. October 11, 1851; d.1874

- - - - -

INGRAHAM

Ingraham, Henry E.*   b. (November 3, 1790)
                            d. (December 20,1852)

wife, CONTENT (Wilson)   b. February 13, 1795
(gmnj)(shaw)(csl - E45)   d. September 14, 1840

Content
Wife of
Henry E. Ingraham
and Daughter of
William Wilson of New York

She died Sept. 14, 1840
Aged 45 Years
Her children arise up, and call her blessed
Her husband also, and he praiseth her

Notes:
--Henry E. Ingraham was b. November 3, 1790 at Hudson, Columbia Co., New York, son of Duncan Ingraham of Boston and Susan Greenleaf. He d. December 20, 1852 at Jubilee, near Kickapoo, Illlinois.
--Henry married Content Wilson July 19, 1815. She was born 13 February 1795, daughter of William Wilson and Agnes Ann Kerr.

--1840 Census: p.268, Orange Twp., NJ
--1850 Census, p.231, Peoria Co., Illinois: Henry E. Ingraham, age 59 b. NY, farmer; Edward H. age 18 b. VA, farmer; "Ducen" (Duncan?), age 12, b. NJ

Children of Henry E. Ingraham and Content Wilson:
Henrietta, b. 17 Jan. 1817, IL; d. Feb. 7,1858, Orange, NJ
    m. April 3,1842, Lewis Condit Lighthipe of Orange
Agnes Ann, b. July 5, 1818 IL; d. July 9, 1820
William, b. May 3, 1820, NY; d. February 3, 1821
Susan Greenleaf, b. April 14, 1822, NY
Janet Suffern, b. April 14, 1822, NY
Anna Kip, b. June 10, 1824 NY; d. November 26, 1893
William Wilson, b. July 24, 1826 NY; d. June 9, 1888
Edward Henry, b. Jan. 25, 1832 NY; d. July 15, 1894
Duncan Greenleaf, b. April 10, 1838
Virginius, b. January 30, 1864, NY; d.August 3, 1860

- - - - -

JACKSON

Jackson, JAMES   b.
(map, Section O)   d. June 12, 1883

Notes:
--Map says: "Section O, Row 5: Negro Burial Ground"
--?James Jackson m. May 8, 1867,Newark: Delilah Howe
--?1880 Census, p.48D, Montclair, NJ: James Jackson, age 56, black, b. NJ, parents b. NJ; Delilah, wife, age 54, black, b. NJ, parents b. NJ

--?1880 Census, p.469.4, East Orange NJ: Elizabeth Scott, age 36, widow, black, b.NJ, father b. MD, mother NJ, housekeeper; Louise Jackson, age 40, widow, black, b. NJ, parents b. NJ, housekeeper; Jane Mason, age 25, single, black, b. VA, parents b. VA, housekeeper (same page as John and Margaret Blanchard, q.v.)

- - - - -

JARVIS

Jarvis, JAMES (gmnj)(shaw)(csl - E16) (map, plot owner,Sect. M)	b. (abt. 1807) d. June 9, 1853 *Aged 46*
wife, Catherine*	b. (abt. 1819) d. (aft. 1880)
Jarvis, WILLIAM (map, Section M)	b. d. March 7, 18_ _
Jarvis, WILFORD (map, Section M)	b. bur. August 31, 1905

Notes:
--1850 Census: p.236, Orange Twp., NJ: James Jarvis, age 35, hatter, b. Ireland; Catherine age 30; Alexander age 12;
Mary Ann age 7; Nelson age 5; William age 2; Catherine age 1 month.
--1860 Census: p.356, 3rd Ward, Orange: Alexander Jarvis age 22, b. Ireland, hatter; Harriet age 29 b. Ireland; Harriet E. age 3 months; Nelson Jarvis, age 24, b. 'Ireland'
--1870 Census, p.472, West Orange: Nelson Jarvis, age 25, b. NJ, hatter; at res. of Margaret "McGurk"
--1880 Census: p. 524 A, Newark, NJ: Katheren Jarvis, widow, age 64, b. Ireland; Nelson Jarvis, son, age 34, b. NJ, works in hat factory

Children of James Jarvis and Catherine ....."
Alexander, b. abt 1838; m. Harriet C.Tichenor; m. Sarah ......
Mary Ann, b. abt. 1843
Nelson, b. abt 1845
William, b. abt. 1848
Catherine, b. 1850

- - - - -

JOHNSON

Johnson, CHILD of C.H. b.
(map, Section H) d.

Notes:

- - - - -

JONES
(map, plot of John Allen & John Jones)

Jones, JOHN b.
(map, plot owner, Sect. G) d.

Jones, GEORGE b.
(map, Section G) d. May 1, 1854

Jones, MARTHA b.
(map, Section G) d. March 8, 1854

Jones, ELIZA b. (abt. 1852)
(map, Section G) d. May 14, 1853
Aged 7 months

Jones, CHILD b.
(map, Section G) d.

Jones, CHILD b.
(map, Section G) d.

Williams, SUSAN b.
(map, Section G) d. January 21, 1854

Notes:
--See: John Allen

- - - - -

JONES
(plot of William and Samuel Jones)

Jones, WILLIAM
(map, plot owner Sect. H)
b. (abt. 1845
d. September 9, 1900
Aged 55

Jones, CHILD of W.
(map, Section H)
b.
d. September 5, 1882

Jones, SARAH
(gmnj)(Shaw)(csl-E72)
(map, Section H)
(NJ Will #17349G, 1871)
b. (abt. 1817)
d. August 17, 1871
Aged 53

Jones, WILLIAM
(map, Section H)
b. (abt. 1866)
d. October 14, 1896
Aged 30

Jones, WILLIAM
(map, Section H)
b. (abt. 1896)
d. December 14, 1896
Aged 0.7.28

Jones, RAYMOND J.
(map, Section H)
b.
d. July 10, 1909

Jones, DOROTHY E.
(map, Section H)
b. (abt. 1912)
d. August 26, 1912
Age 4 mos. 14 days

Jones, MARY
(map, Section H)
b.
d. May 27, 1914
Aged _yr.6 mos. 1 day

Gardner, MARY J.
(map, Section H)
b. (abt. 1851)
d. August 20, 1873
Aged 22 years

Notes:
--?1850 Census, p.239, Orange Twp: Caleb Condit, age 53, farmer b. NJ; Betsy, age 55; Sarah Jones, age 28; William Jones, age 10
--?1860 Census, p.394, 3Wd, Orange: Caleb Condit age 63, b. NJ, farmer; Sarah Jones, age 40, b. Ireland; Mary Jones, age 23 b. Ireland; William Jones, age 19 b. Ireland

--?1870 Census: p.477, West Orange, NJ; Caleb Condit, age 74, b. NJ, farmer; Sarah Jones, age 49 b. Ireland, domestic servant
--?1870 Census, p.471, West Orange, NJ: William Jones, age 29, b. Ireland, house painter; Mary, age 27 b. Ireland; Samuel, age 7, b. NJ; William, age 4, b. NJ; Caleb, age 1, b. NJ
--?1880 Census, p.264.1, West Orange, NJ: William Jones, age 40, b. Ire, house painter; Mary J., age 37, b. Ire.;Samuel, age 17, hatter apprentice; William, age 14; Caleb C. age 11; Robert age 8; Alonzo age 6; Walter age 3; son, b. July 1880; all children b. NJ
--?1900 Census, p.1B, West Orange, NJ: William Jones, b. Apr. 1843, Ire., house painter; Mary J. b. Apr. 1845, Ire.; Caleb C., b. Dec. 1868 NJ, hat pouncer; Alonzo, b. Jan 1874 NJ, hat finisher; Walter K., b. Aug. 1877 NJ, house painter; Benjamin F. b. June 1883, NJ, hat pouncer;

Children of William Jones and Mary J. ......:
Samuel, b. abt. 1863
William, b. abt. 1866
Caleb Condit, b. abt. Dec. 1868; m. Frederica Knapp
Robert, b. abt. 1872
Alonzo, b. abt. Jan. 1874; m. Catherine A. .....
Walter K. b. abt. Aug. 1877; m. Matilda H. .....
son, b. July 1880
Benjamin F., b. abt. June 1883; m. Mary A. ......

- - - - -

KENT

Kent, JACOB N.	b. (April 13, 1811)
(map, plot owner, Sect. J)	d. (February 11, 1893)
wife, SARAH A. (Condit)	b. (July 11, 1816)
(map, Sect. J)	d. (July 8, 1885)
daughter, PHEBE J.	b. (November 29, 1835)
(wife of Stephen M. Tompkins)	d. September 7, 1852
(csl - E60)(map, Sect. J)	d. August 7, 1854
	In 17th year
Kent, GEORGE	b.
(map, Section J)	d.

Kent, CHARLES C. b.
(map, Section J) d. June 18, 1889

Kent, WM. MORRIS b. (abt. 1863)
(map, Section J) bur. May 3, 1908
Aged 45

Notes:
--He married, October 22, 1833, Sarah A. Condit, daughter of Jeptha Condit and Charlotte Smith.
--1850 Census, p.213&214, Orange Twp: Jacob Kent, age 43, hatter; Sarah A. age 34; George, age 16, cigar maker; Silas, age 14; Phebe, age 15; Henry, age 8; all b. NJ
--1850 Census, p.105, Livingston Twp., Essex Co. NJ: Stephen W. Tompkins, age 21, b. NJ, shoemaker; William Tompkins, age 1, b. NJ; at res. of Thomas N. Sharp, b. England, farmer
--1860 Census, p. 352, 1 Wd., Orange: Jacob N. Kent, age 49, b. NJ, hatter; Sarah, age 44 b. NJ
--1870 Census, p.222, East Orange: Jacob Kent, age 60, hatter, b. NJ; Sarah, age 55, b. NJ
--1880 Census, p.506.1, East Orange: Jacob Kent, age 68, works at hatting; Sarah, age 62

Children of Jacob N. Kent and Sarah A. Condit:
George B., b. August 29, 1834, m. Sarah H. Pierson
Phebe J., b. November 29, 1835, m. Stephen M. Tompkins
Silas W. , b. April 26, 1837, d. Civil War, Sept. 12, 1865
    Co. F, 19th Illinois Inf., d. Tennessee
Ruth C., b. May 12, 1840, d. August 8, 1841
Charlotte, b. December 10, 1841, d. June 25, 1842
Henry C., b. May 18, 1842
Hannah, b. August 5, 1843, d. September 21, 1844
Mena D., b. January 21, 1845, d. July 25, 1845
Nancy, b. November 25, 1847, d. August 1, 1849
Chancellor, b. January 10, 1854, d. August 7, 1854

- - - - -

KILBURN

Kilburn, JOSIAH b. (abt. 1813)
(map, Section A) d. February 28, 1856

Notes:

--Note: Daniel Kilburn, wife Harriet and two daughters were bur. in the Old Burying Ground and removed to Rosedale in 1841.
--1850 Census, p.234, Orange Twp: Elizabeth Smith 49, b. NJ; George Smith, age 27 b. NJ, shoemaker; Joseph Smith, age 23 b. NJ, shoemaker; Moses Smith, age 20 b. NJ, shoemaker; George Clay, age 30 b. NY, shoemaker; Elizabeth Clay,age 28 b. PA; Pierson Bond, age 23, b. NJ, shoemaker; Elias Sindler, age 20 b. NJ, shoemaker; Josiah Kilburn, age 27 b. NJ, shoemaker; Elizabeth Smith,age 26, b. NJ; Thomas J. Smith, age 3 b. NJ; Joseph W. Smith, age 1, b. NJ; Mary A. Dorr, age 14, b. Ireland

- - - - -

KYLE

Kyle, James?*   b.
    d.

wife, CATHARINE(Clara M)   b. November 6, 1879
(gmnj)   d. January 29, 1903
(map, Sect. H:"Clara M. (Willis) Kyle")

Notes:
--See: map, Section H, plot of Alexander Willis

- - - - -

LAW

Law,(?), MAGDELENA   b.
(map, Section I)   d.

Notes:
--bur, map, Section I, plot illegible)

- - - - -

Law, Mrs. (Martha)*   b. (abt. 1808)
(map, plot owner, Section G)   d. (aft. 1880)

Law, JOHN   b. (abt. 1807)
(map,Section G)   d. May 19, 1853
    Aged 46

Law, GEORGE b.
(map, Section G) d. July 29, 1849

Law, MATHIAS b.
(map, Section G) d. December 2, 1843

Linsley, INFANT of Wm. b.
(map, Section G) d.

Notes:
--See: Isaac Stone
--1850 Census, p.222, Orange Twp., NJ: John Law, age 43, b. England, hatter; Martha, age 42, b. Eng.; Harriet, age 21, b. Eng.; Charlotte, age 18, b. Eng.; George, age 11, b. Eng.; Mary J., age 10, b. Eng.; Eliza A., age 6, b. Eng.; Sophia, age 5, b. NJ; Martha, age 3, b. NJ; John M., age 1, b. NJ; 4 boarders, hatters, b. England
--1860 Census, p.422&433, 2 Wd, Orange, NJ: Martha Law, age 53, Eng.; Harriet, 29, Eng. hat trimmer; Charlotte, 27, Eng. machine operator; George, 23, Eng.; Mary J. 20. Eng; Eliza, 18, Eng. hat trimmer; Sophia, 16, b. NJ, hat trimmer; Martha 13 NJ; John 11 NJ; Joseph, 25, b. Eng., hatter
--1870 Census, p.354, 2Wd, Orange, NJ: Martha Law, age 64, b. Eng.; Harriet, age 32, works felt hat factory; Charlotte, 29, works felt hat factory; George, age 28, no occ.; Mary J., age 26, dressmaker; Eliza, 24, works at felt hat factory; Martha, age 20; John, age 19 b. NJ, printer; Mary A., age 9, b. NY
--1880 Census, p.112A, Orange, NJ: Martha Law, widow, age 74, b. England, keeping house; res. of Morris Hammel

Children of John Law and Martha .....:
Harriet, b. abt. 1829;
  bpt. Apr.1830, Dewsbury, Yorkshire, England
Charlotte, b. abt. 1832
George, b. abt. 1839
Mary J., b. abt. 1840
Eliza A., b. abt. 1844
Sophia, b. abt. 1845
Martha, b. abt. 1847
John M., b. January 7, 1849

- - - - -

LEADBEATER

Leadbeater, CATHERINE A. b.
  dau. of Wm. Leadbeater d.
(map, grave owned, Sect. I)

CHILD of Wm. Leadbeater b.
(map, grave owned, Sect. I) d.

CHILD of Wm. Leadbeater b.
(map, grave owned, Sect. I) d.

Notes:
--William Leadbeater m. March 1858, Sarah Jane Dunlap
--1860 Census, p.394, 3Wd, Orange, NJ: William Leadbeater, age 26, b. England, shoemaker; Sarah J., age 21, NJ; Sarah L., age 1. NJ
--1870 Census, p.479&480, West Orange, NJ: Wm. Leadbeater, age 38, b. England, pedlar; Sarah, age 34, b. NJ: Sarah L., age 11; George H. age 7; Wm. E., age 3; Samuel D., age 9 months; all children b. NJ; Emma Thorp, age 20, hat trimmer, b. NJ; Patrick Collins, age 35, b. Ireland
--1880 Census, p.245.3, West Orange, NJ: Wm. L..... (Leadbeater), age 46, England, huckster; Sarah J. age 43 NJ; Sarah L. 21; George B. 16, laborer; William 13; Samuel, 10; Lydia, 6; Martha, age 4, b. NJ
--1900 Census, p.9A, West Orange, NJ: William Leadbeater b. Jan. 1833, England, stage driver; Sarah, b. July 1836 NJ; 6 born 5 living

Children of William Leadbeater and Sarah Jane Dunlap:
Sarah L, b. abt. 1859
George H., b. abt. 1863; m. Ruth .....
William E., b. abt. 1867; m. Mabel E. .....
Samuel D., b. abt. 1869
Lydia, b. abt. 1874
Martha, b. abt. 1876

- - - - -

LECLERC

LeClerc, Phebe C. b.
  d. (May 24, 1928)

Note:
--bur. map, Section M, plot of Joseph Edwards, q.v.

- - - - -

LENNOX

Lennox, JAMES (civ. Sect. K, Plot 1, Grave 4) (map, plot owner, Sect. K) (gmnj)(csl - E40)(nps)	b. (1830) d. February 8, 1872 d. (December 2, 1872) *Co. H and D, 39th NJ Inf.*
first wife, ALMIRA (Personett) (csl - E41)(map, Sect. K)	b. (January 18, 1833) d. October 29, 1857
second wife, ELLEN (Personett)(map, Sect. K)	b. (abt. 1840) bur. March 5, 1899
daughter, EMMA IRENE (csl - E41) (map, Sect. K) (above stones visible in 2000)	b. July 13, 1852 d. August 29, 1853
son, CHARLES WILLARD (map, Section K)	b. (September 18, 1860) d. April 22, 1901 *Aged 41*
Cahill, JESSIE ADELE (map, Section K)	b. (abt. 1879) d. November 7, 1881

Notes:
Served: Civil War, Co. H, 39th NJ Inf.,Pvt.(nps)
Served:(?) also, Civil War: Co. D,26th NJ Inf.
Gov't headstone provided: d. 'February 12, 1872'
--James m. first, Almira, December 25, 1850 at Paterson, Passaic Co., NJ. She was daughter of John Personett, q.v., and Fannie Harrison.
--James m. July 9, 1860 at Newark, NJ, as his second wife, Ellen, sister of his first wife; she was daughter of John Personett, q.v., and Fannie Harrison.
--Carpenter; Prop. James Lennox Construction Co.

--1850 Census, p.74B, Caldwell Twp., Essex Co., NJ: James Lennox, age 20, works at cotton mfg., b. Ireland; at res. of John Bowden, age 61, cotton mfr.;adj. to John Personett

--1860 Census, p.18, Harrison, Hudson Co., NJ: James "Lemacks" (Lennox) age 28 b. Ireland; Ellen age 19 b. NJ; "Alonson" (Alonzo) age 11, b. NJ
--1870 Census, p.350A, 2 Wd Orange, Essex Co., NJ: James Lennox, age 40, carpenter, b. Ireland; Ellen, age 29, b. NJ; Wm. age 10; Harry, age 8 b. Canada(?); Elmer, age 6; Frank age 3; Almira, age 7 mos; Mary Personett, age 16,b. NJ, works hat factory; Ada Brower, age 17, b. NJ; Alonzo Lennox, age 21, NJ, carpenter; Alfred Personett, 20, b. NJ, carpenter; Robert Personett, age 14, b.NJ at school; John Personett, age 65, b. NJ, works hat factory
--1880 Census, p.540.2, East Orange, (Long Street), NJ: Ellen Lennox, widow, age 39, Willard, age 19, works hat mfg.; Harry, age 18, works at grist mill; Jessie, age 1, (Jessie Adele Cahill)

Children of James Lennox and Almira Personett:
Alonzo P. Lennox, b. January 10,1849; m.Mary A. Blauvelt
    Served: Civil War, Musician, Co.H, 39th Reg't. NJ
    (He was child of Almira Personett, before her marriage to James.)
Emma Irene, b. July 13,1852; d. August 29, 1853

Children of James Lennox and Ellen Personett:
Charles Willard, b. September 18, 1860; d. Apr. 22, 1901
Harry, b. abt 1862; d. aft 1910
James Elmer, b. May 1864; d. aft. 1900; m. Mary A. .....
Frank Clarendon, b. January 6, 1867; m.Rhetta Hendershot
Almira, b. November 1869

- - - - -

LIGHTHIPE

Lighthipe, Charles A.* b. (October 11, 1824)
(*New York Times*) d. (February 14, 1905)
(map, plot owner, Sect. K) *Aged 80*

wife, Sarah* (Smith) b. (abt. 1828)
  d. (1880-1900)

Notes:
(Charles A. Lighthipe was active at **St. Mark's Church** but may have been buried elsewhere, e. g. Rosedale Cemetery.)
Obituary - *New York Times*, February 15, 1905

"Charles A. Lighthipe of Orange, twice a member of the New Jersey State Legislature and an officer of Newark and Orange financial institutions, died at 5 o'clock yesterday morning at his home, on Main Street. Orange. He had been critically ill since last Friday, but two years ago suffered a paralytic stroke at his Newark office. He was eighty years of age. Mr.
Lighthipe was born in the old Lighthipe homestead on Main Street on Oct. 11, 1824. He organized a hat firm and early made use of labor-saving devices, introducing hot forming. He was associated with the late Llewellyn S. Haskell in the development of (Llewellyn?) Park. He was a Director of the Essex Railroad until it was leased to the Lackawanna. For nearly forty years he was a Director of the American Insurance Company of Newark, and had been identified with the Citizens' Gas Company of Newark from its organization. He was also in the organization of the United States Industrial Insurance Company which was absorbed by the Prudential Insurance Company. He was actively interested in the welfare of **St. Mark's Episcopal Church,** West Orange. Six children - Charles F.; Florence I.; Sarah M.; Arthur; and, Ernest. The funeral will be held on Friday afternoon in **St. Mark's Church.**"

--1850 Census, p.234, Orange Twp: Charles "Sithepe" age 26, hatter; Sarah age 23; Florence age 1 month; all b. NJ (near Maria "Sithepe", age 62 or 82, b. NJ)
--1860 Census, p.396, 3Wd. Orange: Chas. A. "Lightpipe" age 35, hat manufacturer; Sarah F. age 32; Florence age 10; Charles F. age 7; Sarah L. age 5; Arthur 3; Herbert 1; all b. NJ; 3 servants
--1870 Census, p.394, 3Wd, Orange: Charles A. Lighthipe, age 45, manufacturer of hat bodies; Sarah age 43; Florence 18; Charles 17; Sarah 17; Arthur 13; Herbert 12; Ernest 3; 2 servants
--1880 Census, p.170.3, Orange: Charles A. Lighthipe, age 55, President, Orange National Bank; Sarah, age 52; Flornce 30; Sarah M. age 25; Arthur N. age 23, bank clerk; Herbert
age 21, bookkeeper foreman; Ernest age 12; Mary A. Smith, age 70, single, sister-in-law; all b. New Jersey; 1 servant
--1900 Census, p.6A, 3Wd, Orange: "Chardy" Lighthipe b. Oct. 1824, widower, Pres.(?) insurance co.; Florence daughter single b. April 1850, capitalist; Sarah M., daughter, single, b. Feb 1855, capitalist; Arthur N. son, single, b. Dec. 1856, capitalist; all b. NJ; 3 servants

Children of Charles A. Lighthipe and Sarah Smith:
Florence, b. abt. 1850
Sarah M., b. abt 1855

Arthur N., b. abt 1857
Herbert, b. abt. 1859
Ernest, b. abt. 1868

- - - - -

Lighthipe, Lewis Condit*   b. (May 26, 1815)
(map,plot owner, Sect. K) d. (April 3, 1900)

wife, HENRIETTA (Ingraham) b. (abt. 1828)
(map, Section K)   d. (abt. 1858?)

Lighthipe, EDWARD   b.
(map,Sect. K)(child of Wm.) d. d. 18 _ _

Lighthipe, ELECTA(?)   b.
(map, Section K)   d.

Lighthipe, CHILD of Wm.   b.
(map, Section K)   d.

Lighthipe, THOMAS H.   b.
(map, Section K)   d. 188_

Notes:
--Lewis was son of Charles Lighthipe and Maria Smith Condit
--Lewis m. April 3, 1842 at Jubilee College Chapel, Jubilee, Peoria, IL, Henrietta Ingraham
--1850 Census, p.234 Orange Twp., NJ: Lewis 'Sithepe' age 34 merchant; Henrietta, age 32; 'Lenn H.' age 7; Agnes, age 4; Abby, age 1; ALice Condit, age 56; all b. NJ; Bridget Kenney, age 20 b. Ire.; Peter Daley, age 24, b. Ire.,laborer
Maria 'Sithepe' age 62; Oscar, age 32, clerk; Mary A., age 20
--1860 Census, p. 384, 3Wd, Orange, NJ: Lewis C. Lighthipe, age 45, b. NJ, merchant; Maria, age 71 (mother); Oscar, age 43, (brother) shoemaker; Mary A. age 30 (sister); Lewis H., (son) age 17; Agnes C., age 14, (dau.); Abby B., age 10 (dau.); William J. age 7 (son); Margaret S., age 5; (dau.) James A., age 2 (son); all b. NJ; 1 servant
--1870 Census: p.393, 3Wd, Orange, NJ: Lewis Lighthipe, age 54, sup't, hat forming mill; Oscar, age 53, foreman at hat finishing shop; Mary, age 40; Agnes, age 24; William, age 17, clerk in bank; Margaret, age 15; Alfred, age 12; all b. NJ: John Bessel, age 26, b. England, r.r.

paymaster; Abby Bessel, age 21, b. NJ; George Bessel, age 1 b. NJ; 1 servant
--1880 Census, p.169B, Orange, NJ: Lewis C. Lighthipe, widower, age 65, works in hat forming mill; Agnes, dau., age 34, teacher; Margaret, dau., age 25, teacher; James, A. son, age 22, telephone employee; Oscar, brother, age 63 b. NJ, farmer; Mary A., sister, age 50, b. NJ; Max E. Bulter, age 30 b. NY, architect; Mary E. Reddington, age 25 b. NY, housework
--1900 Census, p.37B, Manhattan, NYC: William Lighthipe, b. May 1855 NJ, banker; Lydia, b. May 1855 NJ, parents b. England, 6 born 3 living; Marie, b. March 1877 NY; John, b. March 1888 NY; Esther b. March 1890 NY; 1 servant

Children of Lewis Condit Lighthipe and Henrietta Ingraham:
Lewis Henry, b. Jan. 24, 1843
Agnes C., b. abt. 1846
Helen McFarlane, b. abt. 1847
Abby Bennett, b.Sept.17,1849;d.Jan.6, 1915; m.John Bessel
William J., b. abt. 1853; m. Lydia .....
Margaret S., b. abt. 1855
James A., b. abt. 1858

- - - - -

LORD

Lord, GILBERT b. (abt. 1855)
(map, grave owned, Sect. I) d.

Lord, WILLIAM b. (abt. 1850?)
(map, grave owned, Sect. I) d.

Lord, MRS. (Carolina E.) b. (abt. 1855)
(map, grave owned,Sect. I) d.

Gilman, MRS. b.
(map, bur. w/ Mrs. Lord) d.

Notes:
--1870 Census, p.328&329, 1Wd. Orange, NJ: William Lord, age 19, painter, b. Ireland; Gilbert Lord, age 14, b. Ireland, apprentice shoemaker; at res. of William and Eliza Crosby

--1880 Census, p.61A, Orange, NJ: William Lord, age 30, b. England, painter; Carrie E., wife, age 25, b. NJ, parents b. Germany; Carrie E., dau., age 7 b. NJ; William, son, age 5, b. NJ; Minnie, dau.,age 1 b. NJ; Gilbert, brother, age 25, b. NJ, shoemaker

--1910 Census, p.8B, 2Wd. Orange, NJ: William Lord, age 56, m.37 yrs., b. England, painter & decorator; Carolina E., age 55 b. NJ; Caroline E. Jr. age 35, bookkeeper at paint shop; William F., age 34, son, m.7 yr., painter & decorator; Mary, age 34, dau.-in-law; Minnie, age 30, dau., bookkeeper at factory; Gilbert, age 26, son, bookkeeper at telephone office

Children of William Lord and Carolina E. ......:
Carolina E., b. abt 1873
William F., b. abt. 1875; m. Mary .....
Minnie, b. abt. 1879
Gilbert, b. abt. 1884

- - - - -

LOWDEN

Lowden, Samuel	b. (abt. 1850)
	d.
1st wife, Emma E.(Townley)	b. (abt. 1850)
	d. (bef. 1920?)
Lowden, CHILD of S.	b.
(map, Section A)	d.
(plot of Caleb Townley,q.v.)	

Notes:
--Emma was dau. of Henry Townley and Eleanor Jacobus.
--1850 Census, p.210 Orange Twp.NJ: Henry Townley age 27, shoemaker; Eleanor age 27; Adolphus age 6; Emma age 6 mos. all b. NJ
--?1850 Census, p.88, Chester Twp., Burlington Co. NJ: Joseph E. Lowden, age 28, b. NJ, boat builder; Maryann, age 27 b. MD; Elizabeth age 5; Benjamin F. 3; Samuel, age 1
--?1860 Census, p.1001, Mt. Holly, Cinnaminson Twp., Burlington Co., NJ: Joseph P. Lowden, age 36, ship carpenter; Mary A., age 36; Samuel, age 11; 6 other children; all b. New Jersey

--1870 Census, p.349, 2Wd, Orange, NJ: Henry Townley, age 49, works at hat factory; Eleanor, age 47; Emma, age 21; Adolphus age 27, works felt hat factory; Mary, age 24; William, age 3; Mary, age 2; all b. NJ
--1870 Census, p.242, 3Wd, Orange, NJ: Samuel Lowden, age 19, b. NJ, apprentice carpenter; at res. of Rufus S. and Elizabeth Hooper
--1880 Census, p.95.1, Orange, NJ: Samuel Lowden, age 31, church sexton; Emma E., age 30; Henry D., age 3 months, b. March 1880), son; all b. NJ (adj. to Adolphus and Henry Townley)
--1900 Census, p.4A, 1Wd, East Orange, NJ: Adolphus Townley b. June 1843, m.20, hat finisher; Emma E. Lowden b. Dec. 1850,sister, m.23, 4 born 3 living; Henry B. Lowden b. Mar 1880, nephew,order clerk; Retta B. Lowden, 'niece' b. June 1883, order clerk; Ernest T. Lowden, b. June 1883, nephew,; all b. NJ
--?1900 Census, p.3A, Colwyn, Delaware Co., PA: Samuel Lowden, age 51, b. NJ, father b. 'MD', mother b. NJ; boarder, married 24 years, builder
--1910 Census, p.6B, 1Wd, West Orange, NJ: 'Adolphes' Townley, age 66, widower, b. NJ, hatter; Emma Lowden, sister, age 59, widow, 4 born 3 living; Henry Lowden, age 30 b. NJ, florist for private family; Ernest Lowden, age 23, b. NJ, house painter
--?1920 Census, p.8B, Colwyn, Delaware Co.,PA: Samuel Lowden, age 70 b. NJ, carpenter at club; Henneratte A., age 49, wife, b. England; Anna M., age 18 b. PA, laundress at club; Helen E., age 15 b. PA, clerk mfg. 'auto tokin'; Harriet A. Childs, age 21, b. PA, dau.; James C. Childs, age 23, son-in-law, age 23, cluffer & corker at locomotive works; Heneeritte A. Childs, age 1 month; all b. PA; 1 boarder

Children of Samuel Lowden and Emma E. Townley:
Henry D., b. March 1880
?Retta B., b. abt. June 1883
Ernest T., b. abt. November 1886; m. Etta ....., b. abt. 1884
Child, (bur. St. Mark's Cemetery)

- - - - -

LYNDE

Lynde, WILLIAM (map,ch.property, Sect. H)	b. d.
Lynde, MARY (map, ch. property, Sect. H)	b. d.

Notes:

- - - - -

Lynde, GEORGE   b.
(map, Section M)   d. 1882

Notes:
--bur. plot of Samuel Graham, q.v.

- - - - -

LYON

Lyon, Abby*   b.
(map, Section L)   d. (February 28, 1859)

Notes:
See: bur. plot of Samuel Fairchild, q.v.)

- - - - -

MARKWITH

Markwith, JOHN   b. (May 6, 1809)
(map, Sect. B, plot owner)   d. March 19, 1900

wife, MARGARET (Hall)   b. March 19, 1817
(gmnj)(shaw)(csl-E187)   d. November 3, 1887(?)
(map, Section B)   d. February 23, 1883(?)

daughter, SUSAN   b. (abt. 1846)
wife of Stephen Cole   d. November 3, 1887
(map, Section B)

son, IRA   b. (abt. 1849)
(map, Section B)   d. March 21, 1894

Notes:
--John Richard Markwith, b. May 6, 1809, Essex Co., NJ, son of John C. Markwith and Elizabeth Muchridge.(IGI)

--1840 Census: p.266, Orange Twp.

--1850 Census, p.229, Orange Twp: John "Margrush" age 33, shoemaker; Margaret 33; John 12; George 8; Susan A. 4; Ira age 6 months; James Hall, age 28, laborer; all b. NJ
--1860 Census: p.371, 3Wd, Orange, NJ: John Markwith age 52, shoemaker; Margaret age 43; George age 18, boot fitter; Susan age 13; Ira age 11; Mary age 8.
--1870 Census, p.322, 1Wd, Orange: John Markwith age 52, works boot/shoe factory; Margaret age 53; Ira age 20, works boot/shoe factory; Mary, age 18, works at felt hat factory; all b. New Jersey
--1880 Census: p.67B, Orange, NJ: Jno.Markwith, age 63, b. NJ, shoemaker; Margaret, wife, age 63, b. NJ; Ira, son, age 31, shoemaker; Susan Cole, dau.'single', age 34, b. NJ, at home; Arthur Cole, grandson, single, age 13,at school; Mary Cole, granddaughter, age 3

Children of John Markwith and Margaret ......:
John Jr., abt. 1838; m. Eleanora Wilber
George, b. abt 1842
Susan A., b. about 1846, m. Stephen B. Cole
Ira, b. about 1849
Mary, b. abt. 1852

- - - - -

MATTHEWS

Matthews, ALBERT
(gmnj)(shaw)(csl-E174)
(map, Section B)
(NJWill #17377G, 1871)

b. (December 7, 1814)
d. February 11, 1860
Aged 45.2.4

wife, Mary Ann* (Cary)

b. (September 9, 1806)
d. (aft. 1880)

son, JOSEPH HOBART
(csl - E170)(map,Sect. B)

b. (abt. 1833)
d. May 28, 1863

daughter, MARY EMILY
(csl - E172)(map,Sect. B)

b. (August 16, 1835)
d. July 16, 1865
Age 29.11.0

son, WILLIAM EDGAR
(csl - E171)(map,Sect. B)

b. (August 10, 1836)
d. December 10, 1864(?)
Aged 28.4.0

son, DAVID CLEMENT
(csl - E173)(map,Sect. B)
b. (July 31, 1839)
d. August 25, 1840
Aged 1.0.25

daughter, ANZONETTE C.
(csl - E173)
b. (June 1842)
d. August 12, 1842
Aged 2 months

son, FREDERICK H.
(csl - E170)(map, Sect. B)
b. (March 28, 1862)
d. December 28, 1863
Aged 1.9.0

Notes:
--Albert Matthews b. Orange, NJ m. Mary Ann Cary. She was daughter of Clement Cary and Phebe Jennings. (IGI) Mary Ann was born September 9, 1806.

--1850 Census: p.224&225, Orange Twp., NJ: Albert Matthews age 45, farmer b. NJ; Mary A. age 44; Joseph H. age 17, clerk; Mary E. age 14, Anzinette L. age 5. (?William E. age 12, at res. of Michael Crane)
--1860 Census: p.403, Orange, NJ: Mary A. Matthews, age 53, keeps boarding house, Emily, age 24; William E. age 23, carpenter; Annetta L. age 15. Adj. to Caleb Matthews, age 56, shoemaker.
--?1860 Census, p.823, 9Wd, Newark: Joseph Mathews, age 27, b. NJ, no occupation listed; at res. of Henry Bertram, cigar maker
--1870 Census, p.403, Orange: Mary A. Mathews age 68; A. Laveria 24; William 15; Frank 13; all b. NJ; 10 boarders
--1880 Census: p.197.1, Orange, NJ: Mary A. Mathews, widow, age 73, b. NJ; Leverna, dau. single, age 34, b. NJ;Albert F. Matthews, grandson, single, age 23, b. Michigan, at college.

Children of Albert Matthews and Mary Ann Cary:
Joseph Hobart, b. abt 1833; d. 1863
Mary Emily, b. 1835; d.1865
William Edgar, b. 1836; d. 1864
David Clement, b. 1839; d.1840
Anzonette C., b. 1842; d. 1842
Anzonette Laverna, b. abt 1846; d. aft. 1930
William, b. abt 1855
Frank, b. abt 1857
Frederick H., b. 1862; d. August 7, 1894

- - - - -

Matthews, Caleb* b.
(map, Section A, plot owner) d.

Notes:
--?Caleb H. Matthews: b. abt. 1803; d. 3Wd Orange,May 1870
--?1860 Census, p.363, 3Wd.Orange, NJ: Caleb Matthews, age 56, shoemaker; Phebe, age 40; Hannah, age 38; all b. NJ

- - - - -

Matthews, John* b. (abt. 1808)
(map,plot owner, Sect. A) d.

wife, Elvina* ..... b. (abt. 1810)
  d.

child,GRACE MATTHEWS b.
(map, Section A) d. August 1, 1864

child, HARRY MATTHEWS b.
(map, Section A) d.

child, J. H. MATTHEWS b.
(map, Section A) d.

Notes:
--1850 Census, p.236, Orange Twp., NJ: John H. Matthews, age 42, b.NJ,farmer; 'Elima' age 40; Charlotte age 18; Sarah, age 16; Ambrose, age 14; John H., age 8; Caleb, age 6; Alfred, age 4; Arthur, age 1;all b. NJ; Emma Blanchard, age 12, B, b. NJ; Henry Childs, age 30, b. England, laborer
--1860 Census, p.386, 3Wd. Orange, NJ: John H. Matthews, age 52, hat manufacturer; Elvina, age 50; Ambrose M., age 23, hat manufacturer; Charlotte, age 27; Sarah, age 26; John H., age 18; Caleb F. age 15; Arthur S. age 11; Dewitt C., age 8; also, 1 servant and 1 hatter

Children of John H. Matthews and Elvina .....:
Charlotte, b. abt. 1833; m. 1862, Thomas G. Lindsley
Sarah, b. abt. 1834
Ambrose M., b. abt. 1837; m. 1865, Mary L. Harrison
John H., b. abt. 1842

Caleb F., b. abt 1845
Arthur S., b. abt. 1849
Dewitt C., b. abt. 1853

- - - - -

Matthews, NOAH   b. April 16, 1771
(gmnj)(shaw)(csl-E131)   d. August 3, 1851
(map, Section D)

Noah Matthews
Born April 17th, 1771
Died Aug 3rd, 1851
In the 81st year
of his age

wife, PHEBE (Harrison)   b. March 29, 1774
(csl - E130)(map, Sect. D)   d. January 29, 1835

In
Memory of
Phebe
wife of
Noah Matthews
who was born
March 29, 1776
Died Jan. 29, 1833
Aged 60 years
& 10 months

Notes:
--See: Daniel Babbit
--Noah Matthews m. Phebe Harrison daughter of Simeon Harrison, q.v., and Hannah Crane.
(*Harrison Gen.*, p. 46)
--Their only daughter, Frances Nancy, married Daniel Babbitt, q.v.

--1840 Census: p. 260, Orange Twp.
--1850 Census: p.211, Orange Twp., NJ: Noah Matthews age 79, no occup; William Babbitt age 29?, lawyer; Frances (Nancy) age 24 and Alice age 3 months; all b. NJ; 3 servants; (Adj. to Daniel Babbitt)

- - - - -

Matthews, Simeon H.*　　　　b. (abt. 1817)
(map, Sect. B, plot owner)
(NJ Will #28544G,1900)　　　d. (aft. 1880)

wife, Caroline*　　　　　　　b. (abt. 1819
　　　　　　　　　　　　　　d. (aft. 1880)

daughter, SARAH MARIA　　b. (abt. February 15, 1840)
(gmnj)(csl - E169)　　　　　d. Mary 15, 1851
(map, Section B)　　　　　　*Aged 11.3*

Matthews, JOSEPH　　　　　b.
(map, Section B)　　　　　　d. May 15, 1857

Matthews, SARAH L.　　　　b.
(map, Section B)　　　　　　d.

Notes:
--1850 Census, p.224, Orange Twp: 'Simion H. Mathews' age 33, farmer; Caroline, age 31; Sarah M., age 10; Caroline A., age 8; Simion E. age 6; Frances E., dau.,age 4; Charles B., age 2; all b. NJ; 2 servants
--1860 Census, p.235, Irvington PO, Clinton Twp., Essex Co., NJ: Simeon Matthews age 43, farmer; Caroline age 41; Caroline A., age 18; Simeon E. age 16, teacher; Frances E., age 13; Charles B., age 12; Robert M., age 2; Ella H., age 6 months; all b. New Jersey
--1870 Census, p.311, Passaic, Morris Co., NJ: Simeon H. Mathews age 53, farmer; Caroline age 51; Robert H., age 12; Ellen, age 10; Lucy age 8; 1 servant
--1880 Census: p.292.3, Millington, Morris Co., NJ: Simeon Mathews, farmer, age 63, b. NJ; Caroline Mathews, wife, age 61, b. NJ; Robert H. son, age 21, b. NJ; Ella Mathews, dau. age 20, b. NJ; Lucy Mathews, dau. age 18, b. NJ

Children of Simeon H. Matthews and Caroline ......:
Sarah M., b. abt 1840; d, 1851
Caroline A., b. September 1841; m. Samuel E. Young, q.v.
Simeon E., b. abt. 1844
Frances E., b. abt 1846
Charles B., b. abt 1848
Robert H. b. abt. 1859
Ella H., b. abt 1860
Lucy, b. abt 1862

- - - - -

McCREA

McCrea, NATHAN
(CSL-EC2))(map,Sect.O)
(family information)(nps)

b. (abt. 1827)
d. (September 17,1881)
Co. F. 72nd NY Inf.

wife, Mary Joyce*
(Babbidge)

b. (January 25, 1832)
d. (January 17, 1915)

Notes:
Served: Civil War, Co. F, 72nd NY Inf. (nps) (Co. F. was recruited at Newark, NJ)
Gov't headstone provided: 'd. September 18, 1881'
--Map says: "Section O, Row 5, Negro Burial Ground" (error)
--Nathan was son of Samuel 'McRae' and Mary Rodgers.
Nathan's cause of death was chronic nephritis.
--Nathan 'MacRay' m. Mary J. Babbidge, January 6, 1854, Newark; dau. of Courtney Babbidge and Mercy Joyce; Mary d. of 'cerebral apoplexy'.

--1850 Census: Nathan was boarding in a house where Mary J. was the cook. (information from family)
--1860 Census: p.759, 12 Ward, Newark. Nathan McRay hatter, age 31, b. Maine: Mary, age 27, b. Maine; Samuel, age 6; Nathan age 3; James age 2; Margaret age 4 months
--1870 Census: p.451 11 Ward, Newark: Nathan McRea, age 41, b. Maine, works hat mfg; Mary, age 37 b. Maine; Samuel, age 14, b. NY, works hat mfg; James, age 11, b. NJ; Charles, age 7, b. NJ; William, age 4, b. NJ; Lucy, age 3, b. NJ; Mary, age 5 months b. NJ
--1880 Census: P.179B, Orange, NJ: Nathan McCrea, age 53, b. Maine, hatmaker, father b. Scotland, mother b. Ireland; Mary J. wife, age 48, b. Maine, parents b. Maine; James, age 21, b. NJ, laborer; Charles H. age 17, laborer
William P. age 14; Mary, age 10; Nathan, age 7; Emery A. age 2

Children of Nathan McCrea:
Samuel J., b. May 1854
    m. 1881, Catherine Murphy;dau. of Henry Murphy
    and Julia S. Kelly
Nathan, b. abt. 1858; d. bef. 1873
James, b. October 1858

Margaret, b. 1860
Charles H., b. April 1864; d. aft. 1900; m. Emma J. Wolf
William Penn, b. Dec. 25, 1865; m. Mary Ann Mead
Lucy, b. abt. 1867
Mary, b. March 29, 1870; d. aft. 1900
Nathan C. , b. March 31, 1873; d. aft 1915;m.Gertrude P. .....
Emery Alfred, b. May 1, 1878; d. Sept. 21, 1950
    m. #1, Augusta Hoefner
    m. #2, Mary Jane Lynch

- - - - -

McCULLOUGH

McCullough, JOHN   b.
(map,ch. property, Sect. H)   d. December 22, 1848

- - - - -

McCullough, ELLA   b.
(map, Section H)   d. July 4, 1878

Notes:
--bur. map, Section H, plot of Isaac Baldwin, q.v.

- - - - -

McCullough, Thomas   b.
(map, plot owner, Sect. N)   d.

McCullough, JAMES W.   b.
(map, Section N)   d.

Notes:
--?Supposition: James William McCulloh, often mispelled 'McCulloch' is known to have died in Orange, NJ on June 17, 1861. James was the 1st Comptroller of the U.S. Treasury.(see: *100 Americans Making Consitutional History,* by Melvin I. Urofsky)

- - - - -

McGLEE

McGlee, CAROLINE   b.

(map, ch. property, Sect. N)   d.
                               Aged 3

Notes:

- - - - -

McGLOUGHLIN

McGloughlin, WILLIAM   b.
(map, Section J)   d.

Notes:
--bur. map, Section J, plot of David Bell, q.v.

- - - - -

McKAY

McKay, JAMES   b.
(map, plot owner, Sect. I)   d.

McKay, MARY S.   b.
(map, Sect. I)   d. May 18, 1861

McKay, MOSES   b.
(map, Sect. I)   d. August 11, 1861

Notes:

- - - - -

McMULLIN

McMullin, JOHN E.   b.
(map, Section G)   d. April 28, 1894
                              Aged 4

Notes:
--bur. in or near plot of Eliza Allen, q.v.

--?1895 NJ State Census, p.147: John McMullin, b. Ireland; Mrs. McMullin, b. Ireland; William(?), b. U.S.

MEAL

Meal, JOHN
(map, ch.property, Sect. H)
b.
d. April 18, 1882

Notes:
--?1870 Census, p.489, 12 Wd. Newark, NJ: John Meal, age 58, b. Germany, glass? maker; Eva, age 50, b. Germany; John, age 12, b. NJ

MEEKER

Meeker,
ABRAHAM PIERSON
(gmnj)(csl - E90)
(map, plot owner, Sect. F)
(NJ Will #13968G, 1850)
b. (Abt. 1781)
d. May 7, 1850
In 69th year

wife, ELIZABETH
(gmnj)(shaw)(csl - E91)
(map, Section F)
b. (October 18, 1783)
d. April 3, 1837

To the memory of
Elizabeth
wife of
Abraham P. Meeker
who departed this life
April 3rd, 1837
aged 52 years
5 months
and 16 days

Meeker, MARY
(map, Section F)
b.
d.

Notes:
--Abraham Meeker was born 1781 at Caldwell, NJ, son of Thomas Meeker and Sarah Pierson.

--1850 Census, p.245, Orange Twp: Columbus "Maker" age 35 b. NJ, farmer; Elizabeth age 30, b. NY; Abram age 12; Charles age 9; Susanna 7; Elsey age 5; Emily age 9 months; all children b. New Jersey
--1850 Census, p.236, Orange Twp: John H. Matthews age 42, farmer; "Elima" age 40; Charlotte age 18; Sarah age 16; Ambrose age 14; John H. age 8; Caleb age 6; Arthur age 1; 1 laborer; 1 domestic
--1860 Census, p.906, Twp.5, Range 5E, Moultrie Co. IL: Ambrose Meeker, age 61 b. NJ, farmer; Deborah J. age 48, b. New Hampshire; 2 farm laborers; 1 domestic
--1860 Census, p.654, Union Twp., Union Co., NJ: Albert R. Meeker, age 54, hatter; Susan E., age 49; both b. NJ
--1860 Census, p.386, 3Wd, Orange: John H. Matthews, age 52, hat manufacturer; Elvina age 50; Ambrose M. age 23, hat manufacturer; Charlotte 27; Sarah 26; John H., age 18, clerk; Caleb F. age 15; Arthur S. age 11; DeWitt C., age 8; all b. NJ; 1 servant; 1 boarder
--1860 Census, p.396, 3Wd, Orange: Washington Meeker, age 41 farmer; Phoebe N. age 33; Jane E. 8; Ruth C. age 6; Lowell M. age 4; all b. New Jersey
--1870 Census, p.411, 3Wd, Orange: John H. Mathews, age 62; retired hat manufacturer; real estate $100,000; personal $35,000; "Elinra" age 60; Stewart age 21, clerk; Dewitt age 18; Mary Stetson, age 9, servant; all b. New Jersey

Children of Abraham P. Meeker and Sarah Pierson:
Ambrose, b. abt 1799; m. Deborah .....
Albert Ryerson, b. abt. 1807; m. Susan E. Ball
Elvina, b. abt 1810, m. John H. Matthews
Columbus, b. abt. 1815; m. Elizabeth .....
Washington, b. abt. 1819

'MELLON'

(See: John K. Milne)

METZ

Metz, ROBERT	b.
son of Charles	
(map,ch. property Sect. H)	d. June 27, 1889

Notes:
--?1870 Census, p.388, 3Wd, Orange, NJ: James J. Metz, age 47, b. PA, tinsmith; 'Charles' E. Metz, age 47 b. NJ; Franklin Metz, age 16, b. NJ; Abby Ann Brewster, age 30 b. NJ; Walter Sharp, age 28. b.NJ, expressman

- - - - -

MEYER

Meyer, EDWARD C.
(map, Section H)
b.
d. March 20, 1906
Aged 21 days

Notes:
--Bur. plot of James H. Clark, q.v.

- - - - -

MILLER

Miller, NICHOLAS
(gmnj)
(map, plot owner, Sect. K)
b. February 12, 1827
d. June 4, 1907
Aged 80

first wife, ELIZA
(map, Sect. K)
b. (abt. 1827
d. March 16, 1851

second wife, MARY ANN HOWELL ARBUTHNOT
(Jacobus)
(gmnj)(map, Sect. K)
b. February 17, 1816
d. March 30, 1905
Aged 89

son, CHARLES E.
(gmnj)(csl - E46)(map,Sect. K)
b. May 5, 1851
d. March 14, 1856

Miller, GEORGE A.
(map, Section K)
b.
d. February 24, 1856(?)

Miller, LEWIS
(map, Section K)
b.
d. June _ _, _ _ _ _

Miller, SAMUEL M. JOHN b.
(map, Section K) d. February 17, 18_6

EMMA, child of S. M. Miller b.
(map, Section K) d. May 29, _ _ _ _

SISTER-IN-LAW of Nich. b.
(map, Section K) d.

Notes:
--Nicholas Miller was son of ?Aaron Miller and Lydia Romine.
--Nicholas Miller married #1, Eliza .....
--Nicholas Miller m. Mary Ann Howell Arbuthnot Jacobus, October 25, 1852, Orange Twp., New Jersey
--Mary Ann was daughter of William Arbuthnot (1781-1852) and Mary Howell (1782-1854).
--Mary Ann married first, Monroe Jacobus, Sr.

--1850 Census: p.239, Orange Twp., NJ: Nicholas Miller age 23, hatter, b. NJ; Eliza age 23.
--1860 Census: p.368, 3rd Ward, Orange, NJ: Nicholas Miller age 34, hatter, b. NJ; Mary A. age 40; Stephen age 2.
--1870 Census, p.390, 3Wd, Orange: Nicholas Miller, age 43, works at felt hat factory; Mary A., age 54; Stephen age 12; all b. New Jersey
--1880 Census: p.168.4, Orange, NJ:Nicholas Miller, age 51, b. NJ, works in hat factory;Mary A., wife, age 61, b. NJ; Stephen M. son age 22, florist; Sarah L Jaffary, married, age 31, b. NJ, at home; Frank W. Jaffary, age 12, at school; Eliza B. Senter, age 27, b. MA, canvasser books
--1900 Census, p.8B, 3Wd, Orange: "Nickolas" Miller b. Feb. 1827, r.r. gateman; "May A." b. Jan 1816; (adj. to Stephen Miller, b. April 1858 and his wife, Anna M.)

Children of Nicholas Miller and Eliza .....:
Sarah L., b. abt 1849; m. .....Jaffary
Charles E., b. May 5, 1851; d.March 14, 1856

Children of Nicholas Miller and Mary Ann Howell Arbuthnot:
Stephen M., b. April 1858; m. Anna M. .....

- - - - -

MILLS

Mills, James* b. (abt. 1812)
(map, plot owner, Sect. F) d. (aft. 1880)

wife, CATHARINE H. b. (July 13, 1819)
(gmnj)(csl-E100)(map,Sect.F) d. January 6, 1847

*In
Memory of
Catherine
wife of
James Mills
who Died
Jan.6th,1847
Aged 27 years. 5 mo
& 24 Days*

wife, CHARLOTTE ..... b. (abt. 1831)
(map, Section F) d.

Notes:
--James Mills married #2, Charlotte .....

--1850 Census, p.95&96, 19Wd, New York New York: Jas. Mills, age 38 b. NY, cartman; Charlotte, age 20 b. NJ; Jno. R. age 10 b. NJ; Elias age 8 b. NJ; Jas. D. age 6, b. NJ; Chs. J. age 4 b. NJ; Ann L. Brown, age 17, b. Ireland
--1860 Census, p.307, 11Wd, Newark: James Mills, age 48 b. 'Ireland', hatter; Charlotte age 28 b. NJ; Eliza age 8 b. NJ; Franklin age 6 b. NJ; Elias age 18, b. NJ, hat finisher; Charles, age 13 b. NJ
--1870 Census, p.461, 11Wd, Newark: James Mills, age 58 b. NY, works hat mfg.; Charlotte age 39 b. NJ; Eliza C. age 18 b. NY; Franklin P., age 16 b. NY; apprentice plumber
--1880 Census: p.425.4, Newark, NJ: James Mills, age 68, b. NY, hatter, father b. NJ, mother b. NY; Charlotte, wife, age 49, b. NJ, parents b. NJ

Children of James Mills and Catherine H. .....:
John R., b. abt 1840
Elias, b. abt 1842
James D., b. abt 1844
Charles J., b. abt 1846

Children of James Mills and Charlotte .....:
Eliza C., b. abt 1852
Franklin P., b. abt 1854

- - - - -

MILNE

Milne, JOHN K. (gmnj) (nps) (map, plot owner, Sect. E) (& map, plot owner, Sect. J)	b. June 11, 1836 d. June 4, 1906 *Co.G, 26th NJ Inf*
wife, MARY (Bracken) (map, Section E)	b. March 20, 1840 d. January 10, 1905 *Aged 65.9.20*
daughter, CLARA KEITH (map, Section J)	b. September 15, 1876 d. May 30, 1880 bur. June 1, 1880
son, GEORGE P. (map, Section E)	b. (abt. 1878) d. August 13, 1910 *Aged 31.9.24*

Notes:
Served: Civil War; Co. G, 26th NJ Inf., Pvt. (nps)
--In the plot, Section E, are also: Flora Elizabeth Price, q.v., Geo. Strother, q.v.
--?1860 Census, p.0, Image 230, Pound Ridge PO, Rye, Westchester Co., NY: John Milne, age 21, b. Scotland, moulder; at res. of George A. Downs, moulder
--1870 Census, p.413, 3Wd, Orange: John "Miller" age 38 b. Scotland, laborer; Mary age 28 b. Ireland; William, age 5, b. NY; Mary, age 4, b. NJ; John A., age 2 b. NJ; Louisa age 6 months, b. NJ
--1880 Census, p.189.1, Orange: John "Millon" age 44, b. Scotland, laborer; Mary, age 48 b. Ireland; William age 15, b. NJ, hatter apprentice; Mary, age 14 NJ; John 12 NJ; Louisa, age 10 b. NJ; Matilda age 8 b. NJ; Flora, age 6 b. NJ; George age 1 b. NJ
--1887-1890 Orange Directory: John K. Milne, sexton at Valley Congregational Church

--1900 Census, p.8B, 4Wd, Orange: John K. Milne, b. June 1836, Scotland, immig. 1853, sexton; Mary b. Mar 1839 ' 'Scotland', immig. 1860; William b. Dec. 1864, Staten Island, police officer; Mary b. Mar 1867 NJ, dressmaker; Louisa b. Dec. 1870 NJ, hat trimmer; Matilda J. b. June 1872 NJ, hat trimmer; George P. b. Oct. 1878, NJ, stenographer

Children of John K. Milne and Mary Bracken:
William, b. December 1864; m. Minnie .....
Mary, b. March 1867; unm. in 1930
John A., b. abt. 1868' m. Leola (nee Plumber?)
Louisa, b. December 1870; m. Augustine J. Reinhardt
Matilda J., b. June 1872; unm. in 1930
Flora, b. October 1875; m. John M. Price, q.v.
Clara Keith, b. 1876; d. 1880
George P., b. October 1878; m. Daisy .....

- - - - -

MITCHELL

Mitchell(?), MARGARET b.
(map,ch. property, Sect. H) d. December 16, 1921

Notes:

- - - - -

MORGAN

Morgan, FRANCES L. b.
(map, Sect. B) d. June 9, 1904

Notes:
--See: Plot of Ann P. Browne
--?dau. of John Morgan and Frances Browne

- - - - -

MORRISON

Morrison, ... b.
  d.

wife, SARAH JANE (Oven) b. (February 16, 1844)
(gmnj)(csl - E203) d. September 25, 1869
(map, Section A) *Aged 25.7.9*

Notes:
--Sarah Jane was daughter of George and Jane Oven, q.v.
--1850 Census: p.221, Orange Twp., NJ: George Oven age 39, hatter, b. England; Jane age 32 b. NJ; Martha, age 12; Mary age 10; John age 8; Hannah age 7; Sarah age 5.
--1860 Census: p.401, 2Wd, Orange, NJ: George '"Owen" age 48, hatter. b. England; Jane age 43 b. NY; Martha age 22 b. NJ; Mary age 20, Hannah age 17; Jennie age 15; John age 13; William H. age 10; James A. age 7

- - - - -

MULFORD

Mulford,
BENJAMIN PRINCE b. April 30, 1836
(gmnj)(csl - E50) d. September 29, 1903
(map, Section J) *Aged 66*

first wife, SARAH F. (Dean) b. (December 27, 1839)
(gmnj)(csl - E50) d. February 28, 1864
(map, Section J) *Aged 24.2.1*

second wife, Mary Josephine
(Williams) b. (b. March 1844)
  d. (d. aft. 1900)

son, ALVAH DEAN b. September 5, 1860
(csl - E50) d. March 7, 1864
(map, Section J) *Aged 3 years*

son, CHARLES BEACH b. October 28, 1863
(csl - E50)(map, Sect. J) d. February 4, 1864

Notes:
--See: map, Section J, plot of Isaac M. Dean
--Sarah Frances "Fanny" was the only daughter of Isaac M. and Mary Jane Dean. (q.v.)

--Benjamin Prince Mulford was born April 30, 1838 (sic) at Shelter Island, Suffolk Co., NY, son of Alva Stratton Mulford and Bethiah Horton. Sarah Frances Dean was his first wife. He married second, June 2, 1869, Mary Josephine Williams, daughter of Job Crane Williams and Catherine (Stiles) Tichenor. (IGI)(*Williams Gen.*, p.87)

--1850 Census, p.286, Southold, Suffolk Co., NY: Alvah L. Mulford, age 42, farmer; Bethiah age 39; David 19; Benj. age 14; Mary 9; Chas. 2; Isabel age 7 months; all b. New York
--1860 Census, p.151, 11Wd, Brooklyn, Kings Co.NY: Isaac M. Dean, age 47 b. NJ, sash&blind maker; Mary age 40 b. NJ; William, age 15, b. NJ; David, age 24, b. NJ, lawyer; Benjamin 'Mifred' age 25, b. NY, salesman; Sarah 'Mifred' age 20, b. NJ
--1870 Census, p.373, 12Wd, Dist. 11, New York, NY: Benjamin P. "Mumford" age 34, b. NY, salesman; Mary, age 22, b. "NY"
--1880 Census: p.105.2, Orange, NJ: Benjamin B. Mulford, age 42, b. NY, cotton broker; Mary J., age 34, b. NY; Benjamin P. Mulford, son, age 9, b. NY; Grace W. Mulford, dau., age 6, b. NY
--1900 Census, p.4B, 5Wd, East Orange: B. P. Mulford, b. April 1836 NY, parents b. NY, retired; Mary J. b. March 1844 NJ, parents b. NJ; B. P. Jr. b. March 1872 NJ, collector; Grace W. age 25 b. Feb. 1875, NJ, music teacher; 2 boarders; 1 servant

Children of Benjamin Prince Mulford and Sarah E. Dean:
Alvah Dean, b. 1860; d.1864
Charles Beach, b. 1863; d. 1864

Children of Benjamin Prince Mulford and Mary J. Williams:
Benjamin Prince, Jr., b. March 1872
Grace W. b. February 1875

- - - - -

MURRAY

Murray, RICHARD
(map, grave owned, Sect. I)
b.
d. December 24, 1828

Notes:

- - - - -

NEWMAN

Newman, JAMES
(map,ch.property, Sect. H)

b. (abt. 1832)
d. September 5, 1872
Aged 40

Notes:

- - - - -

NEWTON

Newton, RICHARD T.
(map, plot holder, Sect. H)

b. (abt. August 1834)
d. January 20, 1907
Aged 73

wife, SUSAN
(map, Section H)

b. (abt. November 1836)
d. February 6, 1902

Newton, CHILD of Richard
(map, Section H)

b.
d.

Notes:
--Richard was sexton of **St. Mark's Church.**

--1870 Census: p.468, West Orange, NJ: Richard Newton, age 40, b. England, gardener; Susan, age 35, b. Ireland; George R., age 9, b. NJ; Susan E., age 4, b. NJ
--1880 Census: p.258A, West Orange, NJ: Richard Newton, age 45, b. England, sexton, St. Mark's; Susan, age 40 b. 'NJ'; George, age 19 b. NJ, brush making apprentice; Susan, age 14, b. NJ; Louisa, age '7', b. NJ
--1900 Census, p. 1A, 1Wd. Orange, NJ: Richard Newton, b. Aug. 1864, m.43 years, b. England, 'Pen sexton'; Susan, b. Ireland Nov. 1836; Susan A., b. Apr. 1876 NJ, seamstress; Louisa, b. Jan. 1878, b.NJ, seamstress

Children of Richard T. Newton and Susan .....:
George R., b. abt. 1861; m. 1887, Bessie McGreery
Susan A. b. abt. April 1876
Louisa, b. abt. January 1878
child, b. .....

- - - - -

NORMAN

Norman, JOHN
(gmnj)
(map, plot owner, Sect. L)
(nps)
b. (abt. 1826)
d. February 21, 1899
Aged 73
Co. C, 7th NJ Vol.

first wife, Margaret*
b. (abt. 1835)
d. (aft. 1870)

second wife, ELIZABETH
(map, Section L)
b. (abt. February 1819)
bur. August 29, 1902

Norman, JOHN
(map, Section L)
b.
d. January 31, 1869(?)
Aged 3

Norman, JOSEPH
(map, Section L)
b.
d. 1882(?)

Norman, GEORGE S.
(map, Section L)
b.
d. May 16, _ _ _ _

CHILD of John Norman
(map, Section L)
b.
d. January 20, 1867

DAUGHTER of John Norman
(map, Section L)
b. (abt. 1866)
d. January 3, 1869

DAUGHTER of John Gordon
(map, Section L)
b.
d. June 12, 1882

Notes:
Served: Civil War; Co. C, 7th NJ Inf., Pvt. (nps)
Served: also? Co. I, 7th NJ Inf.
--1860 Census, p.341B, 1st Wd.Orange: John Norman, age 35, laborer, b. Ireland; Margaret, age 24, b. Ireland; William, age 6, b. NJ; Margaret A.,age 4, b. NJ; Mary J., age 2, b. NJ; John, age 6 months
--1870 Census, p.223A, East Orange: John Norman, age 49, labor, b. Ireland; Margaret, age 36, b. Ireland; William, age 18; Margaret, age 13; Mary J., age 12; John, age 10

--1880 Census, p.132D, Orange, NJ: John Norman, age 52, b. Ireland, works on farm; Elizabeth, wife, age 60, b. Ireland; Charles J. son, age 21, b. NJ, works on farm; Joseph, son, age 10, b. NJ; Grace, dau. age 9, b. NJ

--1900 Census,m p.6A, 5Wd, Orange, NJ: Elizabeth Norman b. Feb. 1819, widow, b. Ireland, 1 born 1 living; Charles, b. Dec. 1859, stepson, b. NJ, laborer; Grace, b. Jan. 1872 NJ, stepdau.; Elizabeth Gordon, b. Aug. 1882, granddau., b. NJ, father b. PA, mother b. NJ, servant; Annie P. Gordon, b. Aug. 1893 NJ, father PA, mother NJ

Children of John Norman and Margaret.....:
William, b. abt. 1854; m. Fannie .....
Margaret A., b. abt. 1856
Mary J., b. abt. 1858
Charles John, b. abt. December 1859
Joseph, b. abt. 1870
Grace, b. abt. January 1872

Child of John Norman and Elizabeth .....:
daughter, m. John Gordon

- - - - -

OSBORNE

Osborn, ANN
(gmnj)(shaw)(csl - EC4)
(NJ Will #17400G,1871)
(map, Osborne plot, Section N)

b. (abt. 1788)
d. March 20. 1871
Aged 83

Osborn, CATHERINE
(gmnj)(shaw)(csl - EC4)
(NJ Will#16706G,1868)
(map, Osborne plot, Sect. N)

b. (abt. 1786)
d. September 18, 1868
Aged 82

CHILD
(map, Section N)
(removed to Rosedale Cem.)

b.
d.

Notes:
--1850 Census: p.234, Orange Twp.; Catherine 'Osborne' age 58 b. Ireland; Anna Osborne age 56 b. Ireland; Isabella Douglass, age 12, b. Ireland

--1860 Census: p.368,Orange, NJ: Catherine Osborn age 50, b. NY; Ann Osborn age 54, b. NY. (sisters?); Elizabeth Button, age 12, b. NJ
--1870 Census, p.465, West Orange: Ann Osborn, age 84, b. "NY"; at boarding house of Julia Byerly

- - - - -

OVEN

Oven, GEORGE (map, Section A)	b. (abt. 1811) d. April 30, 1874
wife Jane T.*	b. (abt. 1818) d. (aft. 1880)
daughter MARTHA A. (gmnj)(map,Sect. A)	b. December 13, 1837 d. July 4, 1867
son, WILLIAM H. (map, Section A)	b. (abt. 1851) d. December 20, 1873
daughter, MARY (map, Section A)	b. (abt. 1840) d. May 2, 1906 *Aged 66.4.4*
son JAMES AUGUSTUS (map, Section A)	b. (abt. 1853) d. February 16, 1921 *Aged 68.5.4*
daughter, HANNAH (map, Section A)	b. (abt. 1843) d. April 23, 1927 *Aged 83 years*
Oven, GEORGE (map, Section A)	b. d.

Notes:
--?See: George Oven, christened July 10, 1812, Tideswell, Derbyshire, England, son of John and Sarah Oven (IGI)
--?1832 Nov. 29: Arv. New York from Liverpool, S. S. Ajax; George Oven, age 21, hatter
--1840 Census: p.264, Orange Twp.

--1850 Census: p.221, Orange Twp., NJ: George Oven age 39, hatter, b. England; Jane age 32 b. NJ; Martha, age 12; Mary age 10; John age 8; Hannah age 7; Sarah age 5.
--1860 Census: p.401, 2Wd, Orange, NJ: George '"Owen" age 48, hatter. b. England; Jane age 43 b. NY; Martha age 22 b. NJ; Mary age 20, Hannah age 17; Jennie age 15; John age 13; William H. age 10; James A. age 7
--1870 Census: p.346, 2nd Ward, Orange, NJ: George Oven age 56, felt hat worker, b. England; Jane age 50 b. NY; Hannah age 26, schoolteacher; Mary age 30; John age 23, student; William 19, clerk; Augustus 17.
--1880 Census: p.93.1, Orange, NJ: Jane Oven, widow, age 62, b. NY, father b. Ireland, mother b. NY: Mary, dau., single, age 41, b. NJ, works in hat shop; Hannah, dau., single, age 37, b. NJ school teacher; James A. son, single, age 27, b. NJ, works in carriage factory

Children of George Oven and Jane T. ......:
Martha A., b. 1837; d.July 4, 1867
Mary, b. abt 1840; d. May 2, 1906
John, q.v., b. abt 1842; m. Frances Harriet Raney
Hannah, b. abt 1843; d. April 23, 1927
Sarah Jane 'Jennie', b. abt. 1845; m. ..... Morrison, q.v.
William H., b. abt 1851; d. Dec. 20, 1873 (map)
James Augustus, b. abt 1853; d. February 16, 1921

- - - - -

Oven, John, Rev.   b. (abt. 1842)
                               d. (abt. 1875)

wife, FANNIE   b. September 20, 1843
(Frances Harriet Raney)   d. August 13, 1875
(map, Section A)

Notes:
--bur. map, Section A, plot of George Oven, q.v.
--John Oven was pastor of Trinity Church, Apalachicola, FL
--Rev. John Oven m. abt. 1874 Frances Harriet Raney, dau. of David Greenway Raney and Harriet Frances Jordan
--John and Fannie died when their only child was an infant.

Child of Rev. John Oven and Frances Harriet Raney:
William John Breck Oven;b. abt. 1875;

m. 1910, Bershe Archer Meginnis

- - - - -

PALMER

Palmer, GEORGE   b.
(map, Section J)   d.
                               Aged 53

Notes:
--Bur. plot of Thomas E. Brown, q.v.
--See: ?Mrs. Bentley
--See: ?Benjamin Vincent

- - - - -

PATTERSON

Patterson, JOHN   b.
(map, ch. property,Sect.I)   d. (no dates)

Notes:
(?)Served: Civil War, Co. B, 39th NJ Inf., Pvt. (nps)
(?)Served: Civil War, Co. C, 7th NJ Inf., Pvt. (nps)
(?)Served: Civil War, Co. D, 7th NJ Inf., Pvt. (nps)
--See: Sect. H, Thomas Patterson
--?1870 Census, p.411, 3Wd, Orange: John Patterson, age 24, b. Ireland, stone cutter; Ellen age 26 b. Ireland; James A. age 9 months b. NJ; Jane 'Cathey', age 55, b. Ireland; Thomas Patterson, age 19, b. Ireland, apprentice stone cutter
--?1880 Census, p.481B, Newark: John H. Patterson, age 38 b. Ire, hatter; Ellen, wife, age 38 b. Ire.; Edward, age 17 b. NJ, hatter; Mary A. age 13 b. NJ; Elizabeth age 11 b. NJ; John J., age 4 b. NJ
--?1900 Census, p.9B, 21Wd, Brooklyn, Kings Co. NY: Ellen Patterson b. Oct. 1848, Ireland, widow, 10 born 3 living, immig. 1862; Patrick, son, b. May 1880 NY, labor; John J., son, b. May 1877 NY, soldier 17th Inf. U.S.A.

?Children of John H. Patterson and Ellen Kennedy:
Edward, b. abt. 1863
Mary A., b. abt. 1867
Elizabeth, b. abt. 1869

John Charles, b. Sept. 18, 1871
John Joseph, b. May 7, 1876
Patrick, b. May 30, 1880

- - - - -

Patterson, Thomas* b.
 d.

wife Lettisia* b.
 d.

son, ROBERT JAMES b. January 1872
(gmnj) d. August 19, 1874

Son, THOMAS ALEXANDER b. September 24, 1873
(gmnj) d. August 24, 1874

Patterson, CHILD b.
(map, Section H) d. December 4, 1872

Patterson, CHILD b.
(map, Section H) d.

Patterson, CHILD b.
(map, Section H) d.

Notes:
--?1870 Census, p.411, 3Wd, Orange: John Patterson, age 24, b. Ireland, stone cutter; Ellen age 26 b. Ireland; James A. age 9 months b. NJ; Jane Cathey, age 55, b. Ireland; Thomas Patterson, age 19, b. Ireland, apprentice stone cutter
--?1880 Census: p.454A, Manhattan, New York: Thomas Patterson, age 30, b. Ireland, single, stone cutter; boarder

- - - - -

PAUL

Paul(?), JAMES b.
(map, Section I) d. (illegible)

PEACOCK

Peacock, ARCHIBALD b.
(map, Section H) d. (1863?)

Notes:

PERRY

Perry, MARY E. b.
(map, ch.property, Sect. H) d.

Notes:

PERSONETT

Personett, JOHN b. March 3, 1805
(Death Cert.)(map, Sect. K) d. August 16, 1886
(Undertaker, 'VanBuskirk')

first wife, Fannie* (Harrison) b. (January 15, 1806)
    d. (February 10, 1842)
(bur. Old Burying Ground, Presbyterian Church, Caldwell, NJ)

second wife, Ellen* ..... b. (abt. 1812)
(predeceased John) d. (bef. August 1866)
    bur.(?) St. Mark's Cemetery

Notes:
--John was son of John Personett, Esq. and Elenor Doremus
--Obituary:
    DEATH OF THE OLDEST ORANGE HATTER
  "Mr. John Personett, of this city, probably the oldest hatter in this vicinity, died at the residence of his son-in-law, Mr. George Gardener,

Newark, on Saturday last, at the age of eighty-one years. He was born in Cedar Grove in March 1805 and received the common school education of the day. When about sixteen years of age he was apprenticed to the hatting trade and learned that trade with James Condit, better known as "Boss Jimmy", who kept a shop on Center Street near Main. In those days every apprentice was compelled to learn every part of the business and consequently Mr. Personett became a thorough workman. He worked at the trade up to within two years of his death, a period of about sixty-three years. For some years he kept a buckeye at Cedar Grove, but most of his life was spent at the kettle. He was a man respected by all who knew him. He leaves a family of several grown children, all of whom are married." (*The Orange Chronicle, Orange, NJ*, August 24, 1886)

--1830 Census: Orange Twp., NJ: John Personett:1 male age 20-30-1 female, under age 5; 1 female age 10-15; 2 females, age 20-30;At residence of James Condit, hatter and widow, "Aunt" Polly Condit.
--1840 Census: p.9, Caldwell Twp. (Cedar Grove)NJ: John 'Parsnet" with father, John Personett, Esq.
--1850 Census:p.074 & 75, Caldwell (Cedar Grove), Essex Co., NJ John Personett, 45, hatter, real estate, $800; Ellen, age 38; Almira, age 17; George, age 14; Charles, age 12; Ellen, age 10; John, age 5; Stephen, age 3; Sarah, age 2; Alfred, age 5 mos.; Alonzo 'Noon'(?))son of Almira) age 1 yr.; (Shares homestead with brother George.Real estate value=$800)(near Jacob V. Jerolaman, age 43, hatter, real estate $150)
--1860 Census: p.111, Caldwell (Cedar Grove) Essex Co., NJ. John Personett, age 55, hatter, Real estate value, $1000; Elinor, age 47, b. NJ; John age 15; Stephen, age 13; Sarah, age 12; Alfred age 10; Mary age 7; Robert age 4; Cornelius Jerolaman, 46, hatter, no real estate value. (John shares homestead with niece,Harriet Personett Jacobus and her family.)
--1870 Census, p.350A, 2 Wd Orange, Essex Co., NJ: James Lennox, age 40, carpenter, b. Ireland; Ellen, age 29, b. NJ; Wm. age 10; Harry, age 8 b. Canada(?); Elmer, age 6; Frank age 3; Almira, age 7 mos; Mary Personett, age 16,b. NJ, works hat factory; Ada Brower, age 17, b. NJ; Alonzo Lennox, age 21, NJ, carpenter; Alfred Personett, 20, b. NJ, carpenter; Robert Personett, age 14, b.NJ at school; John Personett, age 65, b. NJ, works hat factory
--1880 Census: p.474A, East Orange, NJ: George Gardner, age 34, b. NJ, painter; Sarah M. (nee Personett) wife, age 27,
b. NJ; Frederic W. Gardner, son, age 7; John Personett, father-in-law, age 75, b. NJ, works in hat shop (unemployed, apoplexy)

Children of John Personett and Fannie Harrison:
Margaret Ann, b. abt. 1828; d.1901
    m. Abram David Brower, q.v.
Lydia, b. July 1830; d. 1909; m. Charles H. Hull, q.v.
Almira, b. January 18, 1833; d. 1857;
    m. as his first wife, James Lennox, q.v.
George, b. March 9, 1834; d.1908; m. Caroline Smalley
    Served: Civil War, Co. K, 25th NJ Inf.
Charles, b. abt 1839; d. aft 1880; m. Hester A. .....
Ellen, b. abt 1840; d. aft. 1880;
    m. as his second wife, James Lennox, q.v.

Children of John Personett and Ellen ......:
John, b. abt 1845; d.1864; Civil War
    buried: National Cemetery, Chattanooga, Tenn.
Stephen, b. abt 1847; d. 1876; r. r. accident
    probably buried at St. Mark's Cemetery
Sarah M., b. Marcy 7, 1848; d.1926; m. George Gardner
Alfred, b. March 11, 1850; d. 1919; m. Sarah Jane Everson
    buried Rosedale Cemetery, Orange, NJ
Mary, b. March 30, 1853; d. aft. 1930;
    m. Charles W. McEntee
Robert Fillmore, b. Dec. 14, 1854; d. 1919;
    m. Annette C. Bernard; bur. Rosedale Cemetery

- - - - -

PETERS

Peters, Martin	b. (abt. April 1846)
	d. (bef. 1910)
wife, Dora (Weidemeyer) (aka Dorothy C.)	b. (abt. June 1848) d. (aft. 1910)
CHILD of C. Peters (map, Section L)	b. d. May 10, 1882
CHILD of C. Peters (map, Section L)	b. d. May 10, 1882

Notes:
--See: map, Section L, plot of Henry Weidemeyer

--1870 Census, p.397, 3Wd, Orange, NJ: Martin Peters, age 23, b. Prussia, painter; 'Dara' age 21; Charles, age 1, b. NJ; Henrietta Shuman, age 20, b. Prussia, works at felt hat factory
--1880 Census, p.165A, Orange, NJ: Henry Weidenmeyer, age 50 b. Schleswig,Holstein, laborer; Anna, wife, age '71' b. Schleswig Holstein; Martin Peters, son-in-law, age 32, b. Bremen, works in hat factory; Dora Peters, dau, age 30 b. Sch. Holstein; Charles Peters, grandson, age 11, b. NJ; Frederick Peters, grandson, age 9, b. NJ; Anna Peters, granddau., age 7 b. NJ; Frank Peters, grandson, age 2, b. NJ
--1900 Census, p.3B, 3Wd, Orange, NJ: Martin Peters, b. Apr. 1846 Germany, immig. 1862,m. 33 yrs. painter; Dora, b. June 1848, 10 born 6 living, b. Germany, immig. 1864; Chas. H., son, b. Dec. 1867, m.3 yr, b. NJ, painter;Fred. H.,son, b. April 1871 NJ, hat finisher; Frank, son, b. Feb. 1878 NJ, upholsterer; Annie M. Shay, dau. b. June 1873 NJ; William F. Shay, b.Sept. 1877 NY, son-in-law, hat finisher; Ferdinand R. Peters, son, b. Nov. 1885 NJ; 'Florence' L. Peters , dau. b. Jul 1888 NJ; Fannie Peters, dau-in-law b. May 1867, VA, m.3 yrs; Chas. M. Shay, b. Jul 1899 NJ, grandson
--1910 Census, p.13B, 2Wd, Orange, NJ: 'Dorothy C.' Peters, age 47, widow, b. Germany, immig. 1870; Charles, son, married, age 42, b. NJ, painter; Frederick, son, single, age 40, b. NJ, hat finisher; Annie Shay, dau., m.13 yrs, 6 born 4 living, age 36 b. NJ; Ferdinand , son, single, age 24, merchant, retail 'animals'; Florence, dau, single, age 21, filament dept. electric lamps; Frank, son, single, age 32, painter; William Shay, son-in-law, m.13 yr, b. NY, age 32, hat finisher; Charles Shay, grandson, age 10 b. NJ; Dorothy Shay, granddau., age 6 b. NJ; Anna Shay, granddau., age 4 b. NJ; Edna Shay, granddau., age 1, b. NJ

Children of Martin Peters and Dora Weidemeyer:
Charles H., b. Dec. 9,1868; m.1897,Fannie ...;
    m. #2, abt. 1925, Rose H...
Frederick H., b. abt. April 1871; unm. in 1910
Annie M., b. abt June 1873; m. abt. 1897,William F. Shay
Frank H., b. abt. Feb. 1878; ?m. abt. 1911, Lillie/Elizabeth ...
Ferdinand R., b. abt. Nov. 1885; m. Minnie .....
Florence L., b. abt. July 1888
Dora, b. July 25, 1888

- - - - -

PETTIT

Pettit, James*   b. (abt. 1817)
(map, plot owner,Sect. F)   d. (before 1870)

wife, Catherine* (Harrison)   b. (January 15, 1820)
                                             d. (aft. 1900)

CHILDREN   b.
(map, Section F)   d.

MARY ALICE   b.
WILMINA   d. (no dates)
(gmnj)

Notes:
--James Pettit m. Catherine Harrison b. January 15, 1820, d. aft. 1900, daughter of Amos A. Harrison, q.v., and Sarah Badgley. (*The Harrisons of New Jersey,* p. 67,96)

--1850 Census, p.263, South Ward, Newark, Essex Co., NJ: James 'Pettet' age 33, trunk maker; Catherine age 30; James C. age 1; Frances Harrison, age 20; George M. Rorback, age 27, trunk maker; all b. New Jersey
--1860 Census, p164, 10Wd, Newark: James Pettit, age 43, trunk manufacturer; Catherine, age 40; James age 11; Frank, age 8; all b. NJ; 2 boarders
--1870 Census, p.262, 9Wd, Newark: Kate "Pollitt" age 50; James C. age 21, bank clerk; Frank, age 17, bank clerk; all b. New Jersey
--1880 Census, p.274.2, Newark: "Katharine Pittit" widow, age 60, b. NJ; James, son, age 31 b. NJ, bank clerk; 1 servant
--1900 Census, p.2B, 5Wd, East Orange: James C. Pettit, b. May 1849, m.15 yr, 2 born 2 living, capitalist; Dorothy, daughter, b. May 1887; Alice C., dau. b. Oct. 1890; Catherine, mother, widow, b. January 1820, 2 born 2 living
--1910 Census, p.3B, 4Wd, East Orange: James C. Pettit, age 60, widower, b. NJ, parents NJ, own income; Alice C., dau., age 20 b. NJ; 3 servants

Children of James Pettit and Catherine "Kate" Harrison:
James C. Pettit b. abt. 1849; m. Mary Hoyt
Frank, b. abt 1852; m. Mary Carson
(*Harrison Gen.*, p.67, p. 84)

- - - - -

PIERSON

Pierson, Zenas*   b. (abt 1766?)
                                          d. (d. before 1850)

wife, CATHERINE
(Townley)   b. August 2, 1784
(gmnj)(shaw)(csl - E33)   d. March 23, 1863
(map, Section K)   *Aged 79*

daughter, ELIZABETH   b. August 2, 1803
(csl - E33)(map, Sect. K)   d. September 18, 1865

Pierson, BETSY   b. (duplicate?)
(map, Section K)   d.

Pierson, CATHERINE   b. (duplicate?)
(map, Section K)   d.

Notes:
--See: plot of Thomas Cottrell
--Zenas was son of Zenas Pierson and Betsey Nixon.
--Catherine was dau. of Henry Townley and Dorcas Williams
--1850 Census: p.209, Orange Twp., Catherine Pierson, age 66, b. NJ; Elizabeth age 45 b. NJ; Joseph, age 43, b. NJ, no occupation
--1860 Census, p.402, 2Wd. Orange: "Cath Person" 76 b. NJ; "Betsy Person" age 56, b. NJ

Children of Zenas Pierson and Catherine Townley:
Moses
John
Mary; m. Abraham Ward
Elizabeth, b. 1803; d.1863
J. Clark
Joseph, b. abt 1807
Jane, b. abt. 1809; m. Thomas H. Cottrell, q.v.

- - - - -

PLATT

Platt, JOHN   b.
(map, grave owned, Sect.I)   d.

Notes:

- - - - -

PRATT

Pratt, CHILD of R.   b.
(map, map, Sect. H)   d.

- - - - -

PRICE

Price, John M.*   b. (January 1872)
    d.

wife, FLORA E. (Milne)   b. 1873 (October)
(gmnj)(map, Sect. E)   d. March 25, 1934
    Aged 60

Notes:
--bur. map, Section E., plot of John K. Milne, q.v.
--1900 Census, p.8B, 4Wd, Orange: John M. Price b. January 1872, m.6 yr, b. England, immig. 1875, farmer; Flora G. b. Oct. 1875 NJ, father b. Scotland, mother Ireland; Marion M. b. November 1894 NJ (adj. to John K. and Mary Milne, q.v.)
--1910 Census, p.23A, 6Wd, Newark: John H. Price, age 38 m. 16 yr, b. England, com'l traveler pianos; Flora E. age 36 b. NJ, father b. Scotland, mother b. Ireland, 1 born 1 living; Marion M., age 15, b. NJ

Child of John H. Price and Flora E. Milne:
Marion M., b. November 1894

- - - - -

PROCTOR

Proctor,
MATTHEW HENRY   b. (31 August 1844)
(map,Sect. B)   d. November 29, 1916

wife, MARGARET   b. (August 10, 1848)

(Cortright)(map, Sect. B)	d. December 17, 1918
daughter, LULU H. (map, Sect. B)	b. (January 1892) d. October 12, 1915 *Aged 12.9.0*
CHILD of Henry (map, Section B)	b. d.
..... MARTHA PROCTOR (map, Section B)	b. d. May 11, 1892
Clark, MILTON PALMER (map, Section B)	b. d. January 27, 1896 *Aged 5* (?)

Notes:.
--Some burial information from family
--Henry was son of Matthew Proctor and Sarah/Hannah Armitage.
--Margaret was daughter of Emanuel Cortright and Rachel Van Why.

--1841 March 25: Arv. New York from Liverpool, England, S. S. Siddons: Mathew Proctor, age 33, cloth maker; Sarah, age 27; Anna age 9; James age 13
--1850 Census, p.133, Middle Smithfield Twp., Monroe Co. PA: Mathew Proctor age 42 b. England, cloth manufacturer; Johnathan Sailor, age 40 b. England, cloth manufacturer; Hannah Sailor age 28 b. England; David Sailor, age 2 b. PA
--1850 Census, p.143&144, Middle Smithfield, Monroe Co. PA: Emanuel Cortright, age 36, farmer; 'Ratcheal" age 35; David 11; William 4; Margret 3; Sarah M. age 3 months; all b. PA
--1860 Census, p.605, Coolbaugh PO, Middle Smithfield, Monroe Co. PA: Emanuel Cortright, age 43, day labor; William 14; "Maryett" age 13; Elizabeth age 12; Sarah, age 11; Charly J. age 3 months; all b. Pa
--1870 Census, p.108, Tobyhanna Mills PO, Middle Smithfield, Monroe Co. PA: Margaret Cortright, age 18, b. PA, at res. of William Depugh, farmer
--1880 Census: p.242.3, Newark, NJ: Henry Procter, age 35, b. NY, grocery clerk, parents b. England; Margaret, wife, age 29, b. PA; Harry, son, age 1, b. NJ
--1880 Census, p.297.2, Middle Smithfield, Monroe Co. PA: Mathew Proctor age 75, b. England, woolen manufacturer; Mary A., (2nd?) wife,

age 53 b. NY, parents b. France; George Gaint, age 53, single, b. England, spinner; 1 servant
--1900 Census, p.10B, West Orange: Henry M. Proctor b. August 1845, m.22 yr, b. NY, parents b. England, clerk at candy (store); Margaret b. Aug. 1847 PA, parents b. PA, 4 born 3 living; Henry M. b. Sept. 1878 NJ, telephone operator; Edward T. b. April 1882 NJ, plaster maker; William P. b. Nov. 1884 NJ; Lula H. b. Jan 1892 NJ
--1910 Census, p.19B, 5 Wd. West Orange: Henry Proctor age 65, m.34 yr. b. NY, parents b. England, salesman at grocery store; Margaret age 63 b. PA, parents b. PA; Harry M. age 32, son, single, b. NJ, ticket agt. at Erie depot; William P., age 25, son, married b. NJ, electrical machinist; Anna Frances, age 23, daughter-in-law, b. NJ, parents b. NJ; William Jr. age 5 months, grandson, b. NJ

Children of Henry Matthew Proctor and Margaret Cortright:
Henry Milton, b. September 26, 1878
Edwin Thompson, b. August 17, 1882; d. August 1966
    m. Mary Amelia Emmons
William P., b. November 1884; m. Anna Frances .....
Lula H. , b. January 1892; d. October 12, 1915

- - - - -

QUIMBY

Quimby, BYRON W. (map, plot owner, Sect. M)	b. (May 21, 1843) d. June 2, 1922 *Aged 90.0.12*
Quimby, MARY L. (Hull) (map, Sect. M)	b. (abt. 1844) d. June 9, 1925 *Aged 80*
daughter, LOTTIE (map, Section M)	b. (May 26, 1867) d. March 18, 1878

Notes:
--Byron Wickliffe Quimby was son of Daniel Wickliffe Quimby and Mary Gray; Byron m.Dec. 23,1866,Mary L. Hull, dau. of Peter V. Hull, q.v.
--1850 Census, p.223, Orange Twp., NJ: Daniel W. 'Quinby' age 32, hatter; Mary, age 33; Byron W., age 7; Edwin Gray, age 64; Hetty E. Gray, age 19; all b. NJ

--1860 Census, p.356, 3Wd, Orange, NJ: 'Margret' Quimby, age 43; Byron W., age 17, apprentice collar maker; Robert N., age 9; George Gager, age 19, apprentice collar maker
--1870 Census, p.400, 3Wd Orange NJ: Byron 'Quinby' age 27, works at felt hat factory; Mary, age 25; Lottie M., age 3; William G., age 7 months
--1880 Census, p.161A, Orange, NJ: Byron W. 'Quinby' age 37, works hat factory; Mary L, wife, age 36; William G., son, age 10; all b. NJ
--1900 Census, p.6A, 3Wd, Orange, NJ: Byron Quimby, age 57, hat finisher; Mary, age 55; William, age 30, carpenter; Cecelia, age 26, dau.-in-law; Charlott, age 1, granddau.
--1910 Census, p.12B, 3Wd, Orange NJ: Byron 'Quinby' age 66, hatter; Mary, age 66; David Hull, age 66, boarder,widower, (bro-in-law) carpenter; all b. NJ
--1920 Census, p.20A, 4Wd, Orange, NJ: William J. Quimby, age 50, carpenter; Cecelia M., age 46; Charlotte M., age 21, teacher; Helen G., age 18, insurance clerk; Wickliffe C., age 16, insurance clerk; Byron W. Quimby, age 76, retired hatter; Mary L, age 75; Emma, age 12, granddaughter
--1930

Children of Byron W. Quimby and Mary Lavinia Hull:
Charlotte May, b. May 26, 1867; d. 1878
William Gray, b. Dec. 5, 1869; m. Cecelia M. .....

- - - - -

Quimby, DANIEL WICKLIFFE b. (March 15, 1818)
(map, Section M) d. February 22, 1856

WIFE of D. W. b. (December 2, 1816)
(map, Section M) d. April 20, 1872

Notes:
--bur. map, Section M, plot of Byron Quimby, q.v.
--1850 Census, p.223, Orange Twp., NJ: Daniel W. 'Quinby' age 32, hatter; Mary, age 33; Byron W., age 7; Edwin Gray, age 64; Hetty E. Gray, age 19; all b. NJ
--1860 Census, p.356, 3Wd, Orange, NJ: 'Margret' Quimby, age 43; Byron W., age 17, apprentice collar maker; Robert N., age 9; George Gager, age 19, apprentice collar maker

Children of Daniel Wickliffe Quimby and Mary Gray:
Byron Wickliffe, q.v., b. May 21, 1843

Robert Williams, b.Dec. 4, 1851; m. Louisa S. Ward

- - - - -

REDDINGTON

Reddington, WILLIAM
(map, plot owner, Sect. L)
(gmnj)(shaw)(csl - E31)
(NJ Will #17149G, 1870)

b. (May 24, 1829)
d. September 24, 1870
Aged 41.4.0

wife, Mary* (McAllister)

b. (abt. 1833)
d. (aft. 1880)

son, ROBERT
(csl - E31)
(map, Section L)

b.(July 22, 1869)
d. September 22, 1870
Aged 1.2.0

son, THOMAS
(csl - E30)
(map, Section L)

b. (abt. 1860)
d. February 7, 1865
Aged 5

son, WILLIAM ARCHIBALD
(csl - E30)
(map, Section L)

b. (May 19, 1858)
d. December 19, 1866
Aged 8.7.0

'Sichinson', WILLIAM
(map, Section L)

b.
d. March 16, 1942
Aged 70.0.11

Notes:

--William Redington m. Mary McAllister, b. about 1833. Ireland. She d. after the 1880 Census.

--1860 Census:p.421, 2nd Ward, Orange, NJ: Wm. Redington age 30, labor, b. Ireland; Mary A. age 27, b. Ireland; Martha J. age 3, William age 2, Thomas age 4 months; Eliza McAllister, age 17, b. Ireland, hat trimmer

--1870 Census: p.372, 3rd Ward, Orange, NJ; William Redington age 41, grocer b. Ireland; Mary A. age 37; Martha
J. age 13, Mary E. age 6; Sarah age 4; Robert age 1.Also Eliza McAlister age 27, felt hat worker b. Ireland.

--1880 Census: p.139.1, Orange, NJ: Mary Reddington, widow, age 47, b. Ireland; Martha , dau. age 23, b. NJ, dressmaker; May E. Reddington, dau., age 16, b. NJ, dressmaker; Sarah, dau., age 14, b. NJ; Robert McAllister, brother, age 44, b. Ireland, boot & shoe manufacturer; Eliza McAllister, sister, single, age 34, b. Ireland, fancy store & millinery; John Drake, single, age 24, b. NJ, carpenter.

Children of William Redington and Mary McAllister:
Martha J., b. abt. 1857
William Archibald, b. 1858; d. 1866
Thomas, b. 1860; d. 1865
Mary E., b. abt. 1864
Sarah, b. abt. 1866
Robert, b. abt. 1869; d. 1866

- - - - -

REEVES

Reeves, William Maxfield*   b. (abt. September 1847)
                                 d. April 12, 1915

wife, Sarah L.* .....   b. (abt. January 1860)
                                 d. April 17, 1934

daughter, CLARA MAY   b. (abt. September 1884)
(map, Sect. B)   d. April 1903
                                 Aged 18

Notes:
--See: map, Section B, plot of Daniel Bond
--1900 Census, p.1A, West Orange, NJ: Maxfield Reeves, b. Sept. 1847, m.16 yrs., house carpenter; Sarah L. b. Jan. 1860; Clara M. b. Sept. 1884; Lucy b. July 1886; Bertha b. May 1888; Alice b. Dec. 1883; Maxfield b. Aug. 1891; all b. NJ
--1910 Census, p.15B&16A, 2Wd. West Orange: William M. "Reuer", age 62, m.26 yr, house carpenter; Sarah L. age 51 b. NJ, parents b. England; Lucy M. age 23; Bertha J. age 21; 'MacHcel W." age 10; Alice E., age 17; all b. NJ
--1920 Census, p.7B, 2Wd, West Orange: William M. Reeves, age 28, single, hat finisher; Sarah L. Reeves, age 60, widow, mother; both b. NJ
--1930 Census, p. 8B, West Orange: Sarah L. Reeves, age 73, boarder at res. of Mary Heggins

Children of William Maxfield Reeves and Sarah L. ......:

Clara M., b. abt. September 1884
Lucy M., b. abt. July 1886
Bertha J., b. abt. May 1888
Alice E., b. abt. December 1893
William Maxfield, b. abt. Aug. 1891

- - - - -

Reeves, WILLIAM b. November 20, 1820
(gmnj) d. October 6, 1884
(map, plot owner, Sect. K)

wife, ELSIE CAROLINE b. (abt. 1825)
(map, Sect. K) d. (aft. 1880)

mother, FANNIE b. (abt. 1800)
(map, Section K) d. (aft. 1860)

son, HORACE b.
(map, Section K) d. (abt. 1870)

son, EDWIN B. b. (January 4, 1849)
(map, Section K) d. May 5, 1916
(removed to Rosedale? Cem.) *Aged 67*

Reeves, ELIZABETH b.
(map, Section K) d. October 9. 1853

Reeves, ADRIANNA(Fesler) b. (abt. 1850)
(wife of Edwin B.) d. November 22, 1905
(map, Section K) *Aged 56.1.30*
(removed to Rosedale? Cem.)

Reeves, CHILD of Edwin b.
(map, Section K) d. January 12, 1878
(removed to Rosedale? Cem.)

Reeves, GEORGE COOK b. (abt. 1891)
(map, Section K) d. December 17, 1900

Reeves, CHILD of Agustus b.
(map, Section K) d. November 23, 1876
(removed to Rosedale? Cem.)

Reeves, INFANT
(map, Section K)
b.
d. October 18, 1904

Reeves, DAVID B.
(map, Section K)
b. (abt. 1861)
d. March 15, 1865
Aged 4

Doggett, CLARENCE L.
(map, Section K)
b. (abt. 1911)
d. August 27, 1916
Aged 4.9.0

Notes:
--William Reeves m. Elcey Caroline Bond November 18, 1845.
--William Reeve was an assessor for West Orange Twp in 1873;chosen freeholder in 1865-66; Justice of the Peace, 1873;(Shaw, p.806)

--1850 Census: p.232, Orange Twp; William 'Reeves' 29, carpenter; Elsey C. age 25; William M. age 4; Edwin B. age 1; Frances, age 50; all b. New Jersey
--1860 Census, p.426, 2Wd, Orange: William 'Reeves' age 39, master carpenter; Elsie age 35; William M. 13; Edwin B. 11; Augustus W. 8; Ella C. 5; Emily T. 2; Fannie, age 60; all b. New Jersey
--1870 Census: p.471, 3rd Ward, Orange, NJ: William Reeve age 49, lumber yard clerk, b. NJ; Caroline E.(Elcey?) age 45; Edwin B. age 21, carpenter; Augustus W. age 18, labor; Ella C. age 15; Emily J. age 11; Horace B. age one month.
--1880 Census, p.251.3; West Orange: Wm. "Reese" age 59; carpenter; Elsie C. age 54; Wm. M. son, age 33 b. NJ, carpenter; Emily T., age 21; all b. NJ

Children of William Reeves and Elsie Caroline Bond:
William M., b. abt 1847; m. Charlotte .....
Edwin B., b. January 4, 1849; m. Addie Fessler
Augustus W., b.abt. 1852;m.Ida Hanson (see Henry Hanson)
Ella C., b. abt 1855
Emily J., b. abt 1859
Horace B., b. 1870; d. 1870

- - - - -

RICKARD

Rickard, Joseph*
b.

widow,
ELIZABETH (ROLLINSON)
(gmnj)(shaw)(csl - E82)
(map, Section G)

d. (before 1850)
b. (abt 1795)
d. December 10, 1870
Aged 75

Notes:
--bur. map, Section G, plot of Richard Whittingham, q.v.
--Elizabeth was aunt of Samuel Osborn Rollinson, q.v.
--Elizabeth was aunt of Mary Ann Rollinson who married Richard Whittingham, q.v.; she was also sister of Charles Rollinson, b. abt. 1789, England and died January 1833, Boston, Mass.
--Elizabeth was daughter of William Rollinson and Mary Johnson who were married May 10, 1782, St. Martin Church, Birmingham, Warwickshire, England.

--1850 Census, p.237 Orange Twp: Maria Williams, age 35 b. NJ; Margaret Williams, age 33 b. NJ; "Eliza Rikard" age 53, b. NY; 1 servant; 1 boarder
--1860 Census, p.418. 2Wd,Orange: Maria Williams age 52 b.NJ; Margaret Williams age 50 b. NJ; "Eliza Ricard" age 63, b. NY; 1 servant
--1870 Census, p.468, West Orange: Margaret Williams, age '48'; Maria Williams age '50"; "Eliza Rickart" age 70, b. NY, no occupation; 2 servants

- - - - -

ROBBINS

Robbins, JAMES P.
(gmnj)(csl - E42)
(map, plot owner, Sect. K)
(NJ Will # 14418G, 1853?)

b.(abt. 1798)
d. January 4, 1854
d. January 5, 1853
In 56th year

widow, MATILDA
(gmnj)(csl - E43)
(map, Section K)

b. (abt. 1801)
d. February 13, 1866
d. February 1, 1866
In 65th year

daughter, SARAH E.
(csl - E44)(map, Sect. K)
m. Henry S. Condit, q.v.

b.
d. December 10, 1850

Notes:
--1850 Census: p.235, Orange Twp., NJ: Henry S. Condit age 30, b. NJ, hatter; Sarah E.Condit, age 27 b. NY; James P. Robbins age 55 b. NY; Matilda Robbins age 40, b. NY; Eliza Babb age 18, b.NY; Robert P. Robbins age 10 b NJ; Sarah Aymar age 50 b. England; John (James) Aymar age 52, clerk, b. NY.
--1860 Census, p.813, 20Wd, Dist.4, New York City: Mrs. Robins age 45 b. NY; Robert P. Robins, age 18, b.NJ 'D.G.' (dry goods?) clerk; Jno. J. 'Amays' (Amayr) age 50 b. NY, D.G. clerk; Sarah Amays age 40 b. England; Eliza Babb, age 46 b. NY; Sarah Thomas age 40 b. NY; Chas. Mott, age 19 b. NY, dry goods clerk; Jno. Mott age 17 b. NY, D.G. Clerk; Geo. Mott, age 15, b. NY; 1 servant

Children of James P. Robbins and Matilda ......:
Sarah E., b. abt. 1822; m. Henry S. Condit, q.v.
Robert P., b. abt. 1840

- - - - -

ROLLINSON

Rollinson,
SAMUEL OSBORN b. December 20, 1830
(gmnj)(map, Sect. A) d. August 17, 1891

wife, ABBY MARIA
(Harrison) b. May 7, 1835
(map, Section A) d. February 25, 1892
(NJ Will #24699G,1892)

Notes:
Served: Civil War, Co. H, 7th NY State Militia, Cpl. (nps)
--Samuel was nephew of Elizabeth Rollinson Rickard, q.v.
--Samuel was nephew of Mary Anne Rollinson Whittingham, wife of William R. Whittingham, q.v.
--Samuel was grandson of William Rollinson, b. England 1762, d. 1842. William was "one of the first steel engravers in this country. He came to this country just previous to or during the Revolution (sic) and it said that he engraved the buttons on Washington's military coat. He engraved, in 1808, a portrait on steel of Gen. Alexander Hamilton -- one of the best likenesses of Hamilton, it is said, ever made." (*Founders and Builders of the Oranges, Harrison*

Heritage) William also published in 1801 an aquatint recording New York City from the Battery to about Chambers Street.
--Abby Maria was the only child of Simeon Harrison,q.v. and Abby Maria Condit. She married Samuel Rollinson in 1869.

Obituary: *New York Times*, August 19, 1891: "Samuel Osborne Rollinson, (with) the Atlantic White Lead Company, died on Monday at his residence in West Orange, NJ, after an illness of six months with congestion of the liver. ...He was born in the Seventh Ward of this city (NY). His parents died while he was yet a boy, and he was cared for by an aunt. At the age of fifteen he was an employee of the Celeste Co., who formed a stock company under the name of the Atlantic White Lead Company, and with firm and company he remained for more than forty-five years. ...In 1869 he married the only daughter of Simeon Harrison, a member of one of the oldest (families) in West Orange...Mr. Rollinson was a Democrat, and for many years Chairman of the West Orange Town Committee, ...he was for twenty years a Vestryman of **St. Mark's** Episcopal Church, Orange, and for the last five
years was Junior Warden. ...leader of the boy choir of the same
church...Although he began business at a very early age, he found time to cultivate his mind and became a well read man. His was one of the best libraries in the Oranges and he was a member of the Essex County Country Club. ...His wife and four children survive him. The funeral will take place at **St. Mark's** Church."

--1850 Census, p.232, 7Wd, Dist. 2, New York, NY: Chs. Rollinson, age 23, b. NY, bank clerk; Maria Rollinson, age 53, b. NY; S. J. Williamson(?) age 34, male b. NY, tailor; M. A. Williamson? age 32, female b. NY; M. 'S?' 'Williams', age
3, female b. PA; Eliza Rollinson, age 25 b. NY; S. O. Rollinson, age 20, b. NY, clerk
--1850 Census, p.240, Orange Twp: Caleb "Hamson" age 79 farmer; "Katura" age 80; Phebe, age 48; Simeon age 46, farmer; Abby M. age 15; all b. NJ; 7 labor
--1860 Census, p.383, 3Wd, Orange: Simeon Harrison, age 56, farmer; Phebe age 58; Abby age 25; all b. NJ; 2 farm laborers; 3 servants
--1870 Census, p.466, West Orange: Simeon Harrison,age 66, b. NJ, farmer, real estate value $125,000; Phebe (sister), age 68, b. NJ; Saml. C. Rollinson age 39, b. NY, merchant; Abby M. Rollinson, (dau. of Simeon) age 35, b. NJ
--1880 Census: p.272.1, West Orange, NJ: Samuel O. Rollinson, age 49, b. NY; Cashier in White Lead; Abby M., wife, age 45, b. NJ;Simeon H. son, age 9, b. NJ; Phebe H. age 7, b. NJ; Mary S. age 6; William , age 4,

Phebe Harrison, aunt, single, age 78; Harrison Whittingham, cousin, single, age 41, b. NY; two servants
--1900 Census, p.7B, West Orange: S.('Stephen') H. Rollinson, b. December 1870 NJ, father NY, mother NJ, lawyer; William, b. August 1875, brother b. NJ, lawyer; 'Pheobe' b. September 1872 sister b. NJ; Mary S. b. December 1873, sister, b. NJ; 4 servants
--1910 Census, p.21B, 2Wd, West Orange: Simeon H. 'Rollerson' age 38 b. NJ, father b. NY, mother b. NJ, m. 6 years, lawyer; Ruth, age 32 b. NJ, father b. MA, mother b. CT; Keturah C. age 5; 'Lanson' (Simeon) H., age 1, b. NJ; 'Phoebie' H. age 37, sister, b. NJ; 3 servants
--1920 Census, p.12A, 2Wd, West Orange: (Harrison S. Rollinson, age....; ......, wife; William, age 44, brother, single, b. NJ, father b. NY, mother b. NJ, bank mgr.; Phoebe H. age 47, sister, single, b. NJ; Katurah C., daughter, age 14 b. NJ; parents b. NJ; Harrison S. Jr. son age 10 b. NJ; Frank M. Dusenberry age 46, brother-in-law, b. NY, parents NY, electrical manufacturer; Mary S. Dusenberry, age 46, sister, b. NJ; William R. Dusenberry, age 11, b. IL, nephew; David M. Dusenberry, age 8, nephew, b. NJ; 1 boarder; 1 waitress; 1 cook
--1930 Census, p.3B, West Orange: Simeon H. Rollinson, age 59 b.NJ; m. #1 at age 33, lawyer; Ruth M. age 52, b. NJ; Simeon H. Jr. age 21 b. NJ; William, brother, single, age 55 b. NJ, bank officer; Phoebe, sister, single, age 57 b. NJ; 2 servants

Children of Samuel O. Rollinson and Abby Maria Harrison:
Simeon Harrison, b. December 31, 1870; d. Feb. 13, 1934   m. Ruth M. Small
Phoebe Harrison, b. September 14, 1872; d. April 1967
Mary Stymets, b. December 1873; d. November 18, 1935;
    m. Frank M. Dusenberry
William, b. August 24, 1875

- - - - -

ROSE

Rose, JOHN	b. (abt 1807)
(gmnj)(shaw)	d. September 24, 1861(?)
(map, Section E)	*Aged 54*
widow, MARTHA	
(Musgreave)	b. April 13, 1807
(csl - E116)(map,Sect. E)	d. September 14, 1861

daughter, ELIZABETH (csl - E116)(map,Sect. E)	b. August 16, 1830 d. July 23, 1861
son, HENRY (gmnj)(csl - E115) (map, Section E)	b. (abt 1832) d. January 29, 1854 *In 20th year*
son, JOHN (gmnj)(csl - E114) (map, Section E)	b. (abt 1832) d. November 10, 1872 *Aged 40*
son, JULIUS (gmnj) (map,Section E)	b. June 20, 1835 d. September 16, 1892
daughter, SARAH ANN (gmnj) (map,Section E)	b. abt. 1837 d. December 20,1898 bur. January 2, 1897 *Aged 61*
daughter, MARTHA H. (csl - E113)(map,Sect. E)	b. February 5, 1837 d. January 12, 1885
MISS, Rose (map, Section E)	b. d.

Notes:
--family bur. in plot of Henry Dobridge, q.v.; and Robert Dobridge, q.v.
--1850 Census: p.239, Orange Twp., NJ: Henry A. Dobridge age 50, surgeon, b. West Indies: Sarah A. age 46; Martha M. Ross (Rose) age 43; John S. Dobridge age 42; Selina F. age 39; John Ross age 19, clerk; Elizabeth age 20; Henry age 17; Martha age 13; Sarah W. age 12; all b. West Indies
--1860 Census, p.182&183, 7Wd, Newark: Martha Rose, age 51, b. West Indies; Elizabeth age 24, b. West Indies; Sarah, age 20 b. West Indies; Sarah Hussey, age 13, b. NJ
--1870 Census, p.27, 1Wd, Newark: Ephraim Hall, age 40 b. NY, car .....; Mary A., age 35, b. NY; Anna E. age 15 b. NJ; John H., age 13, b. NJ; John 'Ross' age 38, b. West Indies, clerk at express co.
--1880 Census:, p.247.1, Newark, NJ: Martha H. Rose, single, age 41, b. West Indies, keeping house; Sarah A. Rose, sister, single, age 40, b. West Indies, machine operator; Julius Rose, brother, single, age 44, b. West Indies, unemployed.

RUNYON

Runyon, JAMES WESLEY b. (abt. July 1851)
(map, Section J) d. January 1913
  bur. January 9, 1913

wife, Nettie J. b. (abt. 1859)
  d. (bef. 1900)

Notes:
--bur. map, Section J, plot of Stacy B. Bannister, q.v.
--James was son of Hugh Runyon and Harriet Louisa Haslett.
--1870 Census, p.414, 10Wd, Newark, NJ: Hugh Runyon, age 53, b. NY, works at blacksmith shop; Harriet, age 47; Henry, age 24, works for carpenter; James, age 18, druggist clerk; Edward, age 11; Irene, age 7; all b. NY
--1880 Census, p.290C, Newark, NJ: 'Westly' J. Runyon, age '24' b. NY, druggist; Nettie J., wife, age 21, b. NJ; Lillie, dau., age 4 mos. b. NJ
--1900 Census, p.8B, 10Wd, Newark, NJ: Adelia Jackson b. Oct. 1860, widow, b. NJ, dressmaking; Frances Jackson, dau. b. Oct. 1880 NY, dressmaker; Franklin Sherry, cousin, b. Jan 1864 NJ, widower, jeweler; George G. Runyon, b. Sept. 1874 NJ, boarder, jeweler; Wesley Runyon, b. July 1851, widower, b. NY, boarder, druggist
--?1910 Census, p.3A, 10Wd, Newark, NJ: 'John' Runyon, age 57 b. NJ, father NY, mother NJ, m. 5 yrs., salesman at grocery store; Clara, age 55, b. NJ, parents b. NJ

Children of James Wesley Runyon and Nettie J. ......:
Lillie, b. 1880

SCHLICHTING

Schlichting, WILLIAM b.
(map, Section M) d.

Schlighting, ... b.
(map, Section M) d.

Notes:
--bur. map, Section M, plot of Aaron VanBuskirk, q.v.
--?1870 Census, p.377, 3Wd, Orange, NJ: Henry Schlicting, age 41, b. Prussia, boot/shoe maker; Christine, age 38 b. Prussia
--?1880 Census, p.141.2, 3 Wd, Orange, NJ: Henry Schlichting, age 51, b. Launsburg, boot/shoe mfg; Christine, age 50, b. Launsburg
--?1900 Census, p.2B, Orange, NJ: Henry Schlichting, b. Feb. 1826 Germany, widower, immig. 1856, shoemaker

- - - - -

SCHOOR

Schoor, JOHANN   b. October 15, 1856
(csl-E67)   d. February 4, 1882
(map, ch. property, Sect. H)

Notes:
--?1867 Mecklenburg-Schwerin Census: Johann Schoor, b. 1853; res. Domanialamt Schwerin, Mecklenburg - Vorpommern
--?1881 May 3: Arrived New York from Bremen, Germany; S. S. Salier: Johann Schoor, age 24, merchant; and Antoinette Schoor, age 24

- - - - -

SEYMOUR

Seymour, MRS. JOHN   b.
(map, Section G)   d.
(removed to St. John's Cemetery)

Notes:
--See: Plot of Ann P. Browne

- - - - -

SHARP

Sharp, JOHN HARRISON   b. October 10, 1832
(gmnj)(map, plot owner,Sect. J)   d. September 16, 1892

widow, MARTHA JANE
(Beach)   b. March 1, 1834

(gmnj)(map, Section J)	d. December 26, 1906 *Aged 72*
DAUGHTER of J. H. (map, Section J)	b. d.
DAUGHTER of J.H. (map, Section J)	b. d.
Sharp, PHEBE S. (Burnet) (gmnj)(shaw)(map,Sect. J) (csl - E5?)	b. March 4, 1804 d. December 12, 1879
	Mother
Sharp, ANSON WALTER (map, Section J)	b. (abt. 1840) d. July 19, 18_ _
Sharp, MRS. WALTER (map, Section J)	b. d. November 11, 1882
Shourne?, SARAH (map, Section J)	b. (abt. 1829) d.
	Negro servant

Notes:
--John Harrison Sharp was born October 10, 1832, son of Jacob Sharp and Phebe Burnet
--John H. Sharp m. Martha Jane Beach, January 27, 1858, Bloomfield Twp., NJ. She was daughter of William Beach and Caroline Smith.
--John H. Sharp was a collector for West Orange Twp., in 1866; Justice of the Peace in 1863; (Shaw, p.806)

--1850 Census, p.234&235; Orange Twp: Jacob A. Sharp, age 52, farmer; Phebe age 47; Susan age 21; John, age 18, laborer; Anson? W., age 10; Mary, age 6
--1860 Census: p.406, 2Wd., Orange, NJ: John H. Sharp age 27, machine operator; Martha J. age 25; Ada age 1. Adj. to Joseph A. Condit.
--1860 Census: p.384, 3Wd. Orange, NJ: Phebe S. Sharp, age 57; Walter age 20, express driver; Mary age 15
--1870 Census: p.465, John H. Sharp. age 37, depot baggage master, b. NJ; Martha J. age 36; Ada age 10, Milly age 3, Phebe age 1.

--1870 Census, p.388, 3Wd, Orange, NJ: James J. Metz, age 47 b. PA, tinsmith; 'Charles' E. Metz, age 47 b. NJ; Franklin Metz, age 16, b. NJ; Abby Ann Brewster, age 30 b. NJ; Walter Sharp, age 28, expressman, b. NJ
--1880 Census: p.250 B., West Orange, NJ: John H. Sharp, age 46, b. NJ, RR Freight Agent; Martha J. wife, age 45, b. NJ; Mildred,dau., age 13, b. NJ; Phebe M. dau., age 12, b. NJ: Mary, dau., age 6, b. NJ; Sarah 'Shourne'(?), black, domestic servant, b. NJ, parents b. NJ;
--1880 Census, p.250.2, West Orange NJ: Walter Sharp, age 40, b. NJ, horse car driver; Elinor, age 37, b. Ireland; Sarah J. age 7 b. NJ; John, age 4, b. NJ

Children of John H. Sharp and Martha Jane Beach:
Ada, b. abt 1860
Walter, b. abt. Nov. 20, 1864; m. Elinor .....
Mildred, b. about 1867
Phebe M., b. abt. 1868
Mary, b. abt. 1874

- - - - -

Sharp, Richard*	b.
	d. (before 1850)
widow, ANN R.	b. September 25, 1787
(gmnj)(shaw)(csl - E197)	d. October 16, 1865

Notes:
--1850 Census: p. 210, Orange Twp: E. B. Smith (Ezekial Beach Smith, q.v.), blacksmith; Mary A., age 43; Walter, age 18, blacksmith; 'Melzer' age 16, son; Alexander, age 11; Joseph, age 9; Ann Sharp, age 62; all b. NJ; 8 other persons listed at this house.

Children of Richard Sharp and Ann R. .....:
Mary A., b. abt. 1807; m. Elias Beach Smith, q.v.

- - - - -

SHELLEY

Shelley, CHARLES V.	b. (December 7, 1822)
(gmnj)(csl - E7)	d. February 7, 1860
(map, Section N)	d. February 9, 1859

Aged 37.2.0

wife MARY ANN
(gmnj)(shaw)(csl - E7)
(map, plot owner Sect. N)

b. (June 25, 1832)
d. July 29, 1870
Aged 38.1.4

Notes:
--1860 Census: p.381, 3Wd.,Orange, NJ: Mary A. Shelly age 30 b. Ireland; Eliza age 5 b. NJ; Mary A. age 4, NJ; William, age 3, b. NJ; Sarah J. age 7 months, b. NJ (posthumous)
--1870 Census, p.442, South Orange: Mary A. Shelly, age 15 b. NJ; at res. of E. P. Bergamini
--1870 Census, p.134, 2Wd, Newark: Eliza Shelley, age 17, b. NJ; at res. of Joseph Johnson
--1880 Census, p.478.3, East Orange: James Coppinger age 57 b. England, works hat shop ('no work and ague'); Anna Coppinger age 58 b. NJ, parents b. NJ; Laura Coppinger, dau. age 24 b. NJ; William H. Shelley, age 22 b. NJ, father b. England, mother b. Ireland, son-in-law, butcher; Sarah Shelley, dau., age 21, b. NJ

Children of Charles V. Shelley and Mary Ann .....:
Eliza, b. abt 1855
Mary A., b. abt. 1856
William H., b. abt. 1857; m. Sarah Coppinger
Sarah J., b. abt 1859

- - - - -

SHERIDAN

Sheridan, CHILD of J.
(map, Section H)

b.
d.

- - - - -

SHIELDS

Shields, ANNA
(map, Section L)

b.
d. March 8, 1872

Notes:
--See: plot of Patrick Coyne

SIDEBOTHAM

Sidebotham, CHARLES
(map, plot owner, Sect. K)
b. (abt. 1827)
d. November 9, 1894

Sidebotham, MRS.
(map, Section K)
b. (abt. 1836)
d.

Sidebotham, ROBERT
(map, Section K)
b.
d. March 10, 1852

Sidebotham, NANCY
(map, Section K)
b.
d. March 24, 1862

Notes:
--1860 Census, p. 420, 2Wd, Orange NJ: Charles "Traebottam" age 33 b. England, hatter; Mary A., age 33, b. England; Harriet, age 4, b. NJ; Mary E., age 2, b. NJ; 'Hannlen', dau., age 5 mos. b. NJ; William Ainsworth, age 42, b. England, hatter; John Nalin, age 32, b. Eng.,hatter
--1870 Census, p.466, West Orange, NJ: Charles Sidebotham, age 44, b. England, hatter; Amelia, age 34, b. England; Harriet, age 14, b. NJ; Mary E., age 12, b. NJ; Anna, age 10, b. NJ; Eliza J., age 6, b. NJ
--1880 Census, p.258.1, West Orange, NJ: Charles "Sidebottam" aage 54, b. England, hatter; Amelia, age 44 b. England; Anna, age 20, b. NJ, works at hat shop; Eliza J., age 16, b. NJ, works at hat shop

Children of Charles Sidebotham and Amelia .....:
Harriet, b. abt. 1856
Mary E., b. abt. 1858
Anna, b. abt. 1860
Eliza Jane, b. Dec. 15, 1863

SILVERIA

Silveria, GEORGE
(map, ch. property, Section H)
b. (abt. 1895)
d. October 26, 1918
Aged 23 years

Notes:

- - - - -

SIMON

Simon, CATHERINE
(map, grave owned Sect. F)

b.
d. February 2, 1854

Simon, CATHERINE
(map, Section F)

b.
d. May 22, 1853
Aged 10 months

- - - - -

SMITH

Smith, DANIEL T.
(map,plot owner, Sect. E)

b. (abt. 1821)
d. December 1894
bur. January 1, 1894
Aged 73

wife, SUSAN ANN (Beach)
(map, Section E)

b. (abt. 1822)
d. May 2, 1910
Aged 87

daughter, MARY EMMA
(gmnj)(csl - 117)
(map, Section E)

b. (abt. 1846)
d. February 5, 1863.
In 17th year

daughter, MAGGIE
(csl - E118)(map, Sect. E)

b. (June 21, 1853)
d. April 21, 1856
Aged 2.10.0

child, 'OUR BABY"
(csl - E118)

b. (November 11, 1844)
d. December 11, 1844
Aged 0.1.0

Notes:
--Daniel T. Smith m. February 21, 1844, Susan Ann Beach

--1850 Census, p.235, Orange Twp: David S. Beach, age 30 b. NJ, shoemaker; Hannah M. Beach, age 26 b. NJ; Maranda S. Williams, age

18 b. NJ; Daniel T. Smith, age 29 b. NY, hatter; Susan A. Smith age 28 b. NJ; Mary E. Smith, age 4 b. NJ;Gertrude Smith, age 2 b. NJ
--1860 Census: p.370, 3 Wd., Orange, NJ: Daniel T. Smith age 39, hat manufacturer, b. NY: Susan A. age 37 b. NJ; Mary E. age 14; Gertrude age 11, Sarah A. age 9
--1870 Census: p.370, 3rd Ward Orange, NJ: Daniel T. Smith age 50, felt hat manufacturer, b. NY; Susan N. age 47 b. NJ; Gertrude 22; Sarah A. age 19.
--1880 Census: p.170.3, Orange, NJ: Daniel T. Smith, age 59, b. NY, works in hat factory; Susan A. age 57, b. NJ; Gertrude, daughter, age 31, b. NY, single, teacher; Margareta A. Beach, sister-in-law, age 52, b. NJ, at home; Frances Ida Dean, grand niece, age 6, b. NY.

Children of Daniel T. Smith and Susan A. Beach:
'Our Baby', b. 1844; d.1844
Mary Emma, b.1846; d. 1863
Gertrude, b. abt 1848
Sarah A., b. abt 1851
Maggie, b. 1853; d. 1856

- - - - -

Smith DAVID ALLEN b. (February 10, 1807)
(gmnj)(shaw)(csl-E175) d. July 3, 1866
(map, Section B) *Aged 59.4.21*

wife, ELIZA ANN b. (abt. 1807)
(map, Section B) d. January 12, 1902
 Aged 92

son, LEMUEL O. b. (abt. 1841)
(csl - E175)(map, Sect. B) d. 1865
 Aged 24

... OLIVER B. SMITH b.
(map, Section B) d. May 12, 1879

Notes:
--bur. map, Section B, plot of Ezekiel Smith
--David Allen Smith was b. February 10, 1807, son of Walter Smith, q.v., and Abigail Allen

--1850 Census, p.97, Livingston, Essex Co. NJ: Ellis Cook age 67, b. NJ, farmer; Rhoda age 60, b. NJ; Ginette E., age 34 b. NJ; Lemuel C. Smith, age 9 b. NJ
--1860 Census: p.80, Rockaway, Morris Co., NJ: David A. Smith, age 55, farmer; Eliza Ann age 53; Lemuel age 19, labor; Hannah Dodd, age 13; all b. New Jersey

Child of David Allen Smith and Eliza Ann (Cook?):
Lemuel C., b. abt 1841; d. 1865

- - - - -

Smith, ELIJAH S.	b. March 16, 1810
(gmnj)	d. February 16, 1875
(map, plot owner, Sect. F)	d. (February 24, 1874?)
(NJ Will #18616G, 1875)	
first wife, LYDIA (Doremus)	b. June 17, 1809
(map, Section F)	d. March 24, 1865
second wife, Hannah*	b. abt. 1827
	d.
daughter, MARY JANE (Reed)	
(map, Section F)	b. (abt. 1839)
	d. March 31, 1903
?Smith, ENOS C.	b.
(map, Section F)	d. September 4, 1845

Notes:
--Elijah was son of William Smith
--Lea Doremus, daughter of Hessel Doremus and Jannetje Demarest, m. Elijah Smith of Parsippany, Morris Co., N.J. They lived at Orange, N.J. She died at Paterson, N.J.

--1850 Census, p.140&141, Hanover Twp., Morris Co. NJ: Elijah S. Smith, age 40 b. NJ, blacksmith; Lydia age 40; William S. age 16, student; John V. age 14; Mary J., age 10; Susan C., age 8; James H. B. age 2; all b. New Jersey
--1860 Census, p.382, 3Wd, Orange: "Elizabeth" S. Smith, age 50, blacksmith; Lydia age 50; Mary J., age 18; Laura C. age 16; James H. B., age 11; all b. NJ

--1870 Census, p.407, 3Wd, Orange: Elijah S. Smith, age 61 b. NJ, blacksmith; Hannah, age 43, b. NY, keeping house; Byron, age 22 b. NJ, works at felt hat factory; Minnie E., age 2, b. NJ

Children of Elijah Smith and Lea Doremus:
?Enos C. Smith, d. September 4, 1845
William S. Smith, b. abt 1834; m. Amanda Otstaats
John V. Smith, b. abt. 1836; m. Louisa Cherry
Mary J. Smith, b. abt 1840; m. M. J. Reed
Susan C. Smith, b. abt 1842
Louisa Smith, b. m. J. Harrison Matthews of Orange, N.J.
Byron (James H. B.) Smith, b. abt 1848; m. Annie Sippell
(*Gen. of the Doremus Family*)

Children of Elijah S. Smith and Hannah .....:
Minnie E., b. abt. 1868

- - - - -

Smith, EZEKIEL BEACH (gmnj)(shaw)(csl-E177)(Sect. B) (?Will #16556G, 1867)	b. December 27, 1804 d. September 18, 1867
wife, MARY ANN (Sharp) (gmnj)(csl-E178)(map sect. B)	b. March 29, 1806 d. November 19, 1885
son, RICHARD ORISON (gmnj)(map, Section B)	b. (abt. 1854) d. February 8, 1859 *In 5th year*

Notes:
--Ezekiel Beach Smith was son of Walter Smith (q.v.)

--1850 Census: p. 210, Orange Twp: E. B. Smith (Ezekial Beach Smith, q.v.), blacksmith; Mary A., age 43; Walter, age 18, blacksmith; 'Melzer' age 16, son; Alexander, age 11;
Joseph, age 9; Ann Sharp, age 62; all b. NJ; 8 other persons listed at this house.
--1860 Census: p.361, 3 Wd.,Orange, NJ: Ezekiel B. Smith age 56, blacksmith; Mary A. age 55; Melzer, age 26; Alexander age 22, livery business; Joseph A. age 19, schoolteacher; Mary Ann Sharp age 13; Martha Smith age 43; Endora age 21, teacher; Amzi age 16, clerk; Oscar age 13.

--1870 Census: p.384, 3rd Ward Orange, NJ: Mary A. Smith age 60; Melzer age 38, blacksmith; Joseph A. age 28, meat dealer; Henry age 23 butcher; Walter E. age 39 real estate agent; Charlotte C. age 35; Helen 9; Jessie age 4.
--1880 Census: p.171.1, Orange, NJ: Mary Ann Smith, widow, age 74, b. NJ, father b. Ireland, mother b. NJ; 'Metsor' Smith, son, single, age 46, blacksmith; James B. Montgomery, single, age 35, b. Maryland, clerk.

Children of Ezekiel Beach Smith and Mary Ann Sharp:
Walter Eugene, b. abt 1831; m. Charlotte C. Rathbone
Melzer, b. abt 1834
Alexander, b. abt 1838
Joseph A., b. abt 1841
Henry, b. abt 1847
Richard Orison, b. abt 1854; d. 1859

- - - - -

Smith,
GEORGE WASHINGTON
(gmnj)(shaw)(csl-E168)
(map, Sect. B, plot owner)
(NJ Will #13888G, 1849)

b. July 6, 1812
d. December 1, 1849
Aged 37

In
Memory of
George Washington
Smith
Born July 6th A.D. 1812
Died Dec.r 1st A.D.1849

wife, REBECCA LOUISA
(Reock) (map, Section B)
(gmnj)(csl - E168)(shaw)

b. (abt. 1812)
d. January 8, 1862
Age 50

daughter, MARY LOUISA
(gmnj)(csl - E168)

b. April 7, 1837
d. April 8, 1837

In
Memory of
Mary Louisa
Infant Daughter of

George W. & Louisa Smith
Born April 7, 1837
Died April 8th 1837
But Jesus said, Suffer little
children, to come unto me, and
forbid them not, for of such is
the Kingdom of Heaven

INFANT son	b.
(map, Section B)	d.

Notes:
--Rebecca was daughter of John Reock and Lucy .....
--U.S. Federal Census Mortality Schedules for persons died in the year ending June 1st 1850: George W. Smith; b. NY; died Essex Co. NJ; December (1849) age 38 ; occupation shoemaker/cordwainer; cause of death "consumption"

--?1840 Census: p.60 Orange Twp: George W. Smith: 3 males age 20 to 30; 1 female age 20 to 30
(adjacent to Daniel Smith: 1 male age 15 to 10; 1 male age 50 to 60; 2 females age 10-15; 3 females age 15-20; 1 female age 20-30; 1 female age 50-60; 1 female age 80-90)
--?1850 Census: p.211 Orange Twp: Daniel Smith age 65 b. NJ; Ann White age 40 b. NY (domestic)
(adjacent to 'Eliza' Smith age 35 b. NJ)
--1850 Census p.145 East Ward Newark: John Reock age 60 b. NJ gentleman; Lucy age 60 b. NJ; Phebe C. age 30 b. NJ

- - - - -

Smith, JOSEPH	b. July 19, 1796
(gmnj)(shaw)(csl-E102)(map E)	d. March 13, 1836
(NJ Will #12740G, 1836)	

Joseph Smith
Born July 19, 1796
Died March 13, 1836

wife, ELIZABETH (Quimby)	b. November 13, 1800
(gmnj)(csl - E102)	d. April 14, 1871
(map, plot owner, Section E)	

(NJ Will #17431G, 1872)

son, GEORGE (map, Section E)	b. (abt. 1823) d. May 12, 1854
son, MOSES (map, Section E)	b. (abt. 1830) d. March 28, 1874
son, JOHN (map, Section E)	b. (abt. 1831) d. (bef. 1870?)
son, JOSEPH (map, Section E)	b. (abt.1836 d.
?Smith, Watson (map, Section E)	b. (abt. 1863) d. June 22, 1936 *Aged 73*
?Smith, ALECIA (map, Section E)	b. (abt. 1850) d. October 1905 *Aged 55*
Smith, LEWIS LEANDER (map, Section E)	b. (abt. 1850) d. May 13, 1894
Smith, CHARLES (map, Section E)	b. (abt. 1853) d.
Smith, MARY (map, Section E)	b. (abt. 1856) d.

Notes:
--Elizabeth was dau. of Caleb Quimby and Rhoda Freeman

--1850 Census, p.234, Orange Twp: Elizabeth Smith 49, b. NJ; George Smith, age 27 b. NJ, shoemaker; Joseph Smith, age 23 b. NJ, shoemaker; Moses Smith, age 20 b. NJ, shoemaker; George Clay, age 30 b. NY, shoemaker; Elizabeth Clay,age 28 b. PA; Pierson Bond, age 23, b. NJ, shoemaker; Elias Sindler, age 20 b. NJ, shoemaker; Josiah Kilburn, age 27 b. NJ, shoemaker; Elizabeth Smith,age 26, b. NJ; Thomas J. Smith, age 3 b. NJ; Joseph W. Smith, age 1, b. NJ; Mary A. Dorr, age 14, b. Ireland

--1860 Census: p.363, 3Wd, Orange, NJ: Elizabeth Smith age 58, runs boarding house; Joseph age 34, shoemaker.
--1860 Census, p.182, 7Wd, Newark, NJ: John Smith, age 29, no occup. listed; Ann, age 27; Leander age 10; Charlie, age 8; Mary, age 4; Frank, age 3; George, age 8 months; all b. New Jersey
--1870 Census: p.393, 3rd Ward, Orange, NJ: Elizabeth Smith age 69; Joseph age 44, boot/shoe maker; Ann M. age 37, felt hat worker; Lewis L. age 18 felt hat apprentice; Charles age 16, sells newspapers; Frank age 14; Mary age 12; George age 10; and several boarders.
--1870 Census: p.393, 3rd Ward, Orange, NJ: Elizabeth Smith age 69; Joseph age 44, boot/shoe maker; Ann M. age 37, felt hat worker; Lewis L. age 18 felt hat apprentice; Charles age 16, sells newspapers; Frank age 14; Mary age 12; George age 10; and several boarders.

Children of Joseph Smith and Elizabeth Quimby:
?son, d. bef. 1850; m. Elizabeth .....
George, b. abt 1823; d. 1854
Joseph, b. abt. 1827
Moses, b. abt 1830; d. 1874
John, b. abt. 1831; m. Anna M......

- - - - -

Smith, MOSES E.   b. (abt. 1831)
(map, Section L)   d. September 7, 1893
(removed to Rosedale Cem.)

wife, Frances Elizabeth*   b. (abt. 1832)
    d. (aft. 1910)
Notes:
--1850 Census, p.234, Orange Twp. NJ: Elizabeth Smith, age 49 b. NJ; George, age 27 b. NJ, shoemaker; Joseph, age 23, b. NJ, shoemaker; Moses, age 20, b. NJ, shoemaker; George Clay (q.v.), age 30 b. NY, shoemaker; Elizabeth Clay, age 28, b. PA; Pierson Bond, age 23, b. NJ, shoemaker; Elias Sindler, age 30, b. NJ, shoemaker; Josiah Kilburn, age 37, b. NJ, shoemaker; Elizabeth Smith, age 26, b. NJ; Thomas J. Smith, age 3 b. NJ; Joseph W., Smith, age 1, b. NJ; Mary A. Dorr, age 14, b. Ireland
--1860 Census, p.773, 9Wd, Newark, NJ: Moses E. Smith, age 29, b. NJ, carpenter; Elizabeth Smith, age 28, b. NJ; at res. of Thomas H. Cottrell, q.v.

--1880 Census, p.206D, Newark, NJ: Moses E. Smith, age 48 b. NJ, carpenter; Frances E., wife, age 48 b. NJ; Herbert A. age 19 b. NJ, office clerk; Nellie H., age 17, b. NJ
--1900 Census, p.1B, 9Wd, Newark, NJ: Frances E. Smith, b. April 1831, widow, b. NJ, 2 born 2 living; Herbert A., b. July 1860, son, b. NJ, secretary at S.... Hardware; Helen H. Tennyson, b. Aug. 1862, dau., widow, school teacher; Wm. Herbert Tennyson, b.Dec. 1888, VA, grandson; Blanche M. Tennyson, b. Apr. 1896 VA, granddaughter; Lulu Harris, age 16, b. NJ, servant
--1910 Census, p.12A, 9Wd, Newark, NJ: Frances E. Smith, age 79, widow; Herbert A., age 49, son, single, accountant .... R.R.; Helen H. Tennyson, age 44, widow, dau., teacher; Blanch M. Tennyson, age 19, granddau., b. VA, father b. MO, mother b. NJ; W. Herbert, age 21, grandson, b. VA, mother MO, mother NJ, clerk life insurance; Lizzie Jones, age 22, b. TN, servant

Children of Moses E. Smith and Frances Elizabeth Cottrell:
Herbert A., b. abt. 1861
Helene H. "Nelllie", b. abt. 1863; m. (William?) Tennyson

- - - - -

Smith, STEPHEN   b. (March 25, 1813)
(csl - E164)(map,Sect. C)   d. February 11, 1855
                         Aged 42

wife, Martha C.*   b. (abt. 1820)
                         d. (aft. 1880)

Notes:
--?Stephen was son of Walter Smith, q.v.

--1850 Census, p.228, Orange Twp: Stephen Smith, age 34, carpenter; Martha C., age 30; Eudora E., age 12; Amzi S. age 6; Oscar, age 3; all b. New Jersey
--1860 Census: p.361, 3 Wd.,Orange, NJ: Ezekiel B. Smith age 56, blacksmith; Mary A. age 55; Melzer, age 26; Alexander age 22, livery business; Joseph A. age 19, schoolteacher; Mary Ann Sharp age 13; Martha Smith age 43; Eudora age 21, teacher; Amzi age 16, clerk; Oscar age 13.
--1870 Census, p.203, East Orange: Amzi Smith, age 26, b. NY, clerk in store; Martha C., age 53, b. NJ; Eudora age 30 b. NJ; Oscar age 23, b. NY, clerk in bookstore

--1880 Census, p.171.1, Orange: Martha C. Smith, age 64, widow, b. NJ; Eudora E. age 32, single, dau., b. NJ
--1900 Census, p.7A, 1Wd. Orange: Oscar Smith b. NY January 1847, widower; Eudora, sister, single, b. October 1838 NJ; Charlotte Lyon, aunt, single, b. June 1821 NJ
--1910 Census, p.9A, 5Wd, East Orange: 'Arnza' Smith age 63, m.34 yrs. b. NJ, 'banker Sub Treasury'; Ellen, age 56, b. NJ, 1 born 1 living; Leonard H., son, age 32, m.2yrs., physician; Edith B., age 31, daughter-in-law, b. Illinois, father b. England, mother b. Illinois; Sylvia age 9 months, granddaughter b. NJ; Eudora, age 72, sister, single, b. NJ

Children of Stephen Smith and Martha C. ......:
Eudora E., b. abt 1838
Amzi S., b. abt 1844
Oscar, b. abt 1847

- - - - -

Smith, WALTER
(gmnj)(csl - E165)
(map, plot owner, Sect. C)
(NJWill #14617G, 1854)

b. (December 20, 1777)
d. April 7, 1854
In 77th year

wife, ABIGAIL (Allen)
(gmnj)(shaw)(csl - E166)
(map, Sect. C)

b. (September 6, 1782)
d. September 30, 1853
In 71st year

son, NATHANIEL MILLER
(csl - E167)(map, Sect. C)

b. (April 8, 1809)
d. September 24, 1844
Aged 35.5.15

In
Memory of
Nathaniel M. Smith
who Died
Sept.r 24th, 1844
Aged 33 years,5 mos
and 15 days

Notes:
--Walter Smith was son of Capt. Isaac Smith and Sarah Meeker.
-- Walter Smith married Abigail Allen, dau. of Samuel Allen and Hannah Beach.

--1850 Census, p.276, Springfield, Essex (now Union Co.) NJ: Walter Smith, age 72, farmer; Abby age 67; Mary, age 39; Noah, age 22, farmer; all b. New Jersey

Children of Walter Smith and Abigail Allen:
Ezekiel Beach Smith, q.v., b. December 2, 1804
?David Allen, b. February 10, 1807
Nathaniel Miller, b. 1809; d. 1844
Havilah Niedlis, b. October 16, 1815, d. July 7,1885
    m. Lettice M. Washburn
George Washington, b. June 25 1817; d. November 24 1895

- - - - -

Smith, WILLIAM   b. (abt. 1771)
(gmnj)(shaw)(csl - E92)   d. October 27, 1851
(map, Section F)

This stone is Erected
By
Ruth C. Tomkins
in grateful remembrance of
her Father
William Smith
who died
Oct.r 27th, 1851
In the 80th year of his age

wife, RUTH C.(Paddleford)   b. (abt. 1773)
(csl - E93)(map, Sect. F)   d. November 20, 1849

Sacred
to the memory of
Ruth
wife of
William Smith
who died
Nov.r 20th,1849
Aged 76 years

Notes:
--bur. map, Section F, plot of Elijah S. Smith, q.v.
--?Ruth was daughter of Edward Paddleford and Hannah Tichenor.

--1850 Census, p.236, Orange Twp: Enos C. Tompkins, age 40, b. NJ, hatter; William Smith, age 78, b. NJ; Ruth C. Tompkins, age 39 b. NJ; Harriet E. Pierson, age 23, b. NJ; William Stone, age 24, b. England, hatter

Children of William Smith and Ruth Paddleford:
Elijah S. Smith, q.v., b. abt. 1810
Ruth Caroline, January 27, 1811; m. Enos C. Tompkins, q.v.

- - - - -

SNOW

Snow(?), ISAAC b.
(map, grave owned, Sect. I) d. November 21, 1852
Aged 5

Notes:

- - - - -

SOMERSET

Somerset, SARAH (Brindly) b. (abt. 1802)
(gmnj)(csl - E22) d. September 18, 1882
(map, Sect. L) *In 80th year*

Our Mother

Notes:
--Bur. plot of William Crosby, q.v.
--1870 Census, p.301&302, Bayonne, Hudson Co., NJ: Sarah Summersett, age 66, b. 'Australia'; Margaret Summersett, age 32, b. Australia, fancy store; adj. to John Summersett
--1870 p.301&302, Bayonne, Hudson Co. NJ: John Summersett, age 32, b. Ireland, upholsterer; Eliza, age 32, b. Ireland; Margaret age 5, b. NJ; Emma, age 3 b. NJ
--1880 Census, p.9.1, Bayonne, Hudson Co., NJ: William Kerr age 37 b. NY, parents b. NY, no occupation listed; Margaret Kerr age 40 b. Australia, father b. 'Eugler'(England?), mother b. Ireland, dealer in fancy goods; Clarence Kerr age 1 yr 11 months b. NJ, father b. NY, mother b. Australia; Sarah "Sornasch" (Somerset), age 74, mother-in-law, widow, b. Ireland, parents b. Ireland

--1880 Census, p.225.3, South Orange: John E. Somerset age 47, b. Ireland, parents b. Ireland, dry goods store; Eliza, age 42, b. Ireland; Anna M. age 15, b. NJ; Emma, age 13 b. NJ; Walter age 6, b. NJ
"John Somerset m. Eliza McCormick. Their daughter Margaret Anna Frances Somerset was born 18 Nov. 1864 in South Orange and died 8 Dec. 1943 in Newark, NJ"
--1910 Census, p.8A, 1Wd, Bayonne, Hudson Co., NJ: Samuel Peyatt, age 47, m.12 yr, b. NJ, father PA, mother NJ, r.r. conductor; Emma L. age 43, b. NJ, parents b. Ireland, 1 born 1 living; Helen L. age 10 b. NJ; John E. Somerset, age 79, father-in-law, widower, b. Ireland

Children of Sarah Somerset:
John E., b. abt 1833, Ireland; m. Eliza McCormick
Margaret, b. abt. 1840 Australia, m. William Kerr

- - - - -

SOPER

Soper, FREDERICK b. (abt. August 1844)
(map, Section A) d. (bef. 1910)

wife, Anna ..... b. (abt. October 1850)
 d. (aft. 1920)

Soper, EDGAR A. b.
(map, Section A) d.

Notes:
Served: Civil War, Co. H, 26th NJ Inf., Pvt. (nps)
(pension to widow, Anna Soper)
--Frederick was son of Platt Soper, q.v.
--1850 Census, p.234, Orange Twp., NJ: Mary Soper, age 41; Sarah A., age 20; Abby A., age 18; Mary E., age 15; Juliet age 12; Frederick P. age 5; Emma C. age 3; Gertrude, age 1; all b. NJ
--1860 Census, p.384, 3Wd, Orange, NJ: Mary Soper, age 50; Mary E., age 25; Julia, age 22; "Edward" age 15
--1870 Census, p.312, 1Wd, Orange, NJ: Mary Soper, age 59; Julia, age 28; Frederick, age 24
--1880 Census, p.118C, Orange, NJ: Frederick P. Soper, age 36, b. NJ, foreman in stone quarry; Anna, wife, age 30 b. NY; Harry, son, age 8 b. NY; Emma, dau.,age 5, b. NJ

--1900 Census, p.8B, 5Wd, Orange, NJ: Frederic P. Soper, b. Aug. 1844, m.30 yr, b. NJ, father NY, mother NJ, super. at quarry; Anna, age 49, b. Oct. 1850 NY, parents b. NJ, 2 born 2 living; Harry P., b. May 1872 NJ, wood polisher; Emma C. b. Jan .1875 NJ
--1910 Census, p.3A, 5Wd. Orange, NJ: Anna Soper, age 58, widow; Howard G. Brehaut, age 38; Emma G., age 35; Frederick S., age 2
--1920 Census, p.6B, 5Wd, Orange, NJ: Howard G. Brehaut, age 47, b. Canada, tool maker; Emma E., age 44, b. NJ; Frederick S., age 11, b. NJ; Anna S., age 69, mother-in-law, b. NJ
--?1930 Census, p.26B, Jersey City, Hudson Co., NJ: Anna J. Soper, age 77, 'single', b. NY, parents NY; Elizabeth Millerick, age 68, single, servant, b. Ireland

Children of Frederick P. Soper and Anna .....:
Harry, b. abt. May 1872
Emma C., b. January 26, 1875, m.Howard G. Brehaut

- - - - -

Soper, Platt (map, plot owner, Sect. A)	b. d. (bef. 1900)
wife, Maria Riker	b. (abt. 1809) d. (aft. 1900)
daughter, GERTRUDE (map, Section A)	b. (abt. 1849) d. April 1, 1851

Notes:
--Platt Soper m. Feb. 4, 1829 at Caldwell NJ, Maria Riker.
--1850 Census, p.234, Orange Twp., NJ: Mary Soper, age 41; Sarah A., age 20; Abby A., age 18; Mary E., age 15; Juliet age 12; Frederick P. age 5; Emma C. age 3; Gertrude, age 1; all b. NJ

- - - - -

SOUTHWICK

Southwick, EVA (map,ch.property, Sect. H)	b. d. October 17, 1880
Southwick, CHILD of Eva (map, ch. property, Sect. H)	b. d. July 21, 1880

Notes:
--?1880 Census, p.107.2, Orange, NJ: Jefferson W. Southwick, age 29 b. NY, physician; Clara, age 22, b. NY

- - - - -

SPEAR

Spear, SAMUEL   b.. (abt. 1799)
(gmnj)(csl - EC1)   d. April 22, 1843
(map, Section O)

To
the
Memory of
Samuel Spear
who Dyed
April 22nd 1843
in the 45th year of his age

Notes:
--Map says: "Section O, Row 5: Negro Burial Ground"

- - - - -

SPEIR

Spier, JOHN   b.
(map,ch. property, Sect. H)   d. February 29, 1882

Notes:

- - - - -

SPRIGG

Sprigg, Anna Mary

Note:
--bur. plot of Joseph Edwards, q.v.

- - - - -

STAGG

Stagg, Amos L.*	b. (abt. 1818)
(map, plot owner Sect.G)	d. (aft. 1880)
wife, Eunice* (Pierson)	b. (abt. 1825
(map, Section G)	d. (aft. 1880)
Stagg, WARREN P.	b. 1848
(gmnj)(map, Sect. G)	d. March 4, 1851

Notes:
--Amos was son of Jacob Stagg and Sarah Tompkins (dau. of Enos Tompkins, q.v.)
--His son, Amos Alonzo Stagg, was the renowned American collegiate coach. He studied at Exeter Academy and Yale University where he was a divinity student, a member of Skull and Bones, and an end on the first All-America Team. He died at the age of 102 at Stockton, California
--1850 Census: p.231, Orange Twp., NJ: Amos L. (Lindsley) Stagg age 32, shoemaker; Eunice age 25; Warren P. age 2. (adj. to Henry D. Condit age 41 shoemaker and Rachel age 40)
--1860 Census, p.391, 3Wd, Orange, NJ: Amos Stagg, age 41, shoemaker; Eunice, age 35; George R., age 9; Sarah E., age 7; Harriet, age 4; Hannah P., age 1
--1870 Census, p.470&471, West Orange, NJ: Amos L. Stagg, age 50, farm laborer; Eunice, age 46; George, age 19, apprentice sash & blinds; Sarah, age 17, hat trimmer; Hattie, age 14, hat trimmer; Paulina, age 11; ALonzo age 7; Ida, age 5; Minnie, age 2; all b. NJ
--1880 Census: p.263C, West Orange, NJ: Amos L. Stagg, age 61, b. NJ, shoemaker; Eunice, age 55, wife, b. NJ; George B. , son, age 29, bookkeeper; Sarah E. daughter, age 27, b. NJ, works in hat shop; Hattie E., dau., age 24, saleslady; Paulina H. dau., age 20, b. NJ, seamstress; Amos A. son, age 17;Mary D. dau., age 15; Minnie E. dau., age 12

Children of Amos Lindsley Stagg and Eunice Pierson:
Warren P., b. abt 1848; d.1851
George B., b. abt. 1851
Sarah E., b. abt. 1853
Harriet E., b. abt. 1856
Paulina Hannah, b. abt. 1860
Amos Alonzo, b. Aug. 16, 1862;d. Mar. 17, 1965;aged 102
Mary Ida., b. abt. 1865
Minnie E., b. abt. 1868

STEINHAUSEN

Steinhausen, MRS.
(map, plot owner, Sect. L)
(removed to Rosedale Cem.)
b.
d. 1871

Steinhausen, F. G.
(csl-E32)
b.
d. January 23, 1857
Aged 23.6.7

Steinhausen, HUGO
(map, Section L)
(removed to Rosedale Cem.)
b.
d. January 26, 1857

Steinhausen, LUDWIG
(map, Section L)
(removed to Rosedale Cem.)
b.
d. May 4, 1854

Steinhausen, LOUIS
son of Ludwig(map,Sect. L)
b.
b. May 4, 1854

Brower, THOMAS
(map, Section L)
b.
d. 1867

Brower, WIFE of Thomas
(map, Section L)
b.
d.

Brower, LOUISA
(map, Section L)
b.
d. January 10, 1857

Pahte, AUGUST
(map, Section L)
b.
d. June 16, 1854 (1884?)

Notes:
--?1880 Census, p.103A, Orange, NJ: Louiz Steinhausen, a ge 35, b. Prussia, harness maker; Hannah J., age 38 b. NJ; Mabel, age 1, b. NJ; at res. of Cecelia Edwards, widow
--?1880 Census, p.114B, Orange, NJ: Charles Beck, age 53, b. Bavaria, harness maker; Fredericka , age 51 b. Prussia; Franciska, dau. age 22 b. NJ, hat trimmer; Henrietta, age 20 b. NJ; Albert, age 14 b. NJ; Mary,

age 9, b. NJ; Ludwig Steinhausen, brother, widow, age 61, b. Prussia, harness maker

------

STEVENS

Stevens, HENRY (map, Section J)	b. (abt. 1845) d.
wife, PHEBE (Dean?) (map, Section J)	b. (January 1836?) d. (aft. 1900)
daughter?, ANNA G. (map, Section J)	b. (abt. June 1873) d. December 24, 1904

Notes:
--See: plot of Charles Dean, Map, Section J)
--1880 Census, p.251.3, West Orange, NJ: Henry Stevens, age 35, b. England, house painter; Phebe, age 36 b. NJ; Anna G., age 7 b. NJ; Harry C., age 4, b. NJ
--1900 Census, p.8B, West Orange, NJ: Emmaline R.(Peck?) Ward, b. Jan. 1825, NJ, widow; Phoebe Stevens, 'sister', widow, b. Jan. 1836 NJ; Anna G. Stevens, b. June 1873, niece, seamstress; Harry C. Stevens, b. Sept. 1875, nephew, day labor;all b. NJ

Children of Henry Stevens and Phebe Dean:
Anna G. b. abt. June 1873
Harry C., b. abt. Sept. 1875

STITES

Stites, William (map, plot holder, Sect. E)	b. d.
CHILD of Albert Stites (map, Section E)	b. d.

Notes:
--?1850 Census, p.239, Orange Twp., NJ: William Stites, age 41, carpenter; Sarah L., age 38; Edwin M., age 16; Laura A., age 10;

William H., age 5; Amos H., age 14; Frederick age 1; all b. NJ (adj. to Peter A. Vanderhoof, q.v.)
--?1860 Census, p.427, 2Wd, Orange, NJ: William Stites, age 52, b. NJ, master builder; Sarah, age 48; Amos H., age 23, 'collow' maker; Laura A., age 19; William H., age 15, carpenter apprentice; Frederick, age 12; James A., age 9; all b. New Jersey
--?1880 Census, p.314D, Linden, Union Co., NJ: William Stites, age 72 b. NJ, retired carpenter; Sarah L., age 68; Harrison, son, single, age 43, r.r. conductor; Laura, dau., single, age 38; all b. NJ

- - - - -

STOKES

Stokes, Henry B.*	b. (abt 1844)
	d.
Catherine E.*	b. abt. 1846
	d.
son, EARNEST B.	b. January 23, 1877
(csl - E23,map, Section L)	d. June 27, 1877
CHILD of Stokes	b.
(map, Section L)	d.

Notes:
--bur. map, Section L, plot of S. A. Fairchild, q.v.
--1870 Census, p.299, Danbury, Fairfield Co., CT: Henry B. Stokes, age 28, b. England, hatter; Catherine, age 25, b. NY; Emily age 5, b. CT; Lulu, age 2 b. CT
--1880 Census: p.168D, Orange, NJ: Henry B. Stokes, age 36, b. England, works in hat factory, father b. Wales, mother b. England; Catherine E., wife, age 34, b. NY; Lulu D., daughter, age 12, b. Connecticut, at school; Albert Barden, single, age 20, b. NY, works in hat factory; Elizabeth Campbell, single, age 16, b. NJ, servant.

- - - - -

STONE

Stone, ISAAC	b. (abt. 1812)
(map, Section G)	d. September 12, 1850

Notes:
--bur, map, Section G, plot of Mrs. Law, q.v.
--1850 Census, p.197&198, Orange Twp., NJ: Isaac Stone, age 38, hatter, b. Ireland; Ann, age 37 b. Ire.; Jacob, age 5, b. NY; William, age 3, b. NY; Margaret, age 7 b. "Ire"; Isaac, age 1 month, b. NJ; Richard Donnelly, age 35, b. Ire.,hatter

Children of Isaac Stone and Ann .....:
Margaret, b. abt. 1843
Jacob, b. abt. 1845
William, b. abt. 1847
Isaac, b. 1850

- - - - -

STOPFORD

Stopford, EDWARD (map, plot owner, Sect. J)	b. (abt. 1838) d. May 23, 1910 *Aged 81*
wife, HANNAH (map, Section J)	b. (abt. 1836) d.
daughter, MARY JANE	b. (August 28, 1856) d.
daughter, JANE (map, Section J)	b. d. January 20, 1864 *Aged 3 and 1/2 years*
son, THOMAS E. (gmnj)(map, Section J)	b. (January 19, 1863) bur. October 24, 1905 *Aged 40*

Notes:
--1860 Census: p.420, 2Wd., Orange, NJ: Edward "Stopforn" age 32, hatter, b. England; Hannah age 36 b. England; Martha age 7 b. Massachusetts; Joseph age 5 b. NJ; Mary age 3 b. NJ.
--1870 Census: p.466, West Orange, NJ: Edward "Stockford", age 42, hat manufacturer, b. England; Anne age 44 b. NJ; Martha E. age 17, hat

trimmer; Joseph, errand boy; Thomas age 7. Also, Charles Dean age 72, shoemaker
--1880 Census: p.188.4, Orange, NJ: Edward Stopford, age 49, b. England, Hat finisher; Hannah, wife, age 49, b. England; Thomas, son, age 17, b. NJ, apprentice. (adj. to William and Martha Mathews. see next)
--1880 Census, p.188D, Orange: William Mathews, age 26 b. NJ, parents NJ, carpenter; Martha, wife, age 26 b. MA; Egbert, son, age 1 b. NJ
--1895 NJ State Census, p.112, 4Wd, Orange: Edward Stopford; Thomas Stopford
--1900 Census, p.4B&5A, 4Wd, Orange: William H. Matthews b. Sept. 1856 m.22 yr. b. NJ; no occupation listed:
Martha E. b. Nov. 1856, NJ, parents b. England; Egbert b. December 1898?; Florence E. b. Sept. 18891 NJ; Mary O. Burt, age 34, single, boarder (census page damaged)
--1910 Census, p.6A, 4Wd, Orange: W. H. Matthews age 55, m.31 yr, b. NJ, parents b. NJ, Chief, fire department; M. E. age 52, wife, b. MA, parents b. England, 3 born 3 living; E. W. son, single, age 30 b. NJ, hat flanger; W. R., son, single, b. NJ, carpenter; F. E. age 17, daughter, single, b. NJ, stenographer at hat factory; E. Stopford, age 80 b. England, father-in-law, own income

Children of Edward Stopford and Hannah .....:
Joseph, b. abt 1855
Martha E., b. November 1856; m. William H. Matthews
Mary Jane, b. abt. 1857
Thomas, b. abt. 1863

- - - - -

STROTHER

Strother, GEORGE b. (abt. November 6,1802)
(map)(Section E & J) d. March 1, 1864
(removed to Rosedale Cem.) *Aged 62*

WIFE of George Strother b. (abt. 1810)
(map, Section E & J) d. September 15, 1874
(removed to Rosedale Cemetery)

Notes:
--Bur: John K. Milne, q.v., plot, Sect. E and Sect. J

--George Strother m. August 16, 1829, Ann Baldwin at Saint John, Wakefield, Yorkshire, England
--1860 Census, p.193, 7Wd, Newark, NJ: Geo. Strother, age 57, b. England, wool 'salter'; Ann, age 50, b. England; Eliza, age 21, b. England; Jane E., age 15, b. NJ; Ann, age 14, b. NJ
--1870 Census, p.155, Newark, NJ: Ann Strother, age 62 b. England; Eliz, age 31, b. England, dressmaker; Jane Crockett, age 25, b. NJ; Clara B. Crockett, age 5, b. NJ; Edwin L. Annin, age 29, b. PA, store clerk; Anna M. Annin, age 24, b. NJ, seamstress

Children of George Strother and Ann Baldwin:
George, b. abt. July 10, 1830, Wakefield, Yorkshire,England
Eliza, b. abt. January 1, 1839, Wakefield, Yorkshire,England
Jane E., b. abt. 1845; m. 1865, Henry E. Crockett
Anna M., b. abt. 1846; m. Edwin L. Annin

- - - - -

STRYKER

Stryker, Henry* (map, plot owner, Sect. D)	b. (December 10,1805) d. (Aft. 1880)
first wife, ANN (Addy) (csl - E137)	b. (August 23, 1802) d. September 13, 1833 *Aged 31.0.21*
2nd wife, ELIZA (Addy) (csl - E138)(map,Sect. D)	b. (August 6, 1806) d. September 17, 1845 *Aged 39.0.37*

*In
Memory of
Eliza Striker
who departed this life
September 17th 1845
Aged 39 years
and 37 days*

third wife, Sophia Amelia* (Dart)	b. (December 23, 1810) d. (January 28. 1885)

Notes:
--See: Thomas S. Addy
--Henry Stryker,Jr. was born December 10, 1805, son of Henry Stryker,Sr. and Esther Harrison. He m. June 28, 1827 #1 Ann Addy; m. April 9, 1835 #2 Elizabeth Addy; m. April 10, 1855 #3,April 10,1855, Sophia Amelia Dart. She was b.December 23, 1810 and d. January 28, 1885. Ann Addy was b. August 21, 1802. Elizabeth Addy was b. August 6, 1806.(Rootsweb.com)
--Henry Stryker married April 10, 1855 at Orange, Sophia A. Brackett (Dart). She was born December 23, 1810 and died January 28, 1885. (IGI) She m. #1, Alonzo Brackett. (There was an Alonzo Brackett of Massachusetts who taught school at Orange from 1840 to 1850.) (Shaw, p.739)

--1850 Census, p.180, Jacksonville, Morgan Co. IL: "H. Striker" age 44, hatter; C., dau age 22; E. dau. age 20; Henry, age 17, student; J. A. 12, dau.; L. age 12, dau; M. age 10, dau.; Caroline age 8; all b. New Jersey
--1860 Census, p.342&343, Jacksonville, Morgan Co. IL: Henry "Strzker" 54 b. NJ, merchant; Sophia age 49 b. NJ; Charlotte age 32 b. NJ; Henry Jr. age 28 b. NJ, lawyer; Louisa age 22 b. NJ; Mariah age 20 b. NJ; Carrie, age 18 b.
NJ; Alonzo 'Braceth' age 11 b. NJ; S. H. 'Braceth', age 1, b. IL
--1870 Census, p.566, 4Wd, Jacksonville, Morgan Co., IL: Henry 'Wm' Stryker age 64 b. NJ, retired hat & cap mfr.; real estate value $27,000; personal $7,500; Sophia age 60 b. CT; Charlotte age 42 b. NJ; Louise age 32 b. NJ; Carrie, age 28 b. IL; Sophia age 11 b. IL; Alonzo Brackett, age 21 b. NJ; 1 servant
--1880 Census: p.189.2, Jacksonville, Morgan Co., Illinois: Henry Stryker, age 74, b. NJ, retired hatter; Sophia A. wife, age 69, b. CT; Charlotte, daughter, single, age 52, at home; Louisa, daughter, single, age 42, b. NJ, at home; Sophia, daughter, age 21, b. Illinois, at home; Alonzo Bracket, step son, single, age 31, b. NJ, collecting clerk in bank; Mary O'Donnell, single, age 24, b. Ohio, servant.

Children of Henry Stryker and Ann Addy:
Charlotte, b. abt. 1828
Elizabeth, b. abt. 1829; m.1852 ..... English
Henry, b. August 1832;
       m. 1866 Elizabeth A.Henshaw? McClure

Children of Henry Stryker and Elizabeth Addy:
Jane Ann, b. 1836; b.1857
Louisa, b. 1837; m. William T. Capps

Maria, b. 1840, m. 1861, ... Pierson
Caroline, b. 1841, m. 1878 ..... White

Child of Henry Stryker and Sophia Amelia Dart (Brackett):
Sophia H. Brackett, b. 1859, m. John A. Bellatti

- - - - -

STUDLEY

Studley(?), A. b.
(map, ch. property, Sect. I) d.

Notes:

- - - - -

SULLIVAN

Sullivan, WILLIAM b.
(map, ch.property, Sect. H) d.

- - - - -

TALBERT

Talbert, LEVI b. (abt. 1812)
(map,ch.property, Sect. H) d. (aft. 1870)

WIFE of Levi Talbert b.
(map, Section H) d.

Notes:
--1860 Census, p.393, 3Wd, Orange, NJ: Levi 'Tolbart' age 48, b. NJ, no occup; Susan, age 48; Martha, age 14; Mary, age 7; Catherine, age 4; all b. NJ
--1870 Census, p.462&463, West Orange, NJ: LEvi 'Talbot' age 60 b. NY, no occup; Susan, age 48 b. NJ; Sarah C., age 13, b. NJ; Isabella, age 9, b. NJ

- - - - -

TAYLOR

Taylor, Edward D.* b. (abt. 1835)
(map,plot owner, Sect. J) d. (aft. 1920)

wife, Anna G.* (Hannah) b. (abt. 1842)
  d. (aft. 1920)

Taylor, FRED C. b.
(map, Section J) d. October 31, 1878

Taylor, ESTHER GERTRUDE b. (abt. 1893)
(map, Section J) d. September 5, 1894
(grandchild?) *Aged 1*

Notes:
--1870 Census, p.413, 3Wd. Orange, NJ: Edward Taylor, age 35, b. MA, painter; Annie age 28 b. NJ; Charles A., age 2 b. NJ; Fannie B., age 8 mos. b. NJ
--1880 Census, p.181.1, Orange NJ: Edward Taylor, age 45, b. MA, painter; Anna G. age 38 b. NJ; Charles A., age 12, b. NJ; Fanny B., age 10 b. NJ; Edward H., age 8 b. NJ
--1900 Census, p.12B, 4Wd, Orange NJ: Edward D. Taylor, b. Mar. 1833 MA., postmaster; Anna G. b. Aug. 1841 NJ; Fannie B. b. Mar 1867, ass't postmaster; Jannie b. June 1880 NJ
--1910 Census, p.3A, 5Wd, Orange NJ: Edward D. Taylor, age 75, m.43 yrs. b. MA, house painter; Hannah G., age 67 b.NJ, 5 born-4 living; Frances B., age 40, post office clerk; Jennett, age 29, school teacher
--1910 Census, p.8B, 4 Wd, Orange NJ: Charles A. Taylor age 41, m. 15 yrs.,b. NJ, father b. MA, hatter; Anna, age 38, b. Scotland; Malcolm age 14 b. NJ; Edward, age 11, b. NJ
--1920 Census, p.2B, 2Wd, Orange, NJ: Edward D. Taylor, age 85 b. MA; 'Emmer L.'(Annie G.), wife, age 77 b. NJ; Chas. Albert, age 55, son, hat curler; Frances B., age 49, PO clerk; Jeannette H., age 39, teacher; Marietta Freeland, age 55, niece, b. MA, teacher

Children of Edward D. Taylor and Hannah G. ......:
Charles Albert, b. abt. 1865; (d. 1975?) m. Anna .....
Frances B., b. abt. March 1867
Fred H., b. Nov. 6, 1875
Jeannette H., b. abt. June 1880
Fred H., b. Nov. 6, 1875

Taylor, FRANCIS b.
(map, Section H) d.

Notes:
(?)Served: Civil War, Co. C, 39th NJ Inf., Pvt. (nps)
--?1870 Census, p.157, 8Wd, Newark, NJ: Frank Taylor, age 38, pattern maker, b. NH; 'Ageline' age 30 b. ME; Edwin,a ge 3, b. NJ; Harland, age 1, b. NJ
--?1880 Census, p.144 C, Newark, NJ: Frank Taylor, age 48 b. NH, engineer; Anna F. Taylor, age 40 b. ME, Edward E. Taylor, son, age 13, b. NJ

- - - - -

THOMAS

Thomas, John* b.
(map, plot owner, Sect. C) d.

wife, Jane* b.
  d.

daughter, SARAH ELLEN b. (abt. 1818)
(gmnj)(csl - E149) d. August 2, 1834
(map, Section C) *Aged 16*

Late of England

'third' daughter, MARY b. (September 2, 1823)
(gmnj)(csl - E148) d. April 2, 1836.
(map, Section C) *Age 12.7.0*

Late of England

Thomas, ADELAIDE b.
(map, Section C) d.

- - - - -

THOMPSON

Thompson, GILBERT
(map, ch.property, Sect. H)

b.
d.

Notes:

- - - - -

THORP

Thorp, HIRAM
(csl - E63)
(civ-Sect.I,Plot 4, Grave 1)
(map, ch. property, Sect. I)

b. (abt. 1842)
d. April 20, 1884
Aged 62
Vol. Navy Yard,Engineer

Notes:
Served: Civil War: Co. D, NY 50th Engineer Reg't.
--bur. map, Section I: near '2 children of William Leadbeater', q.v.
--1850 Census, p.260&261, Sherburne, Chenango Co., NY:
Israel Thorp, age 38 b. NY, farmer; Ann, age 34, b. NY; Hiram, age 7 b. NY
--1860 Census, p.0, im.496, Hannibal Center, Oswego Co., NY: Israel T. Thorp, age 48 b. NY, farmer; Anna Thorp, age 44 b. NY; Eleanor Paddleford, age 66, ... labor, b. CT;
Lydia Dowes, age 77, lady, b. NY; Hiram Thorp, age 17, b. NY, ass't farmer
--1870 Census, p.554, Hannibal, Oswego Co., NY: Tracy Thorpe, age 58 b. NY, farmer,(has 1 male child age 21 & older); Anna Thorpe, age 54, b. NY; Lydia Paddleford, age 76 b. NY, without occupation
--1880 Census, p.166C, Hannibal, Oswego Co. NY: Tracy Thorpe, age 68 b. NY, farmer; Anna, age 64, b. NY

- - - - -

TOMPKINS

Tompkins, ENOS CONDIT
(gmnj)(csl - E94)(map,Sect. F))
(NJ Will #16573G, 1867)

b. (April 4, 1810)
d. March 5, 1867
Aged 58

wife, RUTH CAROLINE
(Smith)

b. January 27, 1811
d. February 27, 1898

(gmnj)(shaw)(map,Sect. F)   *Aged 87*

Notes:
--bur. map, Section F, plot of Elijah S. Smith, q.v.
--Enos C. Tompkins was b. 1810 son of Enos Tompkins and Sarah Condit. (Condit Genealogy, p.26)
--Ruth Caroline was daughter of William Smith, q.v. and Ruth Paddleford.

--1850 Census: p.236, Orange Twp., NJ: Enos C. Tompkins age 40, hatter; William Smith age 78; Ruth C. Tompkins age 39; Harriet E. Pierson age 23.
--1860 Census: p.395, 3Wd., Orange, NJ: Enos C. Tompkins age 50, hatter; Ruth C. age 49
--1870 Census: p.474, West Orange, NJ: Ruth C. Tompkins age 60; servant.
--1880 Census: p.268.2, West Orange, NJ: Ruth C. Tomkins, widow, age 69, b. NJ; John Garniss, single, age 50, b. NY, merchant.

- - - - -

Tompkins,
LUTHER CROWELL   b. July 27, 1794
(gmnj)(csl-E112)(map,Sect.E)   d. October 2, 1852

wife, RHODA (Condit)   b. November 10, 1795
(gmnj)(csl-E112)(map,Sect.E)   d. March 18, 1883.
                            Aged 87

daughter, CAROLINE   b. (abt. 1824)
(gmnj)(csl-E111)(map,Sect.E)   d. November 25, 1848

*In
Memory of
Caroline
daughter of
Luther & Rhoda
Tomkins
who died
Novr.25th 1848
In her 24th year*

son, JOSEPH C.   b. August 22, 1821

(gmnj)(csl-E112)(map,Sect.E)   d. December 25, 1877

dau.-in-law, MARY A.   b. (abt.1823)
(map, Section E)   d. October 10, 1903
                              Aged 80

Notes:
--bur. map, Section E, plot of Zenas Freeman, q.v.
--Luther C. Tompkins was son of Ziba Tompkins and Elizabeth Crowell.
Luther married January 17, 1817 at Orange, Rhoda Condit.
--Rhoda Condit was daughter of Enoch Condit and Mary Tompkins.

--1850 Census: p.237, Orange Twp., NJ: Luther C. Tompkins, age 53, hatter; Rhoda age 53; Joseph C. Tompkins age 27, iron moulder; Mary A. age 26; Horace B. age 1 month.
--1860 Census: p.363, Orange, NJ: Joseph C. Tompkins age 38;Mary A. age 34; Horace B. age 10; Caroline E. age 7; Rhoda C. age 65; John VanNess age 17, hatter apprentice;
Charlotte Tompkins age 40.
--1870 Census: p.369, 3rd Ward, Orange, NJ: Joseph C. Tomkins age 48, constable; Mary A. (nee Bush) age 48; Horace B. age 26, carpenter; Elizabeth, age 17; Rhoda, age 76; Zenas Freeman, age 55, works at boot/shoe factory; all b. NJ

--Children of Luther Tompkins and Rhoda Condit:
Joseph Condit b. August 21, 1821; d. December 25, 1877;
    m. Mary A. Bush
Caroline Condit b. September 19, 1825; d. Nov. 25, 1848

- - - - -

TOWNLEY

Townley, C. W.   b.
(gmnj)(csl - E202)   d.
(civ: Sect. I, Plot 2, Grave 3)   *"Co. A, 134th NY Inf."*

Notes:
See: Caleb W. Townley, map, Section A

- - - - -

Townley, CALEB   b. (abt. 1823)

(map, plot owner Sect. A)	d. April 11, 1875
(bur. Sect. I, Plot 2, Grave 3)	
(csl-E202) (gmnj)	*Aged 52 years*
Townley, ...	b.
(map, Section A)	d. June 16, 1857

Notes:
Served: Civil War, Co.A, 134th NY Inf., Pvt.
Served:also?,Civil War,Co.A,21st Reg't,Vet. Reserve Corps
Gov't headstone provided: d. 'April 11, 1875'
--?Caleb Townley m. abt.1852, Marietta Munson
--?Caleb m. #2, bef. 1870,Anna .....; she m.#2 Martin Huett
--1870 Census, p.243, 3Wd, Newark,Essex Co., NJ: Caleb Townley, age 45, shoemaker; Anna, age 28; Robert, age 15; Willie, age 8; Lizzie, age 3; all b. NJ
--1880 Census, p.170A, Dist.27, Newark, Essex Co. NJ:
Martin Huett, age 41, b. Canada; Anna Huett, wife, age 40 b. NY; William Townley,stepson, age 18 b. 'NY'; Elizabeth Townley, stepdau. age 12 b. 'NY'

?Children of Caleb Townley and Marietta .....:
Robert, b. abt. 1855
?Children of Caleb Townley and Anna .....:
William, b. abt 1862
Elizabeth, b. abt 168

- - - - -

VAN BUSKIRK

VanBuskirk, Aaron	b. (April 1840)
(map, plot owner, Sect. M)	d. (aft. 1900)
wife, Sarah M.*	b. (January 1837)
	d. (aft. 1900)
daughter, EVELINA	b. (abt. 1858)
(gmnj)(csl - E12)	d. January 11, 1865
(map, Sect. M)	*Aged 8.1.9*
Crane, ARAMINTA	b. (abt. 1843)
(map, Section M)	d. March 18, 1906

Aged 63

Notes:
--Aaron was son of David VanBuskirk, q.v., and Charlotte Williams.

--1850 Census, p.245, Orange Twp: David Van Buskirk age 31, shoemaker; Charlotte 27; Aaron age 10; Levi age 5; Ira age 3; all b. New Jersey
--1860 Census, p.357, 3Wd. Orange: Aaron Vanbuskirk age 21, carpenter; Sarah age 22; Eveline age 2; William A. age 4 months; all b. New Jersey
--1880 Census, p.318.1, Pompton Plains, Passaic Co., NJ: Aaron Vanbuskirk, age 39, carpenter; Sarah M. age 43; William A., age 20, carpenter; Alice age 17; Charlotte age 14; Emma age 12; George age 9; all b. NJ; 3 boarders
--1900 Census, p.8B, Morrisville, Bucks Co., PA: Aaron VanBoskirk b. April 1840 m.45 yr, carpenter; Sarah M. b. Jan. 1837, 6 born 5 living; Charlotte A. Buchanon, dau., b. Dec. 1866, widow, 2 born 2 living, rubber worker; Clyde G. Buchanon b. Jun 1886 grandson, b. PA, father b. Scotland, mother b. NJ; Beatrice A. Buchanon, granddaughter b. Nov. 1890, b. PA; Emma A. Williams, b. June 1869, daughter, m. 11 yrs., 0 born 0 living; Alfred W. Williams b. Nov. 1866 NJ, parents b. NJ, son-in-law, works at rubber mill
--1910 Census, p.13B, 11Wd, Newark: George C. VanBuskirk, age 39, m.21 yr, b. NJ, clerk at insurance co; Ella age 41 b. NJ, 5 born 5 living; Mildred B. 19 PA, clerk at insurance co.; Clara, age 14 b. PA; Andrew age 10 b. PA; George H. age 6 b. PA; Dorothy G. age 8 months, b. NJ; Clyde G. Buchanon, age 23, boarder, single, b. PA, father Scotland, mother NJ, clerk at insurance co.

Children of Aaron Van Buskirk and Sarah M. ......:
Eveline, b. abt 1858; d. 1865
William A., b. abt. 1860
Alice, b. abt. 1863
Charlotte A., b. December 1866; m. ..... Buchanon
Emma A., b. June 1869; m. Alfred W. Williams
George C., b. abt. 1871; m. Ella .....

- - - - -

VanBuskirk, David*   b. (abt. 1819)
                           d.

1st.wife, CHARLOTTE
(Williams) (map, Sect. M)
(gmnj)(shaw) (csl - E11)

b. (March 6, 1823)
d. October 13, 1874
Aged 51.7.7

Brundage, GRACE
(map, Section M)
(granddaughter)

b.
d. August 15, 1881

Brundage, SARAH JANE
(dau.)(map, Sect. M)
(removed to Rosedale Cem.)

b. (abt. 1850)
d. June 17, 1911

Notes:
--Charlotte Williams was daughter of Joseph Williams and Mary Kent.(*Williams Gen*.p.36)

--1850 Census, p.245, Orange Twp: David Van Buskirk age 31, shoemaker; Charlotte 27; Aaron age 10; Levi age 5; Ira age 3; all b. New Jersey
--1860 Census: p.369, 3Wd., Orange, NJ: David VanBuskirk age 42, shoemaker; Charlotte age 37; Levi age 15, shoemaker apprentice; Ira age 14; Sarah age 9
--1870 Census: p.389, 3rd Ward Orange, NJ: David VanBuskirk, age 50, boot/shoe worker; Charlotte age 46; John A. Brundage age 25, sash/blind maker; Sarah age 20; Loretta age 2; John age 3 months.
--1880 Census, p.272B, West Orange, NJ: John E. Brundage, age 36 b. NY, father b. NJ, mother b. Scotland; Sarah J., wife, age 25, b. NJ; Sarah J. age 11; John P. age 10; Charlotte age 8; Ella May age 2; Grace, age 3 mos.;

Children of David Van Buskirk and Charlotte Williams:
Aaron, q. v. b., April 1840; m. Sarah M. .....
Levi, b. abt 1845; m. Mary E. Smith
Ira, b. abt 1847; m. Eleanora .....
Sarah, b. abt 1851; m. John E. Brundage

- - - - -

VANDERHOOF

Vanderhoof, CLARENCE W.
(map, Section B)

b.
d. July 20, 1861

wife?, GERTRUDE	b.
(map, Section B)	d.

- - - - -

Vanderhoof, PETER A.	b. (abt. 1817)
(map, Section B)	d. July 2, 1878
wife, CATHARINE	b. (abt. 1820)
(map, Section B)	d. January 21, 1878
Son, ICHABOD CONDIT	b. (November 15, 1841)
(gmnj)(csl - E189)(Sect. B)	d. January 31, 1848

In memory of
Ichabod Condit
son of
Peter & Catharine Vanderhoof
who died Jan. 31, 1848
Aged 6 years.2 months & 13 days

son, ALFRED IRVING	b. (abt. 1850)
(map, Section B)	d.
son, EUGENE CLEMENT	b. (abt. 1846)
(map, Section B)	d.

Notes:
--Bur. map, Section B, plot of Daniel Bond, q.v.
--1850 Census: p.239, Orange Twp., NJ: Peter A. 'Vandxoof' (Vanderhoof) age 33, shoemaker; Catherine age 30; Robert age 6; Clement age 4; Alice, age 2; Irving b. 1850.
--1860 Census: p.426, 2Wd.,Orange, NJ: Peter 'Vandergrof', age 43, shoemaker, b. NJ; Catherine age 39; Robert L. age 16, boxmaker apprentice; Eugene C. 14; Alice C.,12; Albert J., age 10; Catherine J. age 8; Frances A. age 7, Mary L. age 5.

Children of Peter A. Vanderhoof and Catherine ......:
Ichabod Condit, b. 1841; d. 1848
Robert L., b. abt. 1844; m. Sarah E. ......
Eugene Clement, b. abt. 1846;
    Served: Civil War, Co.G, 37th Reg't NJ

Alice C., b. Oct. 22, 1847; m. Whitfield Holloway Hunt Cox
Alfred Irving b. abt 1850
Catherine J., b. abt 1852
Frances A. b. abt. 1853
Mary L., b. abt. 1855

- - - - -

VAN NESS

VanNess, JAMES (?)　　　b.
(map, Section J)　　　　　d. June 11, 1894

VanNess, MABEL　　　　b.
(map, Section J)　　　　　bur. January 27, 1899

Notes:
(?)Served: Civil War, Co. E,39th NJ Inf., Sgt. (nps)
--bur. map, Section J, plot of Stacy B. Bannister, q.v.
--?1850 Census, p.323, West Wd, Newark, NJ: Catherine Doremus, age 46; Simon Doremus, age 18, silver plater; Lavinia Doremus, age 8; James M. VanNess, age 22, blacksmith; Sarah Cummings, age 19; all b. NJ
--?1850 Census, p.64, North Ward, Newark, NJ: Charles Day, age 48, carriage painter; Harriet, age 41; Joseph, age 21, carriage trimming; Phebe, age 23; Clarissa, age 16; Martha, age 14; David, age 12; William, age 10; James, age 8; George, age 3; all b. NJ
--?1860 Census, p.15, 1Wd, Newark, NJ: James M. 'Vaness', age 32, hardware for saddles; Clarissa, age 26; Emily L., age 5; Fred E. age 2; Clarissa, age 8 mos.; Loda Mulford, black, age 17; all b. NJ
--?1870 Census, p.214&215, East Orange, NJ: James Van Ness, age 40, blacksmith; Clara, age 36; Emily age 15; Frederic 13; Clara age 11; Minnie age 8; all b. NJ
--?1880 Census, p.400.1, Newark, NJ: James Van Ness, age 52, blacksmith; Clarrisa, age 45; Emily, age 25; Frederick, age 22, coach lamps; Clara, age 20, clerk; Minnie, age 18, dressmaker; all b. NJ

- - - - -

VanNess, CHILD of R. H.　　b.
(map, Section J)　　　　　　d.
(remains removed to .....)

Notes:
--bur. map, Section J, plot of John H. Sharp, q.v.
--?1850 Census, p.220, Orange Twp., NJ: Simon Vanness, age 44, hatter; Catherine, age 43; Robert, age 12; George, age 10; Eliza A., age 8; Horace, age 6; Sarah, age 4, all b. NJ
--?1860 Census, p.409, 2 Wd, Orange, NJ: Simon Vanness, age 55, hat manufacturer; Catherine, age 53; Robert, age 21, clerk; Sarah, age 14; George, age 19, hatter apprentice; Eliza, age 19; Horace, age 15, clerk; Sarah Brown, age 79; Ruth A. Valentine, age 24, hat trimmer; Mary A. Brown, age 50; all b. NJ

- - - - -

VERMILYEA

Vermilyea, JOHN	b. June 16, 1808
(gmnj)(shaw)(csl-E87)	d. April 14, 1850
(map, Section F)	

wife, HARRIET (Brown)	b. June 3, 1816
(gmnj)(csl - E87)(map,Sect.F)	d. July 26, 1858

Our mother and father

daughter, HELEN L.	b. September 23, 1837
(csl - E88)(map, Sect. F)	d. June 6, 1855

Notes:
--Bur: map, Section F, plot of Charles Brown,q.v.
--John Vermilyea married Harriet Brown, daughter of Kelitah Brown, q.v., and Maria Canfield

--1850 Census, p.336, West Ward, Newark: Harriet 'Vermilyea' age 33 b. NJ: John age 14 b. NJ; Ellen age 12 b. NJ; Anna, age 11 b. NY; William, age 9 b. NJ; Harriet, age 3 b. NJ; Ira E. Brown, age 20 b. NJ, (brother) carpenter; 5 boarders
--1860 Census, p.4, 2Wd, Newark, NJ: John G. 'Vermylea' age 25 b. NJ, tinsmith; Maria, age 24, b. NJ; John D., age 1, b. NJ; Phebe, age 66 b. 'unk'; Caroline Soper, age 12, b. CT
--1870 Census, p. 325, 20Wd, Phildelphia, PA: C. C. Alvord, age 58 b. MA, carpenter and builder; Sarah A. age 56 b. NJ; Chas. H. age 28 b. PA; Harriet E. 'Vermilya' age 23, b. NJ

Children of John Vermilye and Harriet Brown:
John, b. abt 1836
Helen L., b. 1837; d. 1855
Anna, b. abt 1839
William, b. abt. 1841
Harriet, b. abt 1847

- - - - -

VERSOY

Versoy, GEORGE (map, grave owned, Sect. F)	b. d. November 13, 1851

- - - - -

VINCENT

Vincent, Benjamin*	b. (October 5, 1768) d. (July 23, 1819)
wife, Elizabeth* (Stiles)	b. (January 1, 1770) d. (September 7, 1832)
daughter, HELEN PALMER (gmnj)(shaw)(csl - E52) (map, Section J)	b. (February 6, 1804) d. October 6, 1865 *Aged 61.8.0*

Notes:
--bur. map, Section J, plot of Mrs. Bentley, q.v.
--Benjamin Vincent was born October 5, 1758 at Bloomfield and died July 23, 1819 at Jersey City, NJ. He was son of Cornelius Vincent and Phebe Ward. He married September 1786, Elizabeth Stiles who was b. January 1, 1770 at Montville, NJ and died September 7, 1832 at Jersey City. (Charles C. Gardner Collection)

--?1850 Census, p.234, Orange Twp: Sarah M. Cassedy age 50 b. NJ; Helen 'Palmer' age 48 b. NJ
--?1860 Census: p.384, 3Wd, Orange:Sarah M. Cassidy,age 66, b. NJ; Helen 'Palmer' age 55 b. NJ

- - - - -

WALLACE

Wallace, William　　　　　b.
(map, Section M)　　　　　d.

Wallace, Mary　　　　　　b.
(map, Section M)　　　　　d.

Notes:
--bur. map, Section M, plot of Munson Garrabrant, q.v.

- - - - -

WATERS

Waters, FRANK CECIL　　　b.
(map, ch. property, Sect. N)　d. July 29, 1895
　　　　　　　　　　　　　Aged 14 months

Notes:

- - - - -

WATSON

Watson, DAVID　　　　　　b.(abt. 1814)
(gmnj)(shaw)(csl - E99)　　d. February 1849
(map, Section F)

David Watson
who
Died Feb. 1849
aged
About 35 years

Notes:
--bur. Map, Section F, plot of Alexander Bell, q.v.

- - - - -

WEBB

Webb, DANIEL　　　　　　b. (abt. 1821)
(map, plot owner, Sect. H)　d. (aft. 1880)

Webb, WIFE (Mary) of Daniel (map, Section H)	b. (abt. 1817) d. (aft. 1880)
Webb, DANIEL JR. (map, Section H)	b. (abt. 1852) bur. December 5, 1908 *Aged 56*
Webb, CHILD of Danl. Jr. (map, Section H)	b. d.
Webb, CHILD of Danl.Jr. (map, Section H)	b. d.
Webb, CHILD of Danl. Jr. (map, Section H)	b. d.
Webb, CHILD of Danl. Jr. (map, Section H)	b. d.
Webb, GEORGE (map, Section H)	b. (abt. 1900) bur. July 10, 1900(?) *Aged 4 months*

Notes:
--?Daniel m. abt April 1842, Mary Tunis

--1850 Census, p.237, Orange Twp.NJ: Daniel Webb, age 30, laborer; Mary M., age 33; Eliz, age 6; George, age 4; Charles, age 3; all b. NJ
--1860 Census, p.375, 3Wd, Orange: Daniel Webb, age 40, shoemaker; Mary, age 44; Eliza, age 17; George, age 14; Charles, age 12; Daniel, age 9; James M., age 1;
--1870 Census, p.476, West Orange, NJ: Daniel Webb, age 46, farm labor; Mary, age 50; George, age 25, laborer; Daniel C., age 18, butcher; James, age 11
--1880 Census, p.269C, West Orange, NJ: Daniel Webb, age 59, farm laborer; Mary, wife, age 63, 'in asylum'; Daniel C. age 27, laborer; Catherine, dau.-in-law, age 21; William H., grandson, age 11 mos.; all b. NJ

Children of Daniel Webb and Mary M. (Tunis?):
Eliza, b. abt. 1844
George, b. abt. 1846

Charles, b. abt. 1847
Daniel C., b. abt. 1851; m. Catherine .....
James M., b. abt. 1859

- - - - -

WEIDEMEYER

Weidemeyer, HENRY (map, plot owner, Section L)	b. (abt. 1830) d. October 25, 1893
wife, ANNA M. (Canahel) (map, Section L)	b. (abt. 1812) d. August 22, 1880
Jauchen(?), ANNIE (map, Section L)	b. d.

Notes:
--See: map, Section L, August Hepfner
--Anna Canahel m. #1, Henry Wethling; #2, Henry Weidemayer.
--Death Certificate: Anna Canehel Wethling Weidemeyer; b. Isle of Fehmarn, Germany; bur. **St. Mark's** Cemetery.

--1860 Census, p.363, 3Wd, Orange: Henry "Weidmyer", age 33, b. Denmark, laborer; Anna M. age 48; b. Denmark; Anna age 19 b. Denmark; Dora age 11 b. Denmark; Henry age 9 b. Denmark, Charles age 4 months b. NJ
--1870 Census, p.397, 3Wd, Orange: Henry "Wedemeyer" age 40 b. Denmark, laborer; Annie age 58 b. Prussia; Henry age 18 b. Prussia, apprentice to felt hatter; Annie "Venner" (Hepfner) age 30 b. Prussia, works at felt hat factory; Theodore "Venner" (Hepfner) age 8, b. NJ; Catharine Scheltfat, age 65, b. Prussia, no occupation
--1880 Census, p.165.1, Orange: Henry "Weidenmeyer", age 50 b. Schleswig, Holstein, laborer; Anna, wife, age 71, b. Schleswig,Holstein; Martin Peters, son-in-law, age 32 b. Bremen, works at hat factory; Dora Peters, dau., age 30, b. Schleswig, Holstein; Charles Peters, grandson age 11 b. NJ; Frederick Peters, grandson age 9 b. NJ; Anna Peters, granddaughter, age 7 b. NJ; Frank Peters, grandson age 2, b. NJ

Children of Henry Wethling and Anna Canehel:
Anna, b. abt 1841, m. August Hepfner, q.v.
Dora, b. abt 1849, m. Martin Peters, q.v.
Henry, b. abt 1852

Children of Henry Weidemeyer and Anna Canahel:
Charles, b. abt. 1860; d. bef. 1870?

- - - - -

WHARTON

Wharton, Mrs. Mary*   b.
(map, plot owner, Sect. L)   d.

Wharton, A. BENJ(?)   b.
(map, Section L)   d.

Wharton, DANIEL(?)   b.
child of Margaret(?)
(map, Section L)   d. _ _ _ _

Wharton, LOUISA   b.
(map, Section L)   d.

Forck(?), JOSEPHINE   b.
(map, Section L)   d.

Hirsh, LOUISA   b.
(map, Section L)   d.

Lee, MARTHA   b.
(map, Section L)   d.

Notes:
--Map: names are illegible
--?1850 Census, p.344, Acquackanonk, Passaic Co., NJ: William Wharton, age 50 b. England, paper maker; Mary, age 52, b. NY
--?1850 Census, p.114, Belleville, Essex Co. NJ: John Wharton, age 25, b. NJ, hatter; Mary Ann, age 22, b. PA; Josephine, age 1, b. NJ; William, age 20, b. NJ, hatter
--?1860 Census, p.689 Newark, NJ: John 'Worton' age 34, b. NJ, hatter; Mary, age 32 b. PA; Josephine, age 11, b. NJ; Charles age 8 NJ; Mary age 7 NJ; John age 3 NJ; Ida, age 3 mos. NJ; 1 servant
--?1870 Census, p.356, 4Wd, Newark, NJ: Jno Wharton,age 43, b. NJ, hatter; M.A., age 41 b. PA; Josephine, age 20 b. NJ; Charles, age 18; M.L., age 16; Ida, age 10; Ella, age 5; all children b. NJ; Mary Wharton, age 72, b. NY

WHITTINGHAM

Whittingham, Rev. Dr. WILLIAM ROLLINSON

Bishop, Diocese of Maryland

(gmnj)(shaw)(csl - E81) b. December 2, 1805
(map, Section G) d. October 17, 1879

wife, HANNAH (Harrison) b. October 13, 1795
(csl - E83)(map, Sect. G) d. October 17, 1885
(Will NJ #21887G, 1885)

daughter, MARY ANN b. October 22, 1832
(csl - E196) (map, Sect. A) d. April 22, 1834
(on Caleb Harrison stone, q.v.)

Mary Ann
Daughter of
William R. & Hannah
Whittingham
Born Oct. 22nd, 1832
Died April 22nd, 1834

sister, EMILY RICKARD (Richards)
Whittingham (unm.) b. May 1, 1816
(gmnj)(shaw)(csl - E84) d. March 1, 1854
 Aged 38

mother, MARY ANN b. January 4, 1785
(Rollinson)Whittingham d. September 10, 1849

father, RICHARD b. 1776
(map, Section G) d. 1858

Notes:
--map, Section G, plot of Richard Whittingham
--The remains of the Whittingham family were moved to St. Stephen's Cemetery, Millburn, New Jersey. (Or, their names are on a newer monument there.) William R. Whittingham's son married Martha Gilley

Condit, daughter of Israel D. Condit who gave the land for St. Stephen's Church and Cemetery at Millburn.
--William was born in New York City and died at Orange, NJ. For many years before his death he was an invalid. His last official act was performed on November 7, 1878. He was son of Richard Whittingham who was born 1776, Birmingham, Warwickshire, England; William's mother was Mary Ann Rollinson, daughter of William Rollinson and Mary Johnson; she was born January 4, 1785 at Birmingham, England, died September 10, 1849 at New York. William Whittingham and Mary Ann Rollinson were married January 4, 1805 at New York City.
--William was cousin of Samuel O. Rollinson, q.v.
--William was nephew of Elizabeth Rollinson Richards,q.v.
--Rev. William Whittingham m. Hannah Harrison, daughter of Caleb Harrison, q.v., and Keturah Crane. "He married the woman who, in his eyes, ever remained the most lovely woman in the world. ...There never was a more devoted son, a more affectionate husband, a more loving father, a kinder friend, a more humane master. Domestic life was to him the purest and best of earthly joys."*(Life of William Rollinson Whittingham, Fourth Bishop of Maryland,* William Francis Brand, NY, 1883)*)*
--Rev. William Rollinson Whittingham 'took charge of **St. Mark's** Church about June 1, 1829 and was installed rector, December 18, 1829. October 1, 1831 he was elected Rector of St. Luke's Church, New York City. He resigned May 10,1834 and took a voyage to Europe for his health. On September 17, 1840 he was consecrated Bishop in St. Paul's Church, Baltimore.' (The Whittingham Episcopal Library in Baltimore was named in his honor.)
--"At the time of his consecration he was the youngest of the American bishops; at his death he was the oldest but one."

--1850 Census, p.280, 20Wd, Baltimore, MD: Wm. R. Whittingham, age 44 b. NY, Bishop P.E. Church; Hannah age 43; Edw. age 19, student; Mary, age 15; Margt. age 13; Harrison, age 12; all listed as b. 'NY'; 2 servants
--1860 Census, p.0, Image 660, 20Wd. Baltimore, MD: Wm. Whittington, age 55 b. NY, P.E. Clergy, real estate $2,500, personal $12,500; Hannah, age 60 b. NJ, real estate $10,000; personal $15,000; Mary, age 25, b. NJ; Margaret, age 23, b. NY; Harrison, age 22, b. NY, clerk; 1 cook; 1 servant
--1870 Census, p.283, 12Wd, Baltimore, MD: W. R. Whittingham, age 65, Bishop, P.E. Church; 'Sarah' age 60; Mary age 25; all listed as b. NJ; 2 servants

--1880 Census: p.81A, Baltimore, Maryland: Hannah Whittingham, widow, age 84, b. NJ; M. Whittingham, daughter, single, age 44, b. NY; Charles Wilmer, son-in-law, age 50, b. Maryland, bookkeeper; Mary A. Wilmer, daughter, age 46, b. NJ;P. H. Wilmer, granddaughter, age 14, b. Maryland, at school; William R. Wilmer, grandson, age 13, d. MD; E. C. Wilmer, granddaughter, age 11, b. MD;M.C.Wilmer, granddaughter, age 5, b. MD; J. W. Wilmer, grandson, age 3, b. MD; 3 servants

Children of William R. Whittingham and Hannah Harrison:
--Mary Ann, b. October 22,1832,d.April 22, 1834
--Edward Thomas Whittingham, M.D., b. April 22, 1831;
       m. Martha Gilley Condit
--Mary Ann Whittingham,b. abt. 1835; m. Charles Wilmer
--Margaret Harrison, b. abt 1837; unm. in 1880
--Harrison Whittingham, b. abt. 1838; d. February 25, 1889

Note: Whittingham family members were later removed to St. Stephen's Cemetery, Milburn, NJ:
--Mary Ann Rollinson Whittingham, August 30,1849;
(mother of Rt. Rev. Wm. R. Whittingham.The records of All Saints, New York City list her as buried at St. Mark's Cemetery)
--Alice Brevoot Whittingham, April 15, 1967
(daughter of Walton Condit Whittingham)
--Anna Stabler Whittingham, 1945
(m. Wm. Rollinson Whittingham, son of Edward T.)
--Edward R. Whittingham, August 30, 1977
(son of Walton Condit Whittingham)
--Edward T. Whittingham, MD, October 29, 1886
(son of Rt. Rev. Wm. R. Whittingham)
--Elizabeth Whittingham, 1933
--Elizabeth Renwick Whittingham, April 19, 1986
(wife of Walton Condit Whittingham)
--Emily Richards Whittingham, March 1, 1854;
(Sister of Rt. Rev. Wm. R. Whittingham.There is also a burial record for her at All Saints, New York City.)
--Hannah (Harrison) Whittingham, October 17, 1885
(wife of Rt. Rev. Wm. R. Whittingham)
--Martha Condit Whittingham, August 8, 1992 (1991?)
--Martha Gilley Condit Whittingham, December 1, 1911
(wife or Dr. Edward T. Whittingham)
--Richard Whittingham, June 2, 1858
(father of Rt. Rev. Wm. R. Whittingham)

--Richard Harrison Whittingham, May 7, 1964 (1984?)
--Simeon Harrison Whittingham, February 8, 1869
(son of Walton Condit Whittingham)
--Walton Condit Whittingham, March 30, 1906
(son of Dr. Edward T. Whittingham)
--William Rollinson Whittingham, 1937
(son of Dr. Edward T. Whittingham)
--William Rollinson Whittingham, III, 1964
--Rt. Rev. William Rollinson Whittingham, October 17, 1879
--Eliza Rollinson, wife of Joseph Richard, Dec. 10, 1870

- - - - -

WICKES?

Wickes(?), GEORGE
(map, Section J)
b.
d. October 31, 1869
Aged 14

Notes:
--bur. map, Section J, plot of Thomas E. Brown, q.v.

- - - - -

WIESS

Wiess, CHILD of John
(map, Section H)
b.
d.

Notes:
--bur. map, Section H, plot of Isaac Baldwin, q.v.

- - - - -

WILLIAMS

Williams, ABRAHAM
(csl - E132)(map)
(map, plot owner, Sect. D)
b. (September 22, 1799)
d. April 3, 1861
Aged 61.6.11

wife, MATILDA SEARS
(Carter) (map, Sect. D)
(csl - E133)
b. (January 21, 1808)
d. January 28, 1858

Aged 50.0.7

son, WILLIAM AUGUSTUS (gmnj) (shaw)(csl-E134) (map, Section D)	b. (August 10, 1847) d. October 31, 1850 *Aged 3.2.21*
Williams, CHILDREN of H.P. (map, Section D)	b. d.

Notes:
--See: Daniel Williams
--Abraham was b. September 8, 1799, son of Daniel Williams, q.v., and Naomi Dodd. He m. #2, Emeline Condit, daughter of Jonathan Condit and Abigail Baldwin, and widow of Amzi Condit

--1850 Census, p.238, Orange Twp: Abram Williams, age 50, farmer; Matilda, age 42; Abram P. age 10; William A., age 3; Naoma age 70; all b. New Jersey; 1 servant

Children of Abraham Williams and Matilda Sears Carter:
Martha Ann Williams b. March 13 1837 d. March 13, 1837
Abraham Preston Williams b. 15 June 1840
William Augustus Williams b.Aug. 10,1847 d. Oct. 31, 1850

- - - - -

Williams, Albert Squier	b. (January 2, 1834) d. (December 18 1892)
wife, Abby Frances (Townley)	b. (July 13, 1836) d.
daughter, CLARA M. (map, Section A)	b. (March 11, 1854) d. February 11, 1857
Williams, HENRY (map, Section A)	b. d.

Notes:
--bur. map, Section A, plot of Caleb Townley
--see: Henderson, Hull

- - - - -

Williams, AMOS b. (November 6, 1782)
(gmnj)(csl - E141) d. July 30, 1843
(map, plot owner, Section C)
(NJ Will #13321G, 1843)

> *In*
> *Memory of*
> *Amos Williams*
> *He died*
> *As he had ever lived in*
> *the Christian Faith*
> *July 30th 1843*
> *Aged 60 years*
> *The righteous hath hope*
> *in his death*

first wife, PHEBE (Munn) b. (abt. 1787)
(csl - E141)(map, Sect. C) d. June 6, 1823

> *Phebe*
> *wife of*
> *Amos Williams*
> *died*
> *June 6th A.D.1823*
> *Aged 36 years*

second wife, JOANNA
(Campbell) b. (abt 1798)
(csl - E141)(map,Sect.C) d. October 2, 1841

> *Joanna*
> *Wife of*
> *Amos Williams*
> *Died*
> *Oct.r 2nd A.D.1841*
> *Aged 43 years*

son, STEPHEN b. (abt. 1812)
(csl - E141)(map,Sect. C) d. April 27, 1835

> *Stephen William*
> *Son of*

Amos & Phebe
Williams
Died
April 27th A.D. 1835
Aged 23 years

son, WM. WHITTINGHAM   b. May 7, 1834
(gmnj) (shaw)(csl-141)   d. February 2, 1837
(map, Section C)

William Whittingham
Their only child
Born May 7th 1834
Died Feb. 2nd 1837

Williams, EDWARD GRANT   b.
(map, Section C)   d. September 31, 1849

Notes:
--Amos Williams was a founder of **St. Mark's** Church. (Shaw, p.807)
--Amos was son of Benjamin "Governor Ben" Williams and Phebe Crane. He was born 6 November 1782. He m. #1 Phebe Munn, b. 1787, daughter of Samuel Munn. He m. #2
Joanna Campbell, b. 1798, daughter of John Campbell and Rebecca Baldwin.

Children of Amos Williams and Phebe Munn:
James Alfred Williams, D.D., b. 6 September 1809 (q.v.)
Stephen Williams, b. 1812 d. unm.
Maria Williams, b. 1814
Margaret Williams, b. 17 October 1817
Edward Williams, b. 6 October 1821
Children by Joanna Campbell:
William Whittingham Williams b. 7 May 1834.q.v.
(*Williams Gen..* p.30)

Child of Amos Williams and Joanna Campbell:
William Whittingham, b. 1834; d. 1837

- - - - -

Williams, BENJAMIN Sr.   b. (March 4, 1739)
(gmnj)(csl-E157)(map Sect. C)   d. September 4, 1826
(NJ Will #11806G, 1826)

In
Memory
of
Benjamin Williams
who died
Sept.r 11th, 1826
Aged LXXXVII
The upright shall flourish. Prov.14.11

second wife, PHEBE (Crane) b. (November 19, 1748)
(gmnj)(shaw) (csl - E156) d. May 7, 1822
(map, Section C) *In 75th year*

Notes:
--bur. map, Section C, plot of Samuel Williams, q.v.
--Benjamin Williams, Sr. was confirmed a member of Trinity Church in Newark, September 16, 1813. He was a founder of **St. Mark's** Church.(Shaw p.807)
--Benjamin "Governor Ben" Williams was b. March 4, 1739, son of Amos Williams, Esq. and Mary Nutman. He married #1 Elizabeth Condit b. July 12 1742, daughter of John Condit and Joanna Williams. Elizabeth died May 30, 1763, age 20.10.18 and is buried in the Old Ground of the Presbyterian Church. He married #2 Phebe Crane, b. November 19, 1748, daughter of Caleb Crane. (Benjamin and both of his wives are also 'recorded' in the Old Burying Ground.)

Children of Benjamin Williams and Elizabeth Condit:
Elizabeth Williams b. May 26, 1763 - d. April 12, 1784, age 21, bur. Old Ground

Children of Benjamin Williams and Phebe Crane:
Caleb Williams b. January 14, 1767;
    m. Sarah Kilburn, widow of Mr. Beach
Enos Crane Williams b. November 2, 1768;
    m. Abiah Munn, daughter of Samuel
Josiah Williams b. November 5, 1770;
    m. Sarah Harrison, daughter of Ichabod
Phebe Williams b. July 26, 1773
    m. Matthew Williams, son of Thomas Williams
Benjamin Williams, Jr. b. June 11, 1776;
    m. Joanna Williams, dau. of Zenas Williams
Samuel Williams b. June 20, 1778;

  m. Mary Crane, daughter of Joseph Crane
Phillip Williams b. June 23, 1780;
  m. Sarah C. Hedden, daughter of Caleb Hedden
Amos Williams b. 6 November 1782 (q.v.)
Althea Williams b. January 3, 1785
James Williams b. May 7, 1788; m. Sarah Hunt
Mary Elizabeth Williams, b. November 10, 1790
(*Williams Gen.*,p.42)

- - - - -

Williams, Charles H.*	b. (August 10, 1818)
(map, plot owner, Sect. C)	d. (December 1905)
wife, AMELIA F.* (Baldwin)	b. (November 27, 1817)
(map, Section C)	d. (March 23, 1881)
daughter, MARY ALICE	b. (July 7, 1843)
(gmnj)(csl - E154)(map C)	d. September 2, 1843

In memory of
Mary Alice
Daughter of
Charles & Amelia C. Williams
who died Sept.r 2nd
1843
Aged 4 months
and 24 days

daughter, AMELIA	b. (July 26, 1846).
(gmnj)(csl-E155)(map,Sect.C)	d. July 28, 1847

Amelia
Daughter of
Charles & Amelia E.
Williams
Died
July 28th,1847
Aged 1 month/& 2 days
There angels do always be
hold the fate of our Father
in Heaven

daughter, MARY AMELIA   b. (abt. September 1855)
(map, Section C)   d. February 13, 1856 (?)

Notes:
-- Charles Williams was a Warden of **St. Mark's** Church in 1884. (Shaw, p.809)
--Charles Williams was b. 10 August 1818 son of Samuel Williams and Mary Crane. He died December 1905. He m. December 22, 1841, Amelia F. Baldwin b. 27 November 1817, daughter of Jeptha Baldwin. She d. 23 March 1881.

--1850 Census, p.232, Orange Twp: Charles H. Williams, a ge 31, farmer; Amelia age 31; Samuel A., age 5; Jeptha B., age 1; all b. NJ; 1 servant
--1860 Census, p.418, 2Wd, Orange: Charles Williams, age 41, farmer; Amelia F., age 41; Samuel H., 15; Jeptha B. age 11; Virginia age 8; Charles H., age 4; Mary, age 71; all b. New Jersey; 1 servant
--1870 Census, p.465, West Orange: Charles Williams, age 50, farmer; Amelia 50; Samuel A., age 25; Jeptha age 21; Virginia age 18; Charles H., age 14; 1 servant
--1880 Census, p.255.3, West Orange: Charles Williams, age 61, farmer; Amelia F. age 61; Samuel A., age 35, single, farmer; Charles H., age 23, single, gardener; Virginia B., age 28, married during current year; Ezra C., age 31, married during current year, son-in-law, clerk; all b. NJ; 1 servant
--1900 Census, p.15A, West Orange: Chas. Williams b. Aug. 1818, widower, farmer; Samuel A., b. Aug. 1844, single, farmer; Virginia Baldwin, b. Oct. 1835, sister-in-law, single

Children of Charles Williams and Amelia F. Baldwin:
Mary Alice Williams b. July 7, 1843; d. 1843
Samuel A. Williams b. August 13, 1844; unm.
Amelia Williams, b. 26 July 26, 1846; d. 1847
Jeptha Baldwin Williams, b. May 17, 1849
    m. Georgia Elliott
Virginia B. Williams, b. August 13, 1851;
    m. Ezra C. Williams
Charles Harold Williams, b. October 19, 1853, unm.
Mary Amelia Williams, b. September 1856 d. Feb.12, 1857
(*Williams Gen.*, p.56)

- - - - -

Williams, DANIEL　　　　b. (July 25, 1770)
(map, Section D)　　　　 d. August 9, 1836

In
Memory of
Daniel Williams
who died.Augt 9th 1836
Aged 66 years
& 15 days

widow, NAOMI (Dodd)　　b. (February 1, 1780)
(gmnj)(shaw)(csl - E139)　d. January 9, 1851
(map, Section D)

In
Memory of
Naomi
widow of
Daniel Williams
who died
Jan.9th 1851
Aged 70 years 11 mo
and 8 days

Williams, MARTHA　　　 b.
(map, Section D)　　　　 d.

Notes:
--bur. map, Section D, plot of Abraham Williams, q.v.
--Daniel Williams was b. 22 July 1770, son of Eleazar Williams and Mary Ball. Daniel m. Naomi Dodd b. 30 January 1780 daughter of James Dodd.

--1850 Census, p.238, Orange Twp: Abram Williams, age 50, farmer; Matilda, age 42; Abram P. age 10; William A., age 3; Naomi, age 70; all b. New Jersey; 1 servant

Children of Daniel Williams and Naomi Dodd:
Abraham Williams b. September 8, 1799 (q.v.)
Charlotte Williams b. June 15, 1802, died September 20, 1805
(*Williams Gen.*, p.38)

- - - - -

Williams, Eleazar* b. (August 22, 1734)
　　　　　　　　　　d. (October 11, 1814)

wife, Mary (Ball)* b. (March 1, 1736)
(bur. Old Ground) d. (March 11, 1812)

daughter, MARTHA b. (March 12, 1763)
(gmnj)(shaw)(csl - E140) d. January 24, 1845
(map, Section D)

In
Memory of
Martha
daughter of
Eleazer & Mary
Williams
Died Jan 24,1845
Aged 81 years 11 mo.
and 15 days

--Eleazor Williams was b. August 22, 1734 and died October 11, 1814, son of Gershom Williams and Hannah Lampson. He m. Mary Ball, b. March 1, 1736, d. 11 March 1812, daughter of Timothy Ball.

Children of Eleazar Williams and Mary Ball:
Naomi Williams, b. February 24, 1760;
　　　　m. Zenas Williams, son of Nathaniel Williams
Martha Williams b. March 12, 1763
Deborah Williams b. 21 November 1765 d. 3 November 1799
　　　　(bur. Old Ground)
Daniel Williams b. July 22, 1770, q.v.
(*Williams Gen.*, p.17)

- - - - -

Williams, Henry b.
　　　　　　　　d.

wife, Clara M.(Williams) b.
(map, Section A) d. February 3, 1857

Notes:
--bur. map, Section A, plot of Caleb Townley, q.v.

Williams, James b.
(map, plot owner, Sect. C) d.

Notes:
--map has no entries on this plot

- - - - -

Williams,
JAMES ALFRED, Rev. Dr. b. September 6, 1809
(shaw)(?map, Sect. C) d. September 2, 1883
(NJ Will #21167G, 1883)

wife,
ELIZABETH ANN (Condit) b. May 1, 1813
(shaw)(csl - E152) d. March 1, 1860

son, JAMES ALFRED (Jr.) b. (December 19, 1840)
(csl)(shaw) d. October 2, 1862
  Aged 21.9.14

daughter,
ANNA MARGARET b. (December 24, 1845)
(csl - E151) d. March 5, 1856
  Aged 10.2.12

Notes:
--see: map, Section C, James Williams
--James Alfred Williams, D.D. was son of Amos Williams, q.v., and Phebe Munn. He was an Episcopal priest. He m. 4 October 1837, Elizabeth Ann Condit, b. 1 May 1813, daughter of Ichabod Condit and Elizabeth "Betsey" Leonard.
--Rev James Williams was ordained deacon by Bishop Doane, July 10, 1836. At this time, Rev. Benjamin Holmes was rector of **St. Mark's** Episcopal Church at Orange. Rev. Holmes d.
August 4, 1836 and Mr. Willliams was chosen to succeed him, He remained Rector until his death. He was greatly beloved by the church and highly esteemed by all who knew him. He died after a pastorate of forty-seven years.(*Condit Genealogy*, p.104)

--1850 Census: p. 240, Orange Twp., NJ: James A. Williams, Protestant Episcopal clergy, age 40 b. NJ; Elizabeth A. age 37; Maria E. age 12; James A. age 10; Selina age 7; Anna M. age 5; Stephen W. age 3.
--1860 Census, p.419&420, 2Wd, Orange: James A. Williams, age 50, clergyman; Maria, age 20; James A., age 19, student; Saline age 17; Stephen N., age 12; all b. NJ; 2 servants
--1870 Census: p.466, West Orange, NJ: James A. Williams, age 60, clergy; Maria E. age 30, Selina F. age 25; Stephen age 22, divinity student.
--1880 Census: p.251.3, West Orange, NJ: James A. Williams, age 70, widower, b. NJ, clergyman; Maria E. daughter, single, age 41; Selina F. daughter, single, age 37; Stephen W. son, single, age 32, teacher; 2 servants

Children of James Alfred Williams and Elizabeth A.Condit:
Maria Elizabeth Williams,b. September 1838
James Alfred Williams, Jr.,b. 10 January 1841
Selina Frances Williams,b. 9 May 1843 unm.
Anna Margaret Williams,b. 24 Dec. 1846, d.March 5, 1856
Stephen Whittingham Williams,b. abt 1848 unm., **St. Mark's** Sunday-schoool superintendant
(*Williams Gen.*, p.57)

- - - - -

Williams, SAMUEL   b. (June 29, 1778)
(gmnj)(csl - E158)   d. May 19, 1839.
(map, plot owner, Sect. C)
(NJ Will #13014G,1839)

In
Memory of
Samuel Williams
who died
May 19th 1839
Aged 60 years 10 mo
and 20 days
My flesh shall rest in hope

Tablet in the Sanctuary of St. Mark's Church

In the erection of this tablet the Vestry of St. Mark's bear testimony to the unostentatious worth of SAMUEL WILLIAMS one of the original founders of the church while he lived its constant benefactor Possessing an ardent love for the Gospel in the church, he was active, zealous and munificent in his labours to advance its cause and after a useful life of 61 years peacefully expired in the peace of Christ on Whitsunday AD 1839 having the comfort of a religious hope.

widow, PHEBE (Crane)   b. (October 26, 1784)
(gmnj)(shaw)(csl - E159)   d. June 9, 1856
(map, Section C)   *Aged 71.7.14*

Notes:
--see: Benjamin Williams
--Samuel Williams was a founder of **St. Mark's** Church. (Shaw, p.807)
--Samuel Williams was b. June 20, 1778, son of Benjamin Williams, q.v., and Phebe Crane. He m. #1 Mary Crane b. 1789, d. May 3, 1869, daughter of Joseph Crane and Hannah Sampson. Samuel m. #2 Phebe Crane b. October 25, 1784 daughter of John Caleb Crane and Sarah Meyer.

Children of Samuel Williams and Mary Crane:
Charles Williams b. August 10, 1818
(*Williams Genealogy*,p.30)
--1850 Census: p.232, Orange Twp., NJ: Phebe Williams (widow) age 65 b NJ; with Hannah Crane, sister, age 57, b. NJ.

WILLIAMSON

Williamson, JANE   b.
(map, ch. property, Sect. M)   d.

Notes:
--map says 'occupied by George C. Wilson'

WILLIS

Willis, ALEXANDER   b. (abt. 1839)
(map, plot owner,Sect. H)   d. August 23, 1914
                               Aged 75

wife, MARGARET (map, Section H)	b. (abt. 1845) d. October 25, 1917 *Aged 72*
daughter, MARGARET E. (gmnj)(csl - E66)(map,H)	b. November 16, 1870 d. January 5, 1876
son, ROBERT (gmnj)(csl-E66)(map,H)	b. December 8, 1872 d. January 5, 1876
daughter, ELICIE (gmnj)(csl - E66)(map H)	b. March 25, 1875 d. January 2, 1876
Willis, JOSEPH (map, Section H)	b. (abt. 1887) d. April 21, 1912 *Aged 25*

Notes:
--See: Robert Gordon, James Kyle
--Also bur. in this plot: Robert Gordon, q.v.
--1870 Census: p.382, 3Wd, Orange: Alexander Willis, age 27, b. Ireland, laborer; Margaret, age 23, b. Ireland
--1880 Census, p.246.2, West Orange: Alexander Willis, age 38 b. Ireland, laborer; Margaret, wife, age 33 b. Ireland; Lillis, age 3 b. NJ; Clara M. age 6 months, b. NJ; William 'Millen' other, age 28, single, b. Ireland, laborer
--1895 NJ State Census, p.142, West Orange: Alexander Willis; Margaret; Clara; Arthur; Josiah
--1900 Census, p.12A, West Orange: Alexander Willis, b. July 1843, m.31 yr, immig. 1867, coachman; Margaret b. October 1846 Ireland, immig. 1865, 8 born 4 living; Clara M. age 20 b. Nov. 1879 NJ; Josiah, b. August 1885 NJ
--1910 Census, p.8A, 5Wd, West Orange: Alexander Willis, age 68, b. Ireland, m.42 yr., retired; Margaret age 63, b. Ireland, 8 born 3 living; Arthur age 28, son, single, b. NJ, plumber; Josiah age 23, son, single, b. NJ, plumber

Children of Alexander Willis and Margaret ......:
Lillis, b. abt. 1877
Clara M., b. Nov. 1879; m. James? Kyle
Arthur, b. abt. 1882
Josiah, b. abt. Aug. 1885

- - - - -

WILSON

Wilson, BESSIE b. September 3, 1863
(map, ch.property, Sect. I) d. September 11, 1897
(removed to Evergreen Cem., Hillside, NJ)

Notes:

- - - - -

YEOMANS

Yeomans, RICHARD b. (abt. 1768)
(RootsWed: Youmans-L) d. (bef. 1860)

Notes:
--headstone not found
--Son of Samuel Yeomans

Children of Richard Yeomans:
Samuel, b. abt. 1795
Sarah, b. abt. 1797; d. 1864; m.Nathaniel Beach Winans
Mary, b. abt. 1800; m. ...... Foster
Charity, b. abt.1800-1802; m. #1, John Bowman; m.#2 Peter Norris
Phebe, b. abt. 1803; m. ...... Mead? ...... Woods?

- - - - -

YOUNG

Young, SAMUEL E. b. 1844 (February)
(gmnj)(map, Sect. B) d. January 22, 1920
 Aged 75.11.8

wife, Caroline Amelia* b. (September 1841)
(Matthews) (map, Sect. B) d. September 8, 1926
 Aged 24

Notes:
--bur. map, Section B, plot of Simeon Matthews, q.v.
--Samuel was son of Thomas Young and Hannah (Mills?)

--Samuel m. October 25, 166, Caroline Amelia Mathews
--Caroline was daughter of Simeon H. Matthews, q. v. and Caroline
--1850 Census, p.342, Westfield, Essex/Union Co. NJ: Thomas Young age 35 b. Scotland, farmer; Hannah, age 33 b. NJ; Mary Jane 11; Joanna C. 8; Samuel E. 6; Sarah E. 4; Phebe D. 2; William T. 4/12; all children b. New Jersey
--1850 Census, p.224, Orange Twp: Simeon H. Mathews, age 33, farmer; Caroline 31; Sarah M. 10; Caroline A., age 8; Simeon E. 6; Frances E. 4; Charles B. 2; 2 laborers
--1860 Census, p.322, Rahway, Union Co. NJ: Samuel Young, age 17 b. NJ, apprentice blacksmith; at res. of Edward J. Sisco
--1860 Census, p.235, Irvington PO, Clinton Twp., Essex Co., NJ: Simeon Matthews age 43, farmer; Caroline age 41; Caroline A., age 18; Simeon E. age 16, teacher; Frances E., age 13; Charles B., age 12; Robert M., age 2; Ella H., age 6 months; all b. New Jersey
--1870 Census, p.816, Scotch Plains PO, Westfield, Union Co., NJ: Samuel Young, age 26 b. NJ, blacksmith; carrie A., age 28 b. NJ; Fanny, age 2 b. NJ
--1880 Census, p.581.2, Westfield, Union Co. NJ: Samuel E. Young, age 36 b. NJ, father b. Scotland, blacksmith; Caroline A., age 38 b. NJ, parents b. NJ; Fanny B., age 11, b. NJ
--1900 Census, p.12A, South Orange: Samuel E. Young b. Feb. 1843, m.33 yr, b. NJ, father b. Scotland, mother b. NJ, wheelwright; Caroline A. b. Sept. 1841 NJ, parents b. NJ, 1 born 1 living; Fannie B. b. July 1869 NJ, stenographer
--1910 Census, p.12B, South Orange: Samuel Young age 66 b. NJ, father b. Scotland, carriage manufacturer; caroline age 68 b. NJ; Frances, age 35 b. NJ. stenographer
Child of Samuel E. Young and Caroline A. ......:
Frances B., b. July 1869

- - - - -

ZIMMERMAN

Zimmerman, HENRY b.
(map, plot owner?, Sect. H) d. May 15, 1850

Zimmerman, CHARLES b.
(map, Section H) d. February 25, 1856

Zimmerman, ... b.
(map, Section H) d.

- - - - -

Plaques and Stained Glass Windows at St. Mark's Church

(courtesy of Vincent P. Dahmen)
(Head Deacon, Lamb of God Fellowship)

- - - - -

(Corner Stone)
(in the wall of the bell tower)

ST MARK CHURCH
INCORPORATED 1827   ERECTED 1828
HOLINESS TO THE LORD

- - - - -

(plaque behind the organ)

In loving memory of the Reverend Benjamin Holmes, rector of this church, who was born in New York December 16, 1797; and died at the parsonage, August 4th, 1836. From his youth meekness, gentleness, simplicity and godly sincerity marked him the child of God. Through his whole ministry, zeal in his mater's cause tempered by prudence, sustained by integrity and crowed with charity made him a pattern for his brethren and a pillar of the church, of his activities as a missionary, his faithfulness as a preacher, his devotion as a pastor. This church and that of St. Peter's at Morristown both which he founded are the enduring memorials. Their love for the man their admiration for the Christian their gratitude to the honest watchman of their souls the congregation of St. Mark's Church thus mournfully record.

- - - - -

(plaque)

MAURICE MCKNIGHT HILL
LIEUTENANT AVIATION SECTION
SIGNAL CORP USA
BORN RHODE ISLAND JUNE 3RD, 1894
DIED ORLY-SUR-SEINE FRANCE

AUGUST 29TH, 1918
HIS BODY RESTS IN THE AMERICAN CEMETERY
SURESNES, FRANCE

"DYING AND BEHOLD WE LIVE"
-
ROBERT BRINTON HILL
LIEUTENANT ROYAL AIR FORCE
BORN NEWPORT RHODE ISLAND AUGUST 26TH, 1892
DIED ON SALISBURY PLAIN APRIL 29TH, 1918
HIS BODY RESTS IN DURRINGTON CEMETERY
ENGLAND

- - - - -

(plaque)

TO THE GLORY OF GOD
AND IN MEMORY OF
CHARLES ALEXANDER LIGHTHIPE
BORN OCTOBER 11, 1824 - DIED FEBRUARY 14, 1905
VESTRYMAN 1865:1887 - WARDEN 1887:1905
STEADFAST UNMOVABLE ALWAYS ABOUNDING
IN THE WORKS OF THE LORD
ERECTED BY THE RECTOR WARDENS AND
VESTRYMEN
EASTER 1905

- - - - -

(plaque)

TO THE GLORY OF GOD
AND IN GRATEFUL MEMORY OF
STEPHEN VAN RENSSELAER
WHO FOR MANY YEARS SERVED THIS PARISH
AS CHORISTER VESTRYMAN TREASURER AND
WARDEN
BORN OCTOBER 29TH, 1838 DIED JANUARY
20TH, 1904
ERECTED BY THE RECTOR WARDEN AND
VESTREYMEN

AD 1904

(Plaque on the side of the bell tower)

*THE CHIMES IN THIS CHURCH
ARE DEDICATED TO THE MEMORY OF
EDWINE VAN VLECK
BY HER MOTHER AND FATHER
1913 - 1927
HER SOUL IN HEAVEN
STILL CALLS AMONG US*

(plaque)

*TO THE GLORY OF GOD
IN LOVING MEMORY OF
THE REVEREND JOHN LEE WATSON DD
AND OF ELIZABETH HIS WIFE
ERECTED BY THEIR CHILDREN*
1889

(plaque)

*IN MEMORIAM
HARRISON WHITTINGHAM
WHO ENTERED INTO REST
FEBRUARY 25, 1889
HE LOVED THE CHURCH
AND LOYALLY SERVED HER
FOR MANY YEARS AS
CHORISTER VESTRYMAN AND TREASURER
IN ST. MARK'S PARISH
SERVING THE LORD WITH ALL HUMILITY OF MIND*

(Plaque in the sanctuary)

In the erection of this tablet the Vestry of St. Mark's bear testimony to the unostentatious worth of SAMUEL WILLIAMS one of the original founders of the church while he lived its constant benefactor. Possessing an ardent love for the Gospel in the church, he was active, zealous and munificent in his labours to advance its cause and after a useful life of 61 years peacefully expired in the peace of Christ on Whitsunday AD 1839 having the comfort of a religious hope.

- - - - -

(plaque on Baptismal Font)

*TO THE GLORY OF GOD
AND IN MEMORY OF
EDWARD MORTIMER WILMERDING*

- - - - -

Stained Glass Windows at St. Mark's Church
(courtesy of Vincent P. Dahmen)
(Head Deacon, Lamb of God Fellowship)

- - - - -

(window)

ERECTED BY HER HUSBAND IN MEMORY OF JOSEPHINE KISSAM FIELD WHO DIED MAY 16TH, 1887 AND SHE SHALL BRING FORTH A SON AND THOU SHALT CALL HIS NAME JESUS FOR HE SHALL SAVE HIS PEOPLE FROM THEIR SINS

(signed: lower right hand corner: 'Mary Tillinghast, Fecit May 1889; a famous artist of stained glass windows)

- - - - -

(window)

*In Loving Memory of
Caleb Harrison AE 85+
September 10th, 1854
and of
Keturah Harrison, His Wife
AE 85+ April 9th, 1855*

- - - - -

(window)

IN LOVING MEMORY OF PHILIP MESIER LYDIG
AND HIS WIFE
PAULINE HECKSCHER
MARRIED IN THIS CHURCH SEPTEMBER 7TH, 1865
ERECTED BY THEIR SON
PHILP MESIER LYDIG

- - - - -

(window)
(above the front doors)

*To the glory of God and in memory of
Matilda Coster Heckscher
wife of Stephen Van Rensselaer
erected by their children 1839 - 1915
It shall come to pass at evening time it shall be light*

- - - - -

(window)

*In Memoriam
Andrew Whitemore Ward
Born October 3rd, 1840
Died March 17th, 1867*

- - - - -

(window)

*Rata Jan. 4th, 1784: Mary Ann Whittingham
DeRata September 9. 1849*

- - - - -

(window behind the altar)

*Ye Seek Jesus He is Risen He Is Not Here
To The Glory of God In Loving Memory of
William Rollinson Whittingham DD LL D
First Rector of This Church
Fourth Bishop of Maryland*

- - - - -

(window)

*In Memory of Amos Williams
Died July 30th, 1843*

- - - - -

(oldest window, difficult to read)

*To the glory of God
and in memory of Ben Williams
Died Sept. 4, 1826
and Phebe his wife*

- - - - -

Early History of St. Mark's Church
1808-1884

St. Mark's Episcopal Church was added in 1977 to the National Register of Historical Places, #77000868.

1996 - *West Orange Historic Peservation Commission:*
"Situated on 2.5 acres overlooking the center of West Orange, St. Mark's Episcopal Church is an outstanding example of Gothic Revival architecture. The original section of the brownstone church was built in 1827. An 1860-1861 addition, including a steeple, was attributed to renowned architect Richard Upjohn. No significant physical or structural changes have been made to the church in over 90 years. As with many urban churches throughout the state, the congregations as dwindled greatly and the funds are not available for maintenance or restoration."

A sketch of its early history, prepared by the late rector, James A. Williams, D.D.:

"St. Mark's Church, Orange, may be considered as a daughter of Trinity Church, Newark. In the year 1808 the Rev. Joseph Willard, rector of Trinity, reported: 'That he had performed divine service and preached twice at Benjamin William's, Orange, where he had large and attentive congregations; that there were several families who appear to be attached to the Episcopal Church, for whom he had baptized seven or eight children, and who regularly attend at Newark.

"The families thus alluded to who formed the nucleus of the congregation were those of Benjamin Williams, Sr., of his nephew, James Williams, and of his sons, Benjamin Williams, Jr., Josiah Williams, Samuel Williams and Amos Williams.

"These families continued under the pastor a charge of the rector of Trinity Church, and were favored with occasional services from the successive rectors, Messrs. Willard, Bayard and Powers, until measures were taken for a separate organization. It appears that Benjamin Williams, Sr., was confirmed in Newark, September 16, 1813; Benjamin Williams, Jr., May 1, 1817; James Williams and Samuel Williams, May 21, 1819; and Amos Williams, October 17, 1822.

"In the year 1819 these families were brought to the notice of the bishop of the diocese, John Croes, D.D., who visited them and continued from this time until his death to include their neighborhood in his episcopal visitations. In 1825 their neighborhood was made a missionary station and placed under the charge of the Rev. Benjamin Holmes. Mr. Holmes resided at Morristown, and having several other stations under his care, at first gave his services on but one Sunday a month to Orange. About the time of his appointment the hearts of the llittle band of churchmen were cheered by the accession of Caleb Harrison to their number, with his family and several of his relatives. They then felt encouraged to take measures for the formation of a parish, and on April 7, 1827, St. Mark's Church was incorporated according to the laws of the State. The corner-stone of a church edifice was laid May 12, 1828, by the missionary, Mr. Holmes. A building of brown stone, forty feet by sixty, was erected during the year at a cost of seven thousand to eight thousand dollars, some portion of which hung over the parish as a debt for some three or four years. The building was completed so far as to admit of consecration by Bishop Croes, on February 20, 1829. Before this glad event took place, however, death had made sad inroads upon the few church families. The first churchman of the place, the venerable Benjamin Williams, was called away September 4, 1826. James Williams in 1826, and Josiah Williams, July 20, 1828. Soon after the consecration of the church fifty-four pews were sold, the most of them on very easy terms and all free of rent. The faithful and acceptable missionary was consequently enabled, in his annual report, May 27, 1829, to include fifty-four families and pew-holders as the number constituting the parish. It must be observed, however, that the greater portion of these families, as yet, were but nominally attached to the doctrines of the church. Residing in the neighborhood and having contributed somewhat to the erection of the edifice, several families were induced to take pews, especially as they were subject to no rent for the support of the ministrations. The great burden, both in building the church and in supporting its services, fell upon a few individuals, among whom are especially to be named Messrs. Caleb and John Harrison, and Messrs. Samuel, Amos and Benjamin Williams. Having thus organized the parish, erected a church and gathered a flock, Mr. Holmes relinquished the charge of the congregation, and confined his services to St. Peter's Church, Morristown, in the spring of 1829. The parish then ceased to be a missionary station and was enabled to secure the entire services of the Rev. William Rollinson Whittingham, who took charge about June 1, 1829, and immediately began regular morning and evening services on each Lord's Day. Mr. Whittingham was in deacon's orders, but was ordained priest on December 17, and installed rector on December 18,

1829. At the time when he took charge the communicants were thirteen in number. He was called on a salary of four hundred dollars, and was to continue to perform the dutes of editor to the General Sunday School Union. These united offices of rector and editor were filled by Mr. Whittingham to the entire satisfaction of the parish until November 1, 1830, when, to the extreme regret of the congregation, he felt it to be his duty to resign for the purpose of giving his whole attention to the concerns of the Sunday School Union, to the editorship of the 'Standard Works of Church Divines' and to the charge of the Protestant Episcopal press. The zealous labors of Mr. Whittingham wer greatly blessed. During his brief connection with the parish the number of communicants was more than doubled, and much was done in dispelling prejudices and in confirming the attachment of some who had hitherto been but nominal members of the parish. Although retiring from the pastoral charge, Mr. Whittingham did not cease to take interest in its welfare. While retaining his connection with the Protestant Episcopal press, and while a professor in the General Theological Seminary, he frequently visited it and officiated. During the year 1832 he resided in the parish, and until his election to the episcopate of Maryland, and his removal thither in 1840, the congreagation very often enjoyed and profited from his ministerial services.

"Immediately after the resignation of Mr. Whittingham the vestry took measures for the appointment of a successor, and on November 10,. 1830, elected their former pastor, the Rev. Benjamin Holmes, to the vacant rectorship, and pledged him a salary of five hundred dollars per annum. Mr. Holmes accepted the appointment on February 20, 1831, and took charge of the congregation early in the spring, but circumstances prevented his institution until July 4, 1831, when in due form he was put in possession of the rectorship. During the vacancy service was partially sustained in the church by occasional supplies. One of the first acts of the vestry, after Mr. Holmes' instituion, was to build a tower on the church, and procure a bell weighing four hundred and seventy pounds. In September, 1833, an organ was purchased, at an expense of three hundred dollars.

"In promising Mr. Holmes a salary of five hundred dollars the vestry had depended on the uncertain plan of pledges and subscriptions. The consequence was that the modest, retiring and faithful rector received but an irregular supply for his wants, and was forced to endure much privation. Finding that the plan of subscriptions did not succeed, a few members of the parish determined to rise a permanent fund of five thousand dollars, the interest of which should be devoted to the support of the rector. This object was partially accomplished on January 27, 1834. On this day ten individuals (among whom the most prominent were Samuel Williams, Caleb Harrison, John Harrison, Amos Williams and Benjamin Williams) put their names to an instrument pledging themselves and their heirs, respectively, for moneys to the amoung of five thousand dollars, and gave their personal notes for the amounts which they subscribed, with the understanding that these notes could remain so long as the interest was paid. As the subscribers passed away, and in some cases before death, their pledges were redeemed, so that, deducting losses, about four thousand five hundred dollars was eventually secured to the church in real estate and bank stock. In this same year, 1834, a house and lot were purchased for a parsonage, at a cost of one thousand dollars, with moneys included in the above-mentioned fund. This parsonage and lot, however, being incommodious and at a distance from the church, was subsequently sold in 1836.

"Mr. Holmes continued to discharge the duties of his office to the edification of his increasing flock, and to their entire satisfaction, until his death, which sad event took place, after a short illness, on August 4, 1836. He expired universally beloved, and was buried under the chancel of the church as a fitting resting-place for its founder. As a proof of their attachment, the congregation doubled his salary for the year in which he died, and paid the sum over to his widow (Jane Seaman Ogden) and infant daughter. Mr. Holmes' ministrations were very acceptable unto his people. 'His evenness of temper, unaffected modesty and amiable simplicity of manners made him dear to all, while his unshaken integrity, sound judgment and firmness in the discharge of his duty constrained all to respect no less than they loved him.' He was sincerely attached to the peculiar doctrines of the church, declared them with honest sincerity, and preached the truths of the Gospel generally with faithfulness and devotion, while by a consistent private walk he gave energy and value to his public teaching. Under God his labors were blessed in the edification and the spititual conversion of many. By his prudence, his zeal and his self-sacrifice he accomplished much in laying the foundation and in building up the church, and to him the congregation of St. Mark's owes a lasting debt of gratitude. During his ministry as rector for five years and four months ninety-six baptisms took place, forty-one persons were confirmed, and fifty-five were added to the number of communicants."

William Shaw in his *History of Essex and Hudson Counties,* 1882, continues:

"The writer of the foregoing historical sketch, James A. Williams, then a lay member of the parish, was ordained deacon by Bishop Doane, July 10, 1836. After the death of the rector, Benjamin Holmes, the eyes of the congregation were turned to him for a supply of the pulpit and the vacancy in the rectorship. having been brought up in the parish, and being without experience in the duties of the ministerial office, the proposed invitation to the vacancy was limited, at his own suggestion, to a period of six months, dating from August 13, 1836. On the expiration of this period he was unanimously chosen to the rectorship January 25, 1837, on a salary of four hundred dollars and the use of the parsonage, speedily to be built. On September 9, 1837, he was formally installed by Bishop Doane. The parish, however, was considered to be under his ministerial charge from August 13, 1836.

"In 1884 the Rev. Bishop Faulkner was in charge of St. Mark's. The assistant rectorship was vacant. The wardens were Charles Williams and William Cleveland; Vestrymen, Hon. John L. Blake, George Bayles, M.D., J. M. Hare, S.O. Rollinson, Edward Willliams, James W. Field, Esq., Col. George Gray, Charles A. Lighthipe, S.M. VanRensselaer, Harrison Whittingham. The parish owns, besides the large stone church, a mission chapel and rectory, the whole value at one hundred thousand dollars. Communicants in December, 1884, three hundred and fifty. The Sunday-school comprises over four hundred pupils, with Stephen W. Williams, superintendent.

"The Ladies' Benevolent Society and St. Mark's Guild are active and aggressive in all charitable work. The rector is president of the 'House of the Good Shepherd,' a home for old persons, sustained by Episcopal Churches in the vicinity. The church maintains a boy choir noted for its excellence in music, and is in charge of Messrs. Rollinson, Van Rensselaer and Whittingham."

- - - - -

SOURCES

(csl) --"*Inscriptions* (1665-1880) *on tombstones in the old Cemetery at Orange, NJ and in the Episcopal Cemetery adjoining it*" Microfilm of typed photostatic copy at the Connecticut State Library. Undated. Family History Library Film #2999 Item 12 (List of burials by number: E stands for Episcopal Cemetery and it is presumed that EC stands for Episcopal Cemetery common ground)

(gmnj) --*Orange Episcopal Cemetery*. Richard W. Cook. The Genealogical Magazine of New Jersey. Vol. 67, No. 2. May 1992

--*Gravestone Records From Old Burying Ground, Orange, Essex County*. Rev. Warren Patten Coon. The Genealogical Magazine of New Jersey. Vol.IV. No.2. 1928

(map) --Map (undated) of interments and plot owners at St. Mark's Cemetery

(nps) *U.S. Civil War Soldiers, 1861-1865*. National Park Service, Civil War Soldiers and Sailors System, online

--*Card index to Civil War Soldiers Graves*, Microreproduction of records at the New Jersey Historical Society, Newark, N.J. 1862

--*Inscriptions from St. Mark's Churchyard.Orange*. Monumental Inscriptions of Essex County, NJ. Vol II. New Jersey Historical Society Collections. "Collected in 1904"

--On site research: Vincent P. Dahmen, Head Deacon and Property Manager. Lamb of God Fellowship. Orange, N.J.

--Misc.:Original death certificates; Federal
Census Records; International Genealogical
Index; Roots Web.com; family information

--*National Register of Historic Places*
St. Mark's Episcopal Church. (added 1977)

Baldwin, Charles C. *The Baldwin Genealogy.* Cleveland, Ohio: The
    Leader Printing Co., 1881
Brand, William Francis. *Life of William RollinsonWhittingham, Fourth*
    Bishop of Maryland. New York: E.& J.Young & Co., 1883
Childs, Jean H. C. *The Harrisons of New Jersey - A Partial Genealogy.*
    Newville, PA. Typed Manuscript. 1991
Condit, Jotham H. and Even. *Genealogical Record of the Condit*
    Family. Revision. Condit Family Association. 1916
Eberhart, Edith Whitcraft. *The Doremus Family in America.*
    Gateway Press, Inc. Baltimore. 1990
Fretz, Abr. James, Rev. *Genealogical Record of the Descendants of*
    Leonard Headley of Elizabethtown, N.J. Milton, N.J., 1905
Gilmore, Jean Fairchild. *Early Fairchilds in America.* Gateway Press,
    Baltimore 1991
Quimby, Henry Cole. *Genealogical History of the Quinby (Quimby)*
    Family in England and America. New York,1915
Shaw, William H. *History of Essex and Hudson Counties, New Jersey.*
    Phildelphia. Everts & Peck. 1884
Wickes, Stephen. *History of the Oranges in Essex County, New Jersey.*
    Newark, N.J. Ward & Tichenor, 1892
Wickes, Stephen. *Ten Years' History of the First Presbyterian Church,*
    Orange, N.J. Newark, N.J., L. J. Hardham, 1877
Williams, Lyle Keith. *The Williams Families of New Jersey*
    Decorah, Iowa. The Anundsen Publ. Co. 1998

- - - - -

APPENDIX I

"Inscriptions in the Episcopal Cemetery"

(As an aid to relationships these are listed by number assigned in the typescript at the Connecticut State Library.)

EC1	Squier, Argales, son of Benjamin H.
EC3	Bonnell, J. W.
EC2	McCrea, Nathan
EC4	Osborn, Catherine
EC5	Osborn, Ann
EC6	Brown, John Edward, son of James
EC6	Brown, Maria, dau. of James
E7	Shelley, Charles V.
E7	Shelley, Mary Ann, wife of Charles V.
E8	Horn, Sarah Jane, wife of John
E9	Gonzales, Frank L., son of E. B. & V. A.
E10	Hull, Matilda Cusack
E11	Williams, Charlotte, wife of D. VanBuskirk
E12	VanBuskirk, Evelina, dau. of Aaron
E13	Carpenter, Henry
E15	Hull, Peter R.
E16	Jarvis, James
E17	Coyne, Mary A., wife of Patrick
E18	Condit, Adda, dau. of John P.
E19	Condit, Randolph B., son of John P.
E20	Condit, Roland, son of John P.
E22	Brindly, Henry
E22	Somerset, Sarah
E23	Stokes, Earnest B., son of Henry B.
E24	Edwards, T. S.
E25	Condit, Rosena, dau. of David W.
E26	Condit, Cornelia, wife of David W.
E27	Condit, David N.
E29	Daniels, William
E28	Brown, Thomas
E30	Redington, Thomas, son of William
E30	Redington, William Archibald
E31	Redington, Robert, son of William
E31	Redington, Wm.
E32	Steinhausen, C. L.
E32	Steinhausen, F. H.

E33	Pierson, Catherine, wife of Zenas
E33	Pierson, Elizabeth
E34	Brady, James E., son of James S.
E36	Day?, Daniel
E37	Aymar, Sarah, with of John J.
E38	Babb, Eliza, dau. of James
E39	Atchison, John
E40	Lenox, James
E41	Lennox, Almira, wife of James
E41	Lennox, Emma Irene, dau. of James
E42	Robins, James P.
E43	Robins, Matilda, wid. of James P.
E44	Condit, Sarah E., wife of Henry
E44	Robins, Sarah E., dau. of James P.
E45	Condit, Sarah E. F., dau. of Henry
E45	Ingraham, Content, wife of Henry E.
E45	Wilson, Content, dau. of William
E46	Miller, Charles E., son of Nicholas
E47	Atchison, Emily J., dau. of John
E48	Green, Lizzie, wife of William H.
E49	Walls, (?), Walter
E50	Dean, Isaac M.
E50	Dean, Mary Jane, wid. of Isaac M.
E50	Dean, Sarah Frances, dau. of Isaac M.
E50	Mulford, Alvah Dean
E50	Mulford, Charles Beach
E50	Mulford, Sarah Frances, wife of Benjamin
E51	Gilman, Maria
E52	Vincent, Helen Palmer, dau. of Benjamin
E53	Brown, W. T.
E54	Bannister, Deborah
E55	Bannister, Margaret Perry, wife of Stacy B.
E56	Bannister, Gertrude, dau. of Stacy B.
E57	Gist, Margaret S., dau. of Robert F.
E57	Gist, Mary A.
E58	Sharp, Phebe S.
E59	Bannister, Freddie, son of DeWitt & Emily
E60	Kent, Phebe, dau. of Jacob N.
E62	Gage, Rhomanzo
E63	Thorp, Hiram
E64	Patterson, Robert James, son of Thomas
E64	Patterson, Thomas Alex., son of Thomas
E65	Furguson, Ellen

E65	Furguson, Margaret
E66	Willis, Margaret E.
E66	Willis, Robert
E67	Schoor, Johann
E68	Hitchcock, Joel
E69	Cleaveland, Henry Vail, son of S.C. & S.M.
E69	Cleaveland, Samuel C.
E70	Edwards?, A. Edward
E71	Hitchcock, Charles D.
E71	Hitchcock, H. H.
E72	Jones, Sarah
E73	Hertgebe, Dorothea
E74	Bard, Grace Estell
E75	Browne, Ann P.
E76	Browne, Catherine
E77	Browne, Arthur
E78	Bishop, W. S.
E79	Harrison, Wm.
E80	Allen, John, son of John & Sarah
E81	Whittingham, Wm. Rollinson
E82	Rickard, Eliza Rollinson, wid. of Joseph
E85	Condit, Selina Platt, dau of Morris
E86	Condit, Francces Ann, dau. of Morris
E87	Vermilye, Harriet, wife of John
E87	Vermilye, John
E88	Vermilye, Hellen L.
E89	Brown, Mary Eliz'th, wife of Amzi
E90	Meeker, Abraham P.
E91	Meeker, Elizabeth, wife of Abraham P.
E92	Smith, Wm.
E93	Smith, Ruth, wife of William
E94	Tompkins, Enos C.
E95	Brown, Mary
E96	Brown, Amanda, wife of Kelite
E97	Beach, Charles
E99	Bell, Ann, wife of Nich's.
E99	Bell, Alexander
E99	Bell, Cath'ne Eliz'th, dau. of Jno.
E99	Bell, Ellen
E99	Bell, Louise, dau. of Jas. & El'r
E99	Bell, Mary Ann, dau. of Nich.
E99	Buckingham, Mary
E99	Dight, Mary

E99	Dight, Peter, son of Mary
E99	Watson, David
E100	Mills, Catherine, wife of James
E101	Harrison, Nathan S.
E102	Smith, Elizabeth, wife of Joseph
E102	Smith, Joseph
E103	Gray, Theodore H.
E104	Gray, Matilda T., wid. of Theodore
E105	Freeman, Mary Alice, dau. of Zenas
E106	Freeman, Charles Augustus, son of Zenas
E107	Freeman, Mary A., wife of Zenas
E107	Hitchcock, Charles D.
E108	Gray, Thomas Porter, son of Theodore H.
E109	Gray, Mary Ella, dau. of Theodore
E110	'Bella'
E111	Tompkins, Caroline, dau. of Luther C.
E112	Tompkins, Joseph C.
E112	Tompkins, Luther C.
E112	Tompkins, Rhoda Condit, wife of Luther
E113	Rose, Martha H.
E114	Rose, John
E115	Rose, Henry
E116	Rose, Elizabeth, dau. of John
E116	Rose, Martha Musgrave, wid. of John
E117	Smith, Mary Emma, dau. of Daniel T.
E118	Smith, Maggie, dau. of Daniel T.
E118	Smith, Our baby, ch. of Dan'l T.
E119	Dobridge, Julia J.
E120	Dobridge, Henry A.
E121	Dobridge, Robert
E122	Dobridge, Martha, wife of Robert
E123	Condit, J. W.
E124	Condit, Ira (Family Vault)
E125	Babbit, Charlotte
E126	Babbit, Daniel
E127	Matthews, Nancy, dau. of Noah & Phebe
E127	Babbit, Nancy, wife of Dr. Daniel
E128	Babbit, Daniel C., son of Dr. Daniel
E129	Matthews, Noah, son of Dr. Daniel
E130	Matthews, Phebe, wife of Noah
E131	Matthews, Noah
E132	Williams, Abraham
E133	Williams, Matilda S., wife of Abraham

E134	Williams, William A., son of Abraham
E135	Addy, Elizabeth, widow of Thomas
E136	Addy, Jane
E137	Stryker, Ann, wife of Henry
E138	Stryker, Eliza, wife of Henry
E139	Williams, Naomi, wid. of Daniel
E141	Williams, Amos
E141	Williams, Phebe, wife of Amos
E141	Williams, Stephen, son of Amos
E141	Williams, Wm. Whittingham
E142	Condit, Joseph A.
E143	Condit, Harriet Newall, wife of Joseph
E144	Condit, Ichabod, son of Joseph A.
E145	Condit, Harriet Clara, dau. of Joseph A.
E146	Condit, Harriet Clara, dau. of Joseph A.
E147	Condit, Henry Newell, son of Joseph A.
E148	Thomas, Mary, dau. of John & Jane
E149	Thomas, Sarah Ellen, dau. of John
E151	Williams, Anna Margaret, dau. of James A.
E154	Williams, Mary Alice, dau. of Charles
E155	Williams, Amelia, dau. of Charles
E156	Williams, Phebe, wife of Benjamin
E157	Williams, Benjamin
E158	Williams, Samuel
E159	Williams, Phebe, wid. of Samuel
E160	Crane, Hannah
E161	Bodwell, William, son of Philander
E162	Bodwell, Charles A., son of Philander
E163	Bodwell, Philander J.
E163	Bodwell, Sarah, wife of Philander
E164	Smith, Stephen
E165	Smith, Walter
E166	Smith, Abigail, wid. of Walter
E167	Smith, Nathaniel
E168	Reock, Rebeca Louise, dau. of John
E168	Smith, George W.
E168	Smith, Mary Louisa, dau. of George
E168	Smith, Rebeca Louise, wife of George
E169	Matthews, Sarah Maria, dau. of Simeon
E170	Matthews, Frederick H., son of Hobart
E170	Matthews, J. Hobart
E171	Matthews, Wm. Edgar, son of Albert
E172	Matthews, Mary Emily, dau. of Albert

E173	Matthews, Anzonetta Clement
E173	Matthews, David Clement
E174	Matthews, Albert
E175	Smith, David A.
E175	Smith, Lemuel D., son of David A.
E176	Smith, Richard P., son of Ezekiel
E177	Smith, Ezekiel
E178	Sharp, Mary Ann, wid. of Ezekiel
E179	Sharp, Ann R., wid. of Richard
E180	Gardner, Abigail, wife of Moses
E181	Coe, Susanna
E181	Field, James
E181	Field, Phebe, wid. of Hezekiah
E182	Baldwin, Lucy Irwin, dau. of Lewis
E183	Baldwin, Jane Augusta, dau. of Isaac
E184	Baldwin, Nancy, wife of Isaac
E185	Baldwin, Isaac
E186	Markwith, Margaret, wife, of John
E187	Bond, Daniel
E188	Bond, Phebe, wife of Daniel
E189	Vanderhoof, Ichabod C., son of Peter
E190	Bond, Catherine M., dau. of Daniel
E191	Edwards, David
E192	Edwards, Rhoda
E193	Burnside, James W.
E194	Burnside, George
E195	Burnside, Andrew T.
E195	Burnside, Cornelius, son of Andrew
E195	Burnside, Frances S., wife of Thomas
E195	Burnside, Sarah Crane, wife of Andrew
E195	Burnside, Sarah, dau. of Thomas
E195	Burnside, Thomas
E196	Harrison, Abby, wife of John
E196	Harrison, Caleb
E196	Harrison, Hannah, wife of Simeon
E196	Harrison, John
E196	Harrison, Keturah, wife of Caleb
E196	Harrison, Mary, dau. of Caleb
E196	Harrison, Simeon
E196	Harrison, Simeon, son of Caleb
E196	Whittingham, Mary Ann, dau. of Wm. R.
E197	Harrison, Simeon
E198	Harrison, Abby M. Condit, wife of Simeon

E199   Burnside, Arian
E200   Bruen, John F.
E201   Bruen, Hannah, wife of John F.
E202   Townley, C. W.
E203   Morrison, Sarah J., wife of Daniel

- - - - -

APPENDIX II

Transcript of map of St. Mark's Cemetery

(listed by section and plot owners)
(* indicates remains removed to other cemeteries)

This undated (ca. 1927?) map was recently found in the Archives of the Episcopal Diocese of Newark, N. J. and graciously provided for this book.

This map offers assistance in finding almost the exact location of an individual plot owner or grave site. The cemetery is rectangular. Section A begins at the front of the cemetery on Main Street and Section B, C, etc. follow behind it extending to approximately the same depth as the property of the adjacent First Presbyterian Church of Orange, N.J.

Map 1

Section A, Row 1 (at Main Street)
(later moved to Page J)
CALEB TOWNLEY
--
--
--
Lydia Henderson, d.Dec.12,1918, a. 28
Caleb Townley, d. April 1875, age 52
..... Townley, d. June 16, 1857
Henry Williams
Clara M. Williams,d.Feb.3, 1857
GEORGE OVEN
Geo. Oven., d. Dec. 29, 1886
Geo. Oven, d. Apr. 30, 1874
--
Sarah J. Morrison, d. Sept. 25, 1869
William H. Oven, d. Dec. 20, 1873
Martha A. Oven, d. July 4, 1867
--
Fannie Oven,wife of John, d.8/13/1875
CALEB MATTHEWS
--
--
--
--
--
--
--
JOHN MATTHEWS
--
--
--
--
--
--
--
PLATT SOPER
Gertrude A. Soper, d. Apr. 1, 1851
--
--
--

Section A, Row 2
(later moved to Page J)
CALEB TOWNLEY
--
--
--
child of S. Lowden
--
-- ..... Townley
--
--
GEORGE OVEN
Rev John Oven, d. Sept. 6, 1875
--
Mary Oven, d. May 2, 1906, age 66.4.4
--
--
James Augustus Oven, d.2/16/1921,a.68
--
Hannah Oven, d. Apr.23,1927, age 83
CALEB MATTHEWS
--
--
--
--
--
--
--
JOHN MATTHEWS
Grace Matthews, child, d. Aug.1, 1864
Harry Matthews, child
J. H. Matthews, child
--
--
--
--
PLATT SOPER
Edgar A. Soper
Frederic Soper
--
--

Map 2

Section A, Row 3
FRANCIS BURNSIDE
Arian Burnside, d. July 14, 1874, age 66
--
--
--
--
--
JOHN BRUEN
John Bruen
Hannah Bruen
ABIGAIL HARRISON
--
--
--
--
--
--
--
CALEB HARRISON
Mary Harrison
Simeon Harrison
..... Whittingham
--
--
--
--
SIMEON HARRISON
--
--
--
--
--
--
--
--
--
--
--

Section A, Row 4
FRANCIS BURNSIDE
James Burnside
George Burnside, d. Feb. 26, 1861
Cornelius Burnside
Sarah Burnside
Thomas Burnside
Mrs. Phebe Burnside
JOHN BRUEN
--
--
ABIGAIL HARRISON
Josiah Kilburn, d. Feb. 28, 1856
--
--
--
--
Abigail Harrison, d. Jan. 8, 1851
John Harrison
CALEB HARRISON
Simeon Harrison
Hannah Harrison
--
Caleb Harrison, d. Sept. 11, 1854
Katurah Harrison, d. 1855
--
--
SIMEON HARRISON
Simeon Harrison, d. Mar. 29, 1872
Abbey M. Harrison
--
Maria, wife of S.O. Rollinson
--
S. O. Rollinson
--
--
--
Phebe Harrison
--
--
--

Map 3

Section B, Row (1)
JAMES FIELD
--
--
--
Phebe, wife of James Field
James Field, d. Aug. 23, 1863
Phebe Field
Susanna Coe
--
ISAAC BALDWIN
--
--
Lew. Mandeville Baldwin,1/26/1902, 73
Eva Baldwin, d. Feb. 5, 1912, age 77.5.5
--
--
Ella Jane Baldwin, d. July 11, 1928
--
JOHN MARKWITH
Ira Markwith, d. Mar. 21, 1894, age 44
Susan A. Cole, d.Nov. 3, 1887
Margaret Markwith, d. Feb. 23, 1883
--
HENRY PROCTOR
--
Margaret Proctor, d. Dec. 17, 1918
Matthew H. Proctor, d. Nov. 29, 1916
Lulu H. Proctor,d.Oct. 12, 1915, a.12.9.
DANIEL BOND
Gertrude Vanderhoof
Clarence W. Vanderhoof,d.July 20, 1861
Ichabod C. Vanderhoof
Catherine Vanderhoof, d. Jan. 21, 1878
--
Peter Vanderhoof, d. July 2, 1878
Alfred J. Vanderhoof, son Peter & Cath.
Eugene Vanderhoof
DAVID EDWARDS
David Edwards
Rhoda Edwards
--
--

Section B, Row 2
JAMES FIELD
--
--
--
--
--
--
--
--
ISAAC BALDWIN
--
--
Lucy Baldwin, d. Oct. 21, 1861
Jane A. Baldwin
Nancy Baldwin, d. 11/16/1866, age 70
Isaac Baldwin, d. Mar. 19, 1877, age 86
--
--
JOHN MARKWITH
John Markwith, d. Mar.19, 1900
--
Margaret Hall, wife of John Markwith
Mrs.Stephen Cole,dau.of John Markwith
HENRY PROCTOR
Child of Henry Proctor
Martha Proctor, d. May 11, 1892
--
Milton Palmer Clark,d.Jan. 27,1896. a.5
DANIEL BOND
Sarah L. Reeves, d. Apr. 17, 1934,age 75
Daniel Bond. d. Dec. 11, 1877
--
Phebe Mitchell, d. May 16, 1872
--
Wm. M. Reeves, d.Apr. 12, 1915
Bentley? Reeves, a. Apr. 1903,age 18
--
DAVID EDWARDS
--
Abbey Dean,wife of Isaac P. Baldwin
--
--

Map 4

Section B, Row 3
GEORGE W. SMITH
--
Rebecca L. Roeck, d.Jan. 10,1862
 formerly Mrs. George W. Smith
George W. Smith, d. Dec. 3, 1849
Infant son of George W. Smith
--
--
--

SIMEON MATTHEWS
--
Joseph Matthews, d. May 15, 1857
Sarah M. Matthews, d. May 17, 1851
Sarah L. Matthews, d. Apr. 18, 1854
--
--
--
--

ALBERT MATTHEWS
David C. Matthews
Mary E. Matthews
William C. Matthews, d. Dec. 20, 1865
Albert Matthews, d. 1860
--
--
--

EZEKIEL B. SMITH
--
--
--
--
Richard O. Smith
Ezekiel B. Smith
Mary Ann Smith
--
--

MOSES GARDNER
--
--
--
--

Section B, Row 4
GEORGE W. SMITH
--
--
--
--
--
--
--
--

SIMEON MATTHEWS
--
--
--
--
--
--
--
Caroline Amelie Young,d. 9/8/1926, 84
Samuel Young, d. Jan. 22, 1920, age 75

ALBERT MATTHEWS
Joseph H.Matthews,son of Joseph,d.1863
Frederick H. Matthews, d. Aug. 7, 1894
--
--
--
--

EZEKIEL B. SMITH
child of Henry Growney
David A. Smith
Eliza A.L. Smith,d.Jan.12, 1902, age 92
Elemuel O. Smith
Oliver B. Smith, d. May 12, 1879
--
--
--

MOSES GARDNER
child of George Gardner,d.2/18/1872
Sarah Gardner
Moses Gardner
'Clarrisey'(?), wife of Moses Gardner
Abigail A.Gardner, d. Jan 28, 1856

Map 5

Section C Row 1
SAMUEL WILLIAMS
--
Phebe Williams
Benjamin Williams
Samuel Williams
--
Phebe Williams, d. Jan. 11, 1856
Hannah Crane, d. July 13, 1870, age 79
--

CHARLES WILLIAMS
--
--
--
--
--
--
--

CHURCH PROPERTY
--
--
--
--
--
--
--

PHILANDER BODWELL
--
Charles A. Bodwell, d.Mar.25,1862, a.19
... Bodwell
--
Sarah, wife of P. Bodwell, d.Nov. 5, 1870
Philander Bodwell, d. July 14, 1871
--
--

WALTER SMITH
--
Miller Smith
--
--

Section C, Row 2
SAMUEL WILLIAMS
--
--
--
--
--
--
--
--

CHARLES WILLIAMS
Mary A. Williams
Amelia Williams
Mary Williams, d. Feb. 13, 1856
--
--
--

CHURCH PROPERTY
--
--
Mrs. Ira Condit
Mark Condit
Ira Condit
--
--

PHILANDER BODWELL
--
--
--
--
--
--

WALTER SMITH
Stephen Smith, d. Feb. 12, 1855
Walter Smith, d. Apr. 9, 1854
Abigail Smith, d. Oct. 20, 1853

Map 6

Section C, Row 3
AMOS WILLIAMS
--
Whittingham Williams
Joanna Williams
Amos Williams
Phebe Williams
Stephen Williams
--
--
JAMES WILLIAMS
--
--
--
--
--
--
--
JOSEPH A. CONDIT
--
--
--
--
--
--
--
--
--
--
JOHN THOMAS
--
--
--
--
--
--
--
--

Section C, Row 4
AMOS WILLIAMS
--
--
--
--
--
--
--
Edward Grant Williams, d. Sept.31, 1849
JAMES WILLIAMS
--
--
--
--
--
--
--
JOSEPH A. CONDIT
--
--
Joseph A. Condit, d. Nov. 10, 1881
Mrs. Harriet N. Condit, d. Feb. 25, 1880

Ichabod Condit, d. Mar.1, 1870, age 26
Harriet Clarry Condit
--
Harriet C. Condit
Harry N. Condit, d. June 2, 1860
--
--
JOHN THOMAS
--
Adelaide Thomas
Mary Thomas
Sarah E. Thomas
--
--
--
--

Map 7

Section D, Row 1
ABRAHAM WILLIAMS
--
--
--
--

Daniel Williams
Naomi Williams, d. Jan. 10, 1851
Martha Williams
JOEL CONDIT ENTRANCE(?)
--
--
--
--
--
--
--

IRA CONDIT VAULTS
Hannah E. Condit, d. Mar. 6, 1894
--
--
--
--
--
--
--

HENRY STRYKER
--
--
--
--
--
--
--
--
--
--

Section D, Row 2
ABRAHAM WILLIAMS
--
Abram Williams, d. Apr.5, 1861, age 63
--
Matilda Williams, d. Jan. 31, 1858
--
William A. Williams, d. Nov. 5, 1850
--
Children of H. P. Williams
JOEL CONDIT ENTRANCE(?)
--
--
--
--
--
--
--

IRA CONDIT VAULTS
--
--
--
--
--
--
--
--

HENRY STRYKER
Elizabeth Addy
Jane Addy
--
--
Elizabeth Stryker
John Addy, d. Feb. 24, 1851
--
--
--
--
--

Section D, Row 3
CHARLES HAND
--
--
--
--
children of Charles Hand
--
Albert Hand, d. Apr. 10, 1883
JOEL W. CONDIT VAULTS
--
--
C. Harrison Condit, d. Jan.16, 1881
Joel W. Condit
Francis Condit
Julia Condit
Margaret M. Condit
Sarah Condit
ENTRANCE TO IRA CONDIT VAULTS
--
--
--
--
--
--
--
DANIEL BABBITT
infant son of Wm. Babbitt
--
--
--
--
--
--
--
--
--

Section D, Row 4
CHARLES HAND
Mattie F. Hand, d. June 16, 1863
--
--
--
--
John Crowell
--
--
JOEL W. CONDIT VAULTS
--
--
--
--
--
--
--
--
ENTRANCE TO IRA CONDIT VAULTS
--
--
--
--
--
--
--
DANIEL BABBITT
*Charlotte Stryker Babbitt, d. 7/4/1884
Mrs. Phebe Babbitt'
Daniel Babbitt, d. June 19, 1864
Nancy Babbitt
Daniel C. Babbitt
Phebe Matthews
--
--
Noah Matthews, d. Aug. 4, 1851
--
--
--

Map 9

Section E, Row 1
JAMES BELL (transferred,
  1904, to JOHN K. MILNE)
--

John K. Milne, d. June 4, 1906
Mary Milne, d.June 10, 1905, 65.9.20
--
George P. Milne,d.Aug.18,1910,31.9.24
--
--
WILLIAM STITES
--
--
--
--
--
--
--
DANIEL SMITH
--
--
Mary E. Smith, d. 1863
Margaret, dau.of Daniel, d.Apr. 25, 1856
--
Susan Ann Smith,d.May 2,1910,87.5.28
Daniel T. Smith, bur.Jan.1,1894, age 73
--
HENRY A. DOBRIDGE
--
--
Julia J. Dobridge, d. Mar. 21, 1882
--
Selina F. Dobridge
--
Henry Dobridge, d. Oct. 14, 1873
--
ROBERT DOBRIDGE
Robert Dobridge
Martha Dobridge
Sarah Dobridge
--

Section E, Row 2
JAMES BELL (transferred,
  1904, to JOHN K. MILNE)
Flora Eliz.Price,d.Mar.25,1934,60.5.4
--
--
George Strothers, d. Mar. 1, 1864
Wife of Geo.Strothers, d. Sept. 15, 1874
Children of James Bell
--
--
WILLIAM STITES
child of Albert Stites
--
--
--
--
--
--
--
DANIEL SMITH
--
--
--
--
--
--
--
--
HENRY A. DOBRIDGE
Julius Rose
Sarah Ann Rose, bur.Jan.2,1897,age60
Martha A. Rose
--
John Rose, d. Nov. 13, 1872, age 40
--
Miss Rose
--
ROBERT DOBRIDGE
Henry Rose, d. Feb. 3, 1854
Elizabeth Rose, d. July 25, 1861
Martha Rose, d. Sept. 30, 1861
--

Map 10

Section E, Row 3
HORACE CONDIT VAULTS
David Condit, d. July 19, 1851
Sarah Condit
Horace Condit
Fannie Condit
--
--
--
--

ELIZABETH SMITH
'Alucina' Smith, bur. Oct.4,1905, age 55
Watson Smith, d. June 22, 1936, age 73
--
George Smith, d. May 12, 1854
--
Louis Leander Smith, d. May 13, 1894
--
Moses Smith, d. Mar.28, 1874, age 44
ISAAC B. CONDIT
John Grey, d. Apr. 29, 1850
Mary Grey, d. May 3, 1859
Mary J. Wade, d. May 14, 1856
Miss Grey, d. Mar. 16, 1864, age 11
--
Theo. P. Grey, d. Apr. 25, 1872
Mary Grey, d. Feb. 16, 1850

ZENAS FREEMAN
Caroline Tompkins, d. Nov. 27, 1848
Luther Tompkins, d. Oct. 4, 1852,age 59
*Enos Tompkins, d. June 20, 1906
*Rhoda C. Tompkins, d.Mar. 20, 1883
Mary A. Tompkins,d.Oct.10,1903,80.7.3
--
Jos. C. Tompkins, d. Dec. 27, 1873
--

HENRY CONDIT
Henry D. Condit, d. Oct. 31, 1850
Mary E. Dusie
Son of G. Condit, d. June 5, 1883
Charles Condit, b. May 5, 1855
Geo.F.Condit, d. 6/18/1907
Ann E. Condit, d. June 27, 1854

Section E, Row 4
HORACE CONDIT VAULTS
--
--
--
--
--
--
--
--

ELIZABETH SMITH
--
Mary Smith
John Smith
Charles Smith
Elizabeth Smith
Joseph Smith
Elizabeth Smith, d. Apr. 14, 1871
Joseph Smith
ISAAC B. CONDIT
Theo. Grey
Matilda Grey, d. June 12, 1880
Phoebe C. Condit
Oscar J. Condit
..... Condit
Isaac B. Condit, d. Oct. 9. 1848
--
--

ZENAS FREEMAN
child of Zenas Freeman
Charles Freeman, d. Apr. 1, 1866
Mary A. Freeman
Zenas Freeman
--
--
--

HENRY CONDIT
Charles Condit, d. Apr. 16, 1850
Charlotte Jones, d. Feb. 6, 1900
Lucy Condit, d. Aug. 24, 1855
John H. Condit, d. Feb. 28, 1856
Ada Condit

Map 11

Section F, Row 1
ELIJAH S. SMITH
--
--
Enos C. T. Smith, d. Sept. 4, 1845
--
wife of E. S. Smith
Elijah S. Smith, d. Feb. 24, 1874
Mary Jane Reed,bur.Mar.31,1903,age 64
--
JAMES MILLS
Catherine C. Mills, d. June 11, 1856
--
Florence Smith, bur. June 19, 1903,a. 10
--
Catherine H. Mills
Gladys Partlow?,bur.July 14, 1903,2 mo.
--
Charlotte Mills
JAMES PETIT
Nathan S. Harrison, d. June 1, 1849
--
--
--
--
--
--

JOHN BELL
Mrs. M. A. Bell, d. Apr. 17, 1851
Ann Bell, d. Sept. 1888?
--
Ellen Bell, d. Apr. 3, 1852, age 2
Catherine Bell, d. Dec. 31, 1851, age 6
Mary Buchanan
ALEXANDER BELL
--
--
--
--
--

Section F, Row 2
ELIJAH S. SMITH
--
--
William Smith, d. Oct. 29, 1851
Ruth C. Smith, d. Nov. 23, 1849, age 76
--
Enos C. Tompkins,d.Mar.6,1867,age 58
Ruth Caroline Tomkins,d. 2/27/1898, 87
--
JAMES MILLS
Mrs. Hollum, wife of Jacob
Jacob Hollum, d. Feb. 14, 1855
James Hollum, d. Apr. 14, 1872
--
--
--
Aaron Bentley Hollum,d.2/7/1916, a.90
Mary E. Hollum, d.July 17,1914,age 85
JAMES PETIT
--
--
children of James Petit
--
--
--
--

JOHN BELL
--
--
--
--
--
--
ALEXANDER BELL
David Watson
--
--
--
--
--

Map 12

Section F, Row 3
ABRAM P. MEEKER
--
Abram P. Meeker, b. May 9, 1850
Elizabeth Meeker
--
--
--
--
--

CHARLES BROWN
--
--
--
Charles Brown, b. May 10, 1882
Mary Brown
Maria Brown, d. Juan. 14, 1859
Thelita(Kalita) Brown
--

DAVID BEACH
--
--
--
--
*Charles Beach, d. Mar. 1, 1864
--
--
--

MARY DYKES
--
--
--
Mary Dykes, d. Feb. 18, 1872
Mary Dykes, d. Jan. 19, 1858
Peter Dykes
John Dykes, d. July 20, 1860
--

OWNED AS SEPARATE GRAVES
Mary Collins, d. Oct. 13, 1858
Edward Collins, d. June 27, 1853
  George Collins, d. May 19, 1856
Catherine Simon, d. Feb. 2, 1854
Catherine Simon,b.May 22, 1853,10 mo.

Section F, Row 4
ABRAM P. MEEKER
--
--
--
--
--
--
Mary E. Meeker
CHARLES BROWN
Mrs. Vermilye
John Vermily
--
--
Hellen Vermilye
--
--
--

DAVID BEACH
--
--
--
--
--
--
--
--

MARY DYKES
--
--
--
--
--
William Dykes, d. July 31, 1863
--
--

OWNED AS SEPARATE GRAVES
George Versoy, d. Nov. 13, 1851
--
--
--

Map 13

Section G, Row 1
RICHARD WHITTINGHAM
--
*Eliza, wife of Joseph Rickard
  d.Dec. 13, 1870, age 76
*Richard Whittingham,d.Jun 2, 1858, 82
*Mary Ann Whittingham,d.9/12/1849,85
*Emily R. Whittingham, d. Mar.3, 1854
--
--
--
--

HENRY HARRISON
--
--
Henry Harrison, d. June 5, 1853,age 40
William H. Harrison, d. May 6, 1855
... C. Harrison, d. Nov. 5, 1855
--
AMOS L. STAGG
--
--
Warren P. Stagg, d. Mar. 4, 1851
--
--
--
--
--

ELIZA ALLEN
--
--
--
William Allen, d. June 16, 1852, age 26
Mrs. Allen
John E. McMullin, d. Apr.28, 1894

MORRIS CONDIT
Salina P. Condit
Francis A. Condit, d. Nov. 4, 1852
--
--

Section G Row 2
RICHARD WHITTINGHAM
*Bishop Whittingham, d. Nov. 18, 1879
*Hannah, wife of Bishop Whittingham
--
--
--
--
--
--
--

HENRY HARRISON
--
--
--
--
--
--
AMOS L. STAGG
--
--
--
--
--
--
--
--

ELIZA ALLEN
dau. of E. Austin, d. Nov.20, 1866, age 2
--
--
infant, d. July 26, 1845
infant, d. July 26, 1845
child of Peter Sarony, d. May 15, 1859
--
--

MORRIS CONDIT
Louisa Hennessey, d. Apr. 21, 1859
John Bell, d. Nov. 23, 1873, age 70
--
--

Map 14

Section G, Row 3
ANN P. BROWNE
William L. Brown, d. Mar.19,1900
('wrong space'
Ann P. Browne
child in Ann P. Browne grave
Miss Browne
Catherine Browne
Arthur Browne
children of T. Browne
WARREN BISHOP
Phebe E. Bishop
Warren P. Bishop, b. Jan. 9, 1882
Mary A., wife of W.P.,d.May 14, 1871
--
... (Warren S.) Bishop, d. Apr. 7, 1862
--
--
--
W. G. GARDNER
--
--
--
William Gardner, d. Feb. 16, 1895,a. 48
Julia Gardner
Mary A. Gardner, d. Aug. 1, 1858
child
child
JOHN ALLEN & JOHN JONES
child of Wm. Allen
William C. Allen, d. Feb. 22, 1880
--
--
William Allen, d. Apr. 22, 1853, age 70
Mrs. Allen, d. Nov. 23 1873, age 80
child of Jones
child of Jones
MRS. LAW
Mathias Law, d. Dec. 2, 1843
George Law, d. July 29, 1849
John Law, d. May 19, 1853, age 46
--

Section G, Row 4
ANN P. BROWNE
*Mrs. John Seymour
Arthur Browne
Christopher Herold
Mrs. Christopher Herold
--
children of Wm. Browne
William B. Hanold, d. June 3, 1856
Frances L. Morgan, d. June 9, 1904
WARREN BISHOP
--
Rachael Bishop, bur. Dec. 2, 1905, a. 82
--
Emily Bishop, d. Nov. 17, 1851
--
body in this plot
Laura Williams, bur. July 8, 1919, a.76
Joseph King, bur.May 26,1899, a.3 days
WILLIAM HARRISON
--
Rhoda A. Hodge, bur. May 8, 1913
Mary G. Harrison, d.Jan. 16, 1907,a.78
William Harrison
child of Wm. Harrison
Harriet A. Harrison, b. Aug. 22, 1859
--
JOHN ALLEN & JOHN JONES
Susan Williams, d. Jan. 21, 1854
--
George Jones, d. May 1, 1854
Martha Jones, d. Mar. 8, 1854
John Jones
Eliza Jones, d. May 14, 1853, age 7 mo.
--
--
MRS. LAW
Isaac Stone, d. Sept. 12, 1850
--
--
infant of Wm. Linsley

Map 15

Section H, Row 1
DANIEL WEBB
Daniel Webb
Mary, wife of Daniel Webb
child of Daniel Webb, Jr.
child of Daniel Webb, Jr.
child of Daniel Webb, Jr.
child of Daniel Webb, Jr.
--
--
WILLIAM & SAMUEL JONES
William Jones, d. Dec. 14, 1896,a.7 mos.
Raymond J. Jones, d. July 10, 1909
William Jones, d. Oct. 14, 1896, age 30
--
child of W. Jones, d. Sept. 5, 1882
Sarah Jones, d. Aug. 19, 1871, age 53?
Dorothy E. Jones, d. Aug. 26, 1912
Mary J. Gardiner, d. Aug. 20, 1873,a.22
CHURCH PROPERTY
--
--
--
--
--
Ada Courtney, d. Oct. 21, 1862 age 4
--
William Sullivan
Robt. Geo. Daniel, d. Sept. 24, 1863
William Hughes, d. Jan. 17, 1872
Grace A. Bard, d. July 3, 1872
William Hughes, d. Jan, 17, 1872 (dupl.)
--
Mary A. Condor, d. Jan. 17, 1864
--
John McCullough, d. Dec. 22, 1848
--
--
..... Zimmerman

Section H, Row 2
DANIEL WEBB
Daniel Webb, bur. Dec. 5, 1908, Age 56
--
--
--
Andrew J. Furey, bur. Mar.10, 1905,a.72
--
--
George Webb,bur.Jul 10, 1900?, a.4 mo.
WILLIAM & SAMUEL JONES
William Jones, d. Sept. 9, 1900, age 55
--
--
--
--
--
Mary Jones, d. May 27, 1914
--
CHURCH PROPERTY
Margaret Mitchell?, d. Dec. 16, 1921
--
--
--
--
Henry Collinson
child of Henry Collinson
James Newman, d.Sept. 5, 1872,age 40
Mary E. Perry
George Silveria, d. Oct. 26, 1918,age 23
--
son of A. B. Hollum
--
--
--
Charles Zimmerman, d. Feb. 25, 1856
William Lynd & Mary Lynd
Henry Zimmerman, d. May 15, 1850

Map 16

Section H, Row 3
JAMES CLARK
James A. Clark, d. Dec. 17, 1916, age 81
Catherine Clark, June 17, 1899?
--
--
--
Edward C. Meyer,d.Mar.20,1906.21 d.
infant of Jas. Clark, d. Jan. 26, 1865
infant of Jas. Clark, d. Nov. 10, 1859
ISAAC BALDWIN
child
H. Hanson, d. Dec. 21, 1876
unidentified, d. Dec. 2, 1876
2 children of W. Doe
child of R. Pratt
child of J. Sheridan
2 children of B. Dangler, d. 1882
child of J. Hopkins, d. June 29, 1877
child of J. Canning, d. 1877
Mrs. Cochran, d. March 6, 1877
RICHARD NEWTON
child of Richard and Susan Newton
--
--
Susan Newton, d. Feb. 6, 1902
Richard T. Newton, d.Jan. 20,1907,a.73
--
--

CHURCH PROPERTY
Mrs. Joseph Hiert, d. Aug. 12, 1878
John Heally,d.Apr18,1882, 2 children
Eva Southwick, d. Oct. 17, 1880
  & child d. July 21, 1880
child?
child?
Levi Talbert
James Howard, d. Dec. 12, 1878
John H. Duer, d. Mar. 28, 1869
JAMES GRANT
James Grant, d. Apr. 1, 1857
wife of Levi Talbert
child of ..... Ducker
child of C. H. Johnson

Section H, Row 4
JAMES CLARK
--
--
--
--
--
--
--
--
--
ISAAC BALDWIN
child of Jacob Edwards, d. 1872
2 children Patterson
child Patterson, d. Dec. 4, 1872
child of J. Collinson,March 12, 1877
child of Wm. Williamson
Francis Taylor
Ella McCullough, d. July 4, 1878
child of McCullough?
child of John Wiess
child of Chas. Ferguson
ALEXANDER WILLIS
child of Alex. Willis, d. Jan. 3, 1876
2 children of Alex. Willis, d. Jan. 6, 1876
Mrs. Clara M.(Willis)Kyle,d. Feb,2,1903
Joseph Willis, d. Apr. 21, 1912, age 25
Alexander Willis,d.Aug.23, 1914,age 75
Margaret Willis, d. Oct. 25, 1917, age 72
--
Robert Gordon, d. May 14, 1899,a.24?
CHURCH PROPERTY
--
..... Hoffman, d. Sept. 16, 1882
Gilbert Thompson
John Speir, d. Feb. 29, 1882
John Meal, d. Apr. 18, 1882
Robert, s. of Chas. Metz, d.Jun 27, 1889
--
Johann Schoor, d. Feb. 4, 1882
Archibald Peacock, d. 1863?
SAMUEL CLEVELAND
Henry Cleveland
Samuel Cleveland, d. Oct. 27, 1851
--
--

Map 17

Section I, Row 1
OWNED AS SEPARATE GRAVES
John Farley
John Platt
Mrs. Gilman & Mrs. Lord
Wm. Lord & Gilbert Lord
Catherine S., dau. of Wm. Leadbeater
child of William Leadbeater
child of William Leadbeater
W. H. Gill, d. Apr. 14, 1860
CHURCH PROPERTY
Hiram Thorp
Charles Hughes
John Patterson
Mrs. Studley?
--
--
--
--
--
--
--
--
--
--
2 children
--
--
--
--
--
--
--

OWNED AS SEPARATE GRAVES
John C. Cooper, d. ....., 18_ _
Josephine Cooper
Joel Hitchcock, d. July _ _, 18_ _
..... Armstrong, d. _ _ _ _

Section I, Row 2
ABRAM BROWER
Abram Brower
infant of A. Brower
Romanzo Gage
Harriet Ann Brower, d. May 14, 1901
Kate Brower, d. Nov. 22, 1868, Age 20
--
Walter Brower
Lizzie Brower d. Oct. 2, 1879
CHURCH PROPERTY
Henry Cooper
unidentified grave
--
--
--
--
--
--
--
--
--
--
--
--
--
--
--
--
--
--
--
--

OWNED AS SEPARATE GRAVES
Isaac Snow, d. Nov. 21, 1852, age 5
James Armstrong, d. Apr. 22, 1890
Mrs. Armstrong
Richard Armstrong, d. Dec. 22, 1828
Frederick Clark Armstrong

Map
18

Section I, Row 3
JAMES McKAY
--
--
--
Mary S. McKay, d. May 18, 1861
--
--
--
CHURCH PROPERTY
--
--
--
--
--
--
--
--
--
--
--
--
--
ABEL(?) HERRON(?)
--
--
--
--
Mrs. Herron, d. Mar. 29, 1868, age 53?
--
Abel R......., age 52?
ILLEGIBLE PLOT NAME
infant of Pier...?, d. Aug. 15, 1850
infant of Edward H...
infant of Nicholas Bell?
Magdelene Law?
infant of Pierce? d. Apr. 30, 1854
infant of Charles? Hull?

Section I, Row 4
JAMES McKAY
Moses McKay, d. Aug. 11, 1861
--
--
--
--
--
--
--
CHURCH PROPERTY
--
--
--
--
--
--
--
--
--
--
--
--
--
ABEL(?) HERRON(?)
--
--
--
2 children
Mrs. Crawford, d. Oct. 18, 1863
John Hughes
Thomas Bal......, d. Jan. 2_, 1869
small child
ILLEGIBLE PLOT NAME
James Paul ?
--
--
--
James Higginbotham, d. Feb. 28, 18_6
--
--

Map 19

Section J, Row 1
JOHN 'MELLON' MILNE
*George Strothers, d. Mar. 1, 1864, a. 62
*wid. of Geo. Strother, d.Sept. 15, 1874
--
Clara R. 'Mellon'(Milne),d.Jun. 1, 1880
--
--
--
--
JOHN H. SHARP
*Mrs. Walter Sharp, d. Nov. 11, 1882
--
--
Martha J. Sharp, d. Oct. 25, 1906, age 72
--
John H. Sharp, d. Sept. 16, 1892
Mrs. Phebe Sharp, d. Dec. 15, 1879
--
CHARLES DEAN
--
Charles Dean, d. Nov. 23 1872, age 74
Lydia Dean, wife of Charles Dean
--
Phebe Stevens, d. Oct. 25, 1901,age 65
A...... Stevens, d. Dec. 24, 1904
--
Henry Stevens
STACY B. BANNISTER
--

James VanNess, d. June 11, 1894
Mabel VanNess, bur. Jan. 27, 1899

Section J, Row 2
DAVID BELL
William McGloughlin
--
--
--
--
..... Bell
James Bell, d. Jan. 26, 1865.age 17
Isabella Bell, d. Dec. 4, 1860
JOHN H. SHARP
Negro servant
--
Walter Sharp, d. July 19, 1855? 8 mos.
--
daughter of J. H. Sharp
daughter, of J. H. Sharp
--
child of R. H. VanNess
CHARLES DEAN
--
--
--
--
--
--
--
--
STACY B. BANNISTER
Deborah Bannister, d. age 30?

Margaret, wife of Stacy, d. Apr. 6,1872
Gertrude, dau. of Stacy, d. Sept. 10, 1874

Map 20

Section J, Row 3
AARON GREEN
Rutilla, wife of Aaron Green
Aaron Green
--
*Lizzie Green, d. Feb. 1, 1872
--
--
Lafayette Green, d. Apr. 14, 1860
child
ISAAC M. DEAN
Mary J. Dean, wife of I., d. Mar. 6, 1867
Isaac M. Dean, d. Apr. 30, 1867, age 57
child of I. M. Dean
--
--
--
--

GEORGE N. BOYD
--
--
--
--
*Mrs. Gilman (Alecia?)
--
--

THOMAS BROWN
Thomas W. Brown, d.Feb. 1, 1866, a.51
child Brown
Anna G. Brown, d. Sept. 10, 1911.a.74
Thos. E.Brown, Dec. 5, 1916, 81.3.15
Anna Burnett, d. 1882
Mrs. Featherstone
Thomas F. Featherstone
Wm. Featherstone
Mary Palmer, d. Nov. 29, 1869
George Wickes?, d.Oct. 31, 1869, age 14
ROBERT F. GIST
son of Robert Gist
Margaret S. Gist, d. Sept. 2, 1854
Mary A. Gist, d. Aug. 30, 1854
--

Section J, Row 4
EDWARD TAYLOR
--
--
--
--
--
--
Esther Gertrude Taylor, d.Sep.5,1894,a.1
Fred C. Taylor, d. Oct. 31, 1878
ISAAC M. DEAN
--
Sarah P. Mulford, d. Mar.1, 1864, age 25
Alva D. Mulford, age 3 years
Charles B. Mulford
--
--
Benjamin P. Mulford, d.Sept.29,1903, 66
--
MRS. BENTLEY
Charles Benson
--
Mrs. Benson
--
Mrs. Palmer (Helen)
George Palmer, age 53
--
--
EDWARD STOPFORD
Jane Stopford, d. Jan.20, 1864, age 3
--
--
Thomas E. Stopford, bur.Oct.24,1905, age 40
Anna, wife of Edward Stopford
Edward Stopford, d. May 23, 1910, age 81
--
--
ROBERT F. GIST
--
--
--
--

Map 21

Section K, Row 1
JAMES LENNOX
Chas.Willard Lennox,d.4/11/22,1901, 41
Ellen Lenox, bur. Mar.5,1899
--
James Lennox, d. Feb. 8, 1872
Emma J. Lennox, d. Aug.29, 1853
Almira Lennox
Jessie Adele Cahill, d. Nov. 7, 1881
--
JAMES ROBBINS
--
--
--
--
James P. Robbins, d. Jan.5, 1853. a.55
Matilda Robbins, d. Feb. 1, 1866.a.66
Sarah Robbins, d. Dec. 10,. 1850.a.28
Henry S. Condit, d. June 17, 1899,age 79
LEWIS C. LIGHTHIPE
--
--
--
--
--
--
Henrietta Lighthipe, d. Feb. 9,1868?
Electa (or Clara) A. Lighthipe
NICHOLAS MILLER
George A. Miller, d. Feb. 24, 1856?
Lewis Miller, d. June _ _ _ _
Samuel M. J....., d. Feb. 17, 1856
--
Charles E. Miller, d. Mar. 15, 1856
Eliza Miller, d. Mar. 16, 1851?
child of S. M. Miller
Emma L. R ..... d. May 29, _ _ _ _
JOHN ATCHISON
*John Atichison, d. Oct. 25, 1876
--
--
--

Section K, Row 2
CHARLES H. HULL
Harriet,w.of Peter V. Hull,d.Jan.5,1891
--
Charles H. Hull, d. Nov. 28, 1902,age 64
--
Lydia Hull, d. Feb. 6, 1909, age 78
--
John Personett
child of Chas. H. Hull, d. July 14, 1861
JAMES ROBBINS
--
--
--
--
--
Sarah Aymar, d. Apr. 5, 1861
--
Eliza Babb, d. July 8, 1864
LEWIS C. LIGHTHIPE
Thomas H. Lighthipe, 18_ _
Edward Lighthipe,ch. of Wm.18_ _
child of Wm. Lighthipe
--
--
--
NICHOLAS MILLER
--
--
--
Nicholas Miller, d. Jun 6, 1907, age 80
Mary A. Miller, d. Mar.30,1905,age 89?
sister-in-law of Nicholas Miller
--
--
JOHN ATCHISON
*Emily J. Atchison, d. Sept. 6, 18_ _
--
--
--
--

Map 22

Section K, Row 3
THOMAS COTTRELL
--
--
--
--
--
*Henry Cottrell
Catherine Pierson
*..... M. Cottrell, d.Apr. 23, 1904
JAMES BRADY
--
Ellis M. Brady, d. Aug. 15, 1905?, a.48
--
--
--
--
--
--
CHARLES A. LIGHTHIPE
--
--
--
--
--
--
--
WILLIAM REEVES
--
*Edwin B. Reeves, d. May 5, 1916, a. 67
*Adrianna Reeves,d.11/22/1905, 56.1.30
Clarence L. Doggett?,d.Aug. 27, 1916, 4
Elsie Reeves
William Reeves
infant, d. Oct. 18, 1904
Mrs. Fanny Reeves
CHARLES SIDEBOTHAM
Nancy Sidebotham, d. Mar.24, 1862
Robert Sidebotham, d. Mar. 10, 1852
Mrs. Sidebotham (Mary Amelia)
--

Section K, Row 4
THOMAS COTTRELL
*Thomas Cottrell,bur.Mar.19,1900,a. 91
--
--
*Jane Pierson,wife of Thos.d.5/18/1891
--
Betsy Pierson
Catharine, wife of Zenas Pierson
Elizabeth, dau. of Zenas Pierson & Cath.
JAMES BRADY
--
--
F..... Brady. Aug. 15, 186_
Eugene Brady, Feb. 1_,1851?
Marshall Bertrand Brady, d. 11/9/1893
Emily Brady, d.10/17/1917, age 47.10.0
--
--
CHARLES A. LIGHTHIPE
--
--
--
--
--
--
--
WILLIAM REEVES
--
--
*child of Edwin Reeves, b. Jan.12, 1878
Elizabeth Reeves, d. Oct. 9, 1853
David B. Reeves,d. Mar. 15, 1865, age 4
Horace Reeves, d. 1870
*George Cook Reeves, d. Dec. 17, 1900
*child of Agustus Reeves d.11/23/1876
CHARLES SIDEBOTHAM
Charles Sidebotham, d. Nov. 9, 1894
--
--
--

Map 23

Section L, Row 1
WILLIAM DANIELS
--
Emeline, wife of Wm. Daniels
--
William Daniels
--
--
--
--

CHARLES HEER
--
(Charles J. Boehner, d. 18_ _)
(Catherine V. Boehner, d. 1877)
Katherine E. Boehner,d.May 1,1925,a.71
John B.Boehner,d.Aug.23,1933, 84.4.17
--
--
--

WILLIAM REDDINGTON
children of Wm. Reddington
--
William Reddington
--
--
--
William Sich enson,d.Mar.16, 1942,a.70

JOHN NORMAN
Sarah,ch.of John Gordon,Jun 12, 1882
John Norman, bur. Feb. 23 1899
M... Eiz.Norman, bur. Aug.29, 1902
dau.of John Norman,d. Jan.31,1869? a. 3
John Norman, d. Feb. _ _, 18_ _, age _ _
Geo. S.Norman, d. May 16, 18_ _
Joseph Norman, age ?
child of John Norman, d. Jan 20, 1867
MRS. STEINHAUSEN
*Ludwig Steinhausen, d. May 4, 1854
*Mrs. Steinhausen, d. 1871
*Hugo Steinhausen, d. Jan. 26, 1857
--

Section L, Row 2
WILLIAM DANIELS
--
--
--
--
*Moses E. Smith, d. Sept. 7, 1893
--
--
--

CHARLES HEER
--
--
Charles Heer, d. Feb. 7, 1858
Catherine Heer, d. Nov. 20, 1854
--
--
--
--

WILLIAM REDDINGTON
--
--
--
--
--
--
--

MRS. MARY WARTON
Louisa Hirsh
E... Bloom?
A.Eliz. Wharton?
Louisa Wharton
Josephine F.....
Martha Lee
Daniel? Wharton,child of
Mar...,d.11/1876?
MRS.STEINHAUSEN
Thomas Brown,d. Jan.10,1857
wife of Thos. Brown
August Pahte, d. June 16, 1884?
--

Map 24

Section L, Row 3
WIEDEMEYER
--
--
C.Peter's 2 children,d.May 10, 1882
Anna M. Widemeyer, d. Aug. 22, 1880
S. A. FAIRCHILD
Abbey Lyon, d. Feb. 28,1859
Anna Fairchild
--
child of Stokes
PATRICK COYEN
--
--
--
--
--
--

Anna Shields, d. Mar. 8, 1872
THADDEUS EDWARDS
child of T. Bonnell, d. Apr. 15, 1878
T. Higginson, d. Nov. 7, 1881
--
Thaddeus Edwards, d. Jan. 16, 1878
Mary, wife of T. E.d. April 1,1879
Edward,d.Apr.1,1849
--
Charles W.Edwards,d.10/17/1905,a.30
LEWIS CONDIT deeded (1894) to JOHN CONDIT
Miss (Rosena) Condit
Cornelia? Condit, wife of David W.
David W. Condit
--
--
..... A. ....., d.
*Charles? Condit, d. Aug. 3, 1879
WILLIAM CROSBY
Gilbert Crosby, d. Apr.17, 18_9
John Crosby, d. Dec. 9, 1871
--
--

Section L, Row 4
WEIDEMEYER
Henry Weidemayer, d. oct. 25, 1893
*Emma Fairchild, d. Apr. 17,1862
Annie Jauchen?
August Hepfner?, d, Dec, 18, 1894
S. A. FAIRCHILD
--
--
--
--
PATRICK COYEN
--
--
--
--
--
--
--

AGUSTUS EARL
Amanda Meeker, dau. of A. Earl
Theo. A. Farrer, d.Mar.13,1895,age 48
--
Maria, w. of Agustus,d.Nov.1866,age 29
--
Hattie Earl, d.1867, age 14
William Farrer, d. Feb. 1883
--
LEWIS CONDIT,deeded (1894) to JOHN CONDIT
Ada B.dau.of John,Feb.8,1869,18 mo.
Randolph B.son J. &Martha,d.7/4/1878
Roland Condit,
Bentley B. Condit, d. Mar. 25, 1881
--
--
WILLIAM CROSBY
*William Crosby, d. Sept. 22, 1896
Henry Brindley, d. Mar. 29, 1865
Sarah Summersett, d. Sept. 15, 1882
--

Map 25

Section M, Row 1
AARON VAN BUSKIRK
child of Aaron Van Buskirk
--
--
--
--
..... Schlicting
Wm. Schlicting
--
CHURCH PROPERTY
child of H. Carpenter, d. Apr. 12, 1872
Henry Carpenter, d. Jan. 28, 1877
--
--
--
--
--
--
MUNSON GARRABRANT
Munson Garrabrant
William M. Garrabrant, d.Dec. 7, 1880
--
--
William Wallace
Mary Wallace
--
Jane Garrabrant, d. Jan.25, 1920
JOSEPH EDWARDS
Grandchild of Eugene LeClerc
'occupies'
Anna Maria Sprigg (x'out)
--
--
Anna Maria Sprigg, d. Feb. 25, 1910,a16
Phebe C. LeClerc,bur.May 24, 1928, 83?
JAMES JARVIS
William Jarvis, d.Mar.7,18_ _
James Jarvis, d. 1853
--
--

Section M, Row 2
AARON VAN BUSKIRK
Mrs.VanBuskirk, (Charlotte Williams,
  1st wife of David VanBuskirk)
Sarah Jane Brundage, June 17, 1911
(Annie Defano, 2nd wife of David VB)
--
Grace Brundage, d. Aug. 15, 1881
*Araminta Crane, d. Mar.18, 1906, a.63
--
JAMES CROGAN
Robert E. Allen, d. July 10, 1883
--
--
--
--
*Willie Crogan, d. Jan.30, 1876
--
--
CHURCH PROPERTY
*Jane Williamson
('occupied by Geo. C. Wilson)
--
--
--
--
--
--
JOSEPH EDWARDS
--
--
--
--
--
--
JAMES JARVIS
Wilford Jarvis, d.Aug. 21, 1905
--
--
--

Map 26

Section M, Row 3
CHURCH PROPERTY
Miss Dougherty, d. Jan.28, 1869
Frank L. Gonzales, aged 6 mo.
--
--
--
child
child
--

BYRON QUIMBY
wife of J. W. Quimby, d. Apr. 22, 1872
Wickliffe Quimby
--
--
--
Mary L. Quimby, d. June 9, 1925, a. 80
Bryon W. Quimby, d. June 2, 1922
--

GEORGE HULL
--
--
--
--
--
--
--
Lillian Hull, d. Jun 4, 1930, age 61.1.28

MATILDA CUSICK
--
--
--
--
--
--
--
Peter R. Hull, d. Oct. 23, 1874

CHEETHAM
George Cheetham, d. Apr. 20, 1859
Mary A. Cheetham, d. Apr. 11, 1861
--
--

Section M, Row 4
JOHN HORNE
Jane, wife of John Horne
--
--
--
Anton Horne, bur. Mar. 6, 1901, age 65
--
--
--

BYRON QUIMBY
--
--
Lottie Quimby, d. Mar. 18, 1878
--
--
--
--
--

GEORGE HULL
child of George Hull, d. Mar. 29, 1877
Walter Hull, d. Sept. 21, 1881
child of W. Hull
Lillian Fischer Tanfield, 3/30/1924, a.33
William A. Hull, d. Aug. 15 1935, age 77
George A. Hull, d. Jan.25, 1917, age 80
Joseph Hull, d. Apr. 2, 1916, age 52
--

MATILDA CUSICK
--
--
--
Clarissa Cusack, d. Dec. 26, 1895, a.32
Matilda Cusick, d. Sept. 3, 1883
Richard J. Cusack, d. Dec. 9, 1901, a.68
--
Patrick Cusick, d. Feb. 28, 1878

CHEETHAM
--
--
--
--

Map 27

Section N, Row 1
SAMUEL GRAHAM
Anne S.dau of W.P.Green, d. May 1868
George Lynde, d. 1882
Mary Grayham
small child,dau. of S. Graham
OSBORNE
Catherine Osborne, d.Sept. 19,1868,a. 42
Ann Osborne, d.1871, age 84
--

CHURCH PROPERTY
Mrs.Mary Cunningham,3/10/1895,a. 44
Frank Cecil Waters, d.7/29/1895,a.14 m.
Marjorie Arnold, d. Dec. 19,1895,a.35?
Adelaide DeHart,d.Sept. 28,1898,6 days
*Bessie Wilson,b.9/3/1863d.9/11/1897

--
Caroline McGlee?, age 3
--
--
--
--
--
--
--
--
--
--

MARY ANN SHELLEY
Charles Shelley, d. Feb. 9,. 1859
Mary A. Shelley
--
--

Section N, Row 2
SAMUEL GRAHAM
Mrs. Mary Graham, d. Dec. 12, 1878
Samuel Graham, d. June 25, 1883
--
--
OSBORNE
*child
child of Dr. Davis, d. 1880
--
--

CHURCH PROPERTY
Joseph H. Evans, d.9/291902,a.68
Mrs. Elizabeth Evans, d.9/13/1908,a.70
Harriet? F. R.....
Arthur Browne,d.10/4/1908,a.56
--
--
--
--
--
--
--
--
--
--
--
--

MARY ANN SHELLEY
--
--
--

Map 28

Section N, Row 3
KERSHAW CLEGG
child of Kershaw Clegg
child of Kershaw Clegg
child of Kershaw Clegg
--
--
--
--

WILLIAM CLEGG
--
--
--
--

THOMAS McCULLOUGH
James W. McCullough
--
--
--

CHURCH PROPERTY
--
--
--
--
--
--
--
--
--
--
--
--
--

JAMES BROWN
Mary Brown, d. Dec. 28, 1860
John E. Brown, d. Nov. 10. 1861
--
--

Section N, Row 4
SAMUEL CLEGG
child of Samuel Clegg, d. Nov. 21, 1881
child of Samuel Clegg
child of Samuel Clegg
--
--
--

James F. Clegg, d. Aug. 14, 1882
WILLIAM CLEGG
wife of William Clegg
Virginia L. Smith, bur.May 17, 1919, a.1
William Clegg, d. Dec. 11, 1901
Charles L.Smith,d.9/29/1918, age 3 mo.
THOMAS McCULLOUGH
--
--
--

CHURCH PROPERTY
--
--
--
--
--
--
--
--
--
--
--
--
--

JAMES BROWN
--
--
--
--

Map 29

Section O, Row 1
CHURCH PROPERTY
--
--
--
--
--
--
--
--
--
--
--
--
--
--
--
--
--
--
--
--
--
--
--
--
--

GEORGE CLAY
George Clay,
Sarah, 1st wife of George Clay
Joseph L. Clay, d. Feb. 10, 1879
--

Section O, Row 2
CHURCH PROPERTY
--
--
--
--
--
--
--
--
--
--
--
--
--
--
--
--
--
--
--
--
--
--
--
--
--
--

GEORGE CLAY
Mrs. Clay, d. Sept. 3, 1862
 (2nd wife of George Clay)
--
--

Map 30

Section O, Row 3
CHURCH PROPERTY
--
--
--
--
--
--
--
--
--
--
--
--
--
--
--
--
--
--
--
--
--
--
--
MARY A. BONNELL
--
--
--
--

Section O, Row 4
CHURCH PROPERTY
--
--
--
--
--
--
--
--
--
--
--
--
--
--
--
--
--
--
--
--
--
--
--
MARY A. BONNELL
Joseph W. Bonnell
Theodore Bonnell, d. Aug. 5, 1876
2 children of Joseph W. Bonnell
Mrs. J. W. Bonnell
John W. Bonnell, d. Oct. 12, 1890

Map
31

Section O, Row 5 (beyond a pathway)
('N.B. not laid out beyond this')
NEGRO BURIAL GROUND

--

Mrs. Davis

--

Samuel Spear, d. Apr. 14, 1843

--

--John E. Blanchard

--
--
--
--

--John Blanchard (b. abt. 1824)

--
--
--
--
--
--

James Jackson, d. June 12, 1883

--
--
--
--
--
--
--

Salina Cole
Mabel Blake

--

Nathan McCrea, d. Sept.20,1881

--

Thomas Birch, d. July 24, 1879
(b.abt.1849)
Aramintha Grant, d. Mar. 14, 1872
Ann E. Grant, d. Oct. 14, 1882
Amzy Degroot, d. Oct. 24, 1882 (b. abt.1852)

www.ingramcontent.com/pod-product-compliance
Lightning Source LLC
Chambersburg PA
CBHW060109170426
43198CB00010B/827